Planning Curriculum for Learning World Languages

Paul Sandrock
World Languages Education Consultant

Elizabeth Burmaster, State Superintendent
Wisconsin Department of Public Instruction

Madison, Wisconsin

This publication is available from:

Publication Sales
Wisconsin Department of Public Instruction
Drawer 179
Milwaukee, WI 53293-0179
(800) 243-8782 (U.S. only)
(608) 266-2188
(608) 267-9110 Fax
www.dpi.state.wi.us/pubsales

Bulletin No. 3001

© July 2002 Wisconsin Department of Public Instruction

ISBN 1-57337-103-3

The Wisconsin Department of Public Instruction does not discriminate on the basis of sex, race, religion, age, national origin, ancestry, creed, pregnancy, marital or parental status, sexual orientation, or physical, mental, emotional, or learning disability.

Printed on recycled paper

Foreword

Learning world languages is an essential goal for all students. Today's interdependent world economy and our American society require that we interact with people from other cultures. Regardless of the specific languages our students learn, learning another language gives them the tools they need to communicate across cultural borders. This is an invaluable gift.

This curriculum guide is meant to help educators develop curriculum for learning world languages. Curriculum planning gives us the opportunity to reflect upon the goals and nature of education. It is a time when we formulate goals that harmonize the need of a democratic society for educated and productive citizens with the individual needs of students who seek refinement of their capabilities as well as their place in society.

This document describes step-by-step the decisions necessary for designing a curriculum for learning world languages. Although many suggestions for good instructional practices and activities are made, they remain samples. We strongly believe in the professionalism of Wisconsin's teachers, who are well prepared to plan curriculum and to design day-to-day instructional materials as part of an ongoing process in our school districts.

This guide has been created by a statewide task force of educators who teach daily in classrooms from elementary grades through the university level. Special thanks go to this dedicated group that took *Wisconsin's Model Academic Standards for Foreign Languages* and developed a very useful guide to bring those standards into our classrooms through clearly targeted curriculum. The writing task force also worked with standards, curriculum guides, and other materials from across the country. They have drawn upon the expertise of researchers, theorists, and classroom teachers both in writing and reviewing the guide.

Besides this task force, numerous teachers and administrators were involved in developing this guide through workshops and presentations in which key ideas and models were piloted. They provided excellent suggestions to develop standards-led curriculum, assessment, and instructional practices. Their input helped keep this guide true to the reality of Wisconsin's classrooms. We are confident that our readers will find it useful as they plan a curriculum for learning world languages at the beginning of the third millennium.

Elizabeth Burmaster
State Superintendent

Writing Task Force

The Wisconsin Department of Public Instruction expresses its utmost appreciation and thanks to the task force that committed time and knowledge to make this guide possible. Its members spent countless hours discussing how to make *Wisconsin's Model Academic Standards for Foreign Languages* the focus of curriculum for learning world languages. They contributed examples from their teaching experiences, piloted ideas and templates with colleagues and workshop participants, and wrote the material included in this guide. Their dedication to their profession and to raising student achievement is commended.

Donna Clementi
Foreign Language Program Leader
Appleton Area School District
French Teacher
Appleton West High School
Appleton, Wisconsin

Karen Fowdy
German Teacher
Monroe High School
Monroe, Wisconsin

Patricia Hoch
Foreign Language Department Chair
Onalaska School District
Spanish Teacher
Onalaska High School
Onalaska, Wisconsin

Paul Hoff
Professor of Spanish and Foreign Language Education
Department of Foreign Languages
University of Wisconsin–Eau Claire
Eau Claire, Wisconsin

Paul Sandrock
Consultant
World Languages Education
Wisconsin Department of Public Instruction
Madison, Wisconsin

Jody Schneider
French Teacher, K–8
The Woodlands School
Milwaukee, Wisconsin

Acknowledgments

A special thanks goes to many individuals at the Wisconsin Department of Public Instruction and specifically to Connie Haas, Beverly Kniess, Jack Kean, and Sue Grady. Each spent many extra hours assisting with the development of this guide. Without their dedication and energy, this guide would not have been possible.

Division for Academic Excellence
Jack Kean, Assistant State Superintendent
Sue Grady, Director, Content and Learning Team
Gerhard Fischer, Education Program Coordinator
Connie Haas, Program Assistant

Office of the State Superintendent
Victoria Horn, Graphics Designer
Mark Ibach, Publications Editor
Sandi McNamer, Publications Director

Brent Sandrock provided the image representing Wisconsin world languages standards.
Impressions Book and Journal Services, Inc., provided editing services for this publication.

Copyrighted Materials
Every effort has been made to determine proper ownership of copyrighted materials and to obtain permission for this use. Any omission is unintentional.

Contents

Foreword iii
Task Force iv
Acknowledgments v
Introduction ix

PART I — Creating Curriculum 1

CHAPTER 1 — Introduction to Wisconsin's Standards for Learning World Languages 3
What is the Vision of Wisconsin's Standards for Learning World Languages? 3
What Do We Expect Students to Know and Be Able to Do as a Result of Instruction
    in Another Language? 6
Overview to Wisconsin's Standards for Learning World Languages 6
What Is the Bridge from Standards to the Classroom? 14
    Linking Standards-Based Assessment to Curriculum and Instruction 14

CHAPTER 2 — Implications of Standards for Curriculum and Assessment 17
A Standards-Based Curriculum: How Can it Help? 17
A Mind-Set for Curriculum 19
A Mind-Set for Assessment 23
Performance Guidelines Linked to Key Questions: Context 31
Characteristics of Interpersonal, Interpretive, and Presentational Communication:
    Implications for Assessment 35
Characteristics of a Standards-Based Curriculum: A New Basis for Articulation 39

CHAPTER 3 — Creating a Standards-Based Curriculum 43
Introduction: The Curriculum Design Process 46
Implications of a Standards-Based Design in Curriculum Planning: The Mind-Set 48
The Process for Developing Units in a Standards-Based Curriculum 50
Planning for Instruction 58

CHAPTER 4 — Standards-Based Curriculum Units 61
What's Different? 61
Sample Templates for Designing Curriculum 61
Benchmark Examples of Thematic Content Across Language Levels, K–12:
    Work and Career Units 63
Sample Thematic Curriculum Units: Grouped by Level 96

PART II — Issues Impacting Instruction 139

Chapter 5 — The Role of the Student in a Standards-Based Curriculum 141
Instruction Flowing from a Curriculum of Standards-Based Assessment 141
Brain-Compatible Learning 142
Welcoming Brain-Friendly Learning 142

Tuning Teaching to Learning, Memory, Attention, and Motivation................... 143
The Impact of Threat on Inhibiting Language Acquisition 149
The Role of Enrichment in Enhancing Language Acquisition...................... 152
Working with the Brain for World Language Acquisition and Learning 157
Lesson Planning for Brain-Compatible World Language Acquisition 163

CHAPTER 6 **The Role of Methodology in a Standards-Based Curriculum............. 165**
Factors Shaping Language Learning and Teaching Today..................... 165
From Theory to Practice 173

PART III **Issues Impacting Language Programs 175**

CHAPTER 7 **Considerations for Building Effective Programs 177**
Components of High Quality World Language Programs 177
Practical Considerations.. 179
Characteristics of Effective Foreign Language Instruction 180
Program Enrichment Opportunities 182
Considerations for Designing Foreign Language
  in the Elementary School (FLES) Programs 184
Planning for Success: Common Pitfalls in the Planning
  of Early Foreign Language Programs 185

CHAPTER 8 **Related Issues... 191**
Why Language Learning Matters 191
Why Learn Another Language?... 198
Considerations for Heritage Speakers 199
Use of Technology in World Language Instruction......................... 202

Part IV **Resources 215**
Curriculum Planning Template—Blank 218
Annotated Curriculum Planning Template 220
Key Questions: Thematic Topics 222
Wisconsin's Model Academic Standards for Foreign Languages............... 223
  Overview of Foreign Languages 226
  Content and Performance Standards 228
  Wisconsin Performance Guidelines................................... 236
  Sample Student Performance Tasks 241
Language Functions: A Different View of Structures and Vocabulary 255

Introduction

Wisconsin's *Guide to Curriculum Planning in Foreign Language* began a major shift in curriculum, assessment, and instruction in world language classrooms throughout the state and across the nation when introduced in 1986. Teachers were challenged to create curriculum that focused on student performances described as communicative functions rather than one that merely consisted of a list of content to cover. Instructional practices changed to teach in such a way as to achieve these communicative objectives. The focus switched from teaching students to describe language to helping students use that language. During the next decade, first our national *Standards for Foreign Language Learning* (1996) and then Wisconsin's *Model Academic Standards for Foreign Languages* (1997) moved teachers in their curriculum, assessment, and instruction to concentrate even more on what students need to know and be able to do to use a new language.

What has changed? Instead of beginning with a grammatical sequence and lists of vocabulary to learn, curriculum centers on the standards, describing what students can *do with* the target language versus what they can *say about* it. This switch in the unit and lesson-planning cycle is the basis of this new guide to planning curriculum for learning world languages. The value of designing curriculum units beginning from the mind-set of the standards and working backwards to the level of grammatical structures and vocabulary was confirmed by participants in various workshops and summer institutes during the development of this guide, from 1999 through 2001. Participants made clear they didn't want standards that dictated what to teach. Rather, they appreciated standards that provided common goals, a path to follow.

The members of the writing task force were influenced in the development of this guide by their own classroom experiences and reading of research. Documents that influenced this guide included the previous Wisconsin foreign language curriculum guide, our national and state foreign language standards, the oral proficiency guidelines of the American Council on the Teaching of Foreign Languages (ACTFL), ACTFL's Performance Guidelines for K–12 Learners, and standards-based curriculum guides from other states.

A key part of the development process was working with teachers around the state in workshops, institutes, presentations, discussions, and feedback sessions. The curriculum development process and the template for developing curriculum units were piloted with teachers in various venues. The writing task force is deeply indebted to the contributions, comments, suggestions, and examples provided by our teaching colleagues from all over Wisconsin and across the country.

I am personally and deeply grateful to the talented writing task force that brought this guide out of our discussion phase and created the useful document before you. Each team member made major contributions throughout the development process, including lead authorship on particular chapters: Donna Clementi (Chapter 3, "Creating a Standards-Based Curriculum," and Chapter 7, "Considerations for Building Effective Programs"), Karen Fowdy (Chapter 8, "Use of Technology in World Language Instruction"), Pat Hoch (Chapter 8, "Why Learn Another Language" and "Considerations for Heritage Speakers"), Paul Hoff (Chapter 6, "Role of Methodology in a Standards-Based Curriculum"), and Jody Schneider (Chapter 5, "Role of the Student in a Standards-Based Curriculum"). All writing team members worked together to develop the sample standards-based curriculum units (Chapter 4). Through our collaboration we all gained tremendous insight into how standards impact the development of curriculum and influence our assessment and instructional practices.

Why the switch from *foreign* to *world* languages? It's time. "Foreign language" is a commonly recognized title for our subject area, but it has always been problematic. Our professional community continues the debate, but the change has been supported in pilot testing across the state as we strive to move away from *foreign* with its connotation of "alien." The switch to *world languages* emphasizes that languages connect us rather than keep us separated, that languages help us understand the world and participate in multilingual communities. Many people within the United States use in their home or community the languages taught in our schools, so there is nothing foreign about it. At the beginning of the third millennium, we want to emphasize helping students make other languages their own.

This guide will help us design curriculum for learning world languages that will bring the standards into our classrooms. By using it, we will find ourselves, from kindergarten through senior year of college and beyond, on the same path, developing students who can use a second or third language in ways that are valuable in the real world.

Paul Sandrock, Consultant
World Languages Education
Department of Public Instruction
Madison, Wisconsin
July 2002

Part I
Creating Curriculum

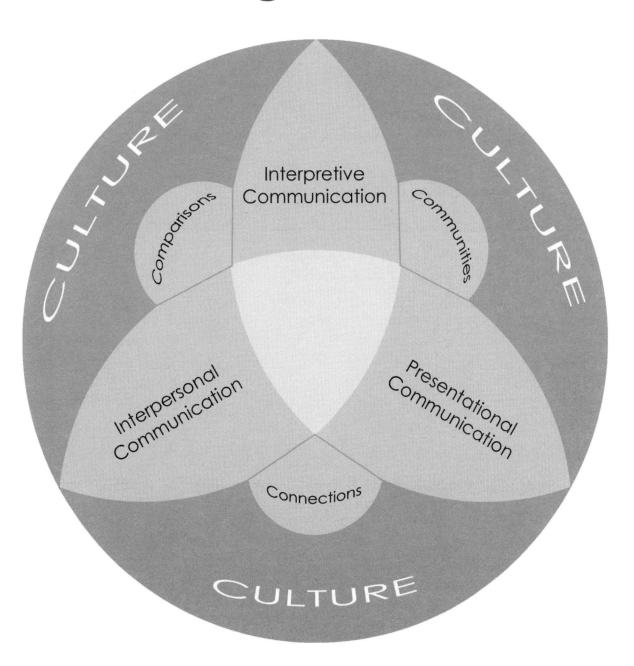

Introduction to Wisconsin's Standards for Learning World Languages

> What is the Vision of Wisconsin's Standards for Learning World Languages?
> What Do We Expect Students to Know and Be Able to Do as a Result of Instruction in Another Language?
> Overview of Wisconsin's Standards for Learning World Languages
>   Communication
>   Culture
>   Connections
>   Comparisons
>   Communities
> What Is the Bridge from Standards to the Classroom?
>   Linking Standards-Based Assessment to Curriculum and Instruction
> References

As citizens of this planet, we see boundaries between countries and cultures rapidly giving way to a new global community, a connected community. Technology is providing this connection, opening the doors to more communication and access to new information. In work, study, and leisure, people are crossing borders, moving several times throughout their lives, changing jobs, and traveling great distances. Children growing up in this interconnected world need more than basic reading, writing, and mathematics skills. The ability to understand and communicate in more than one language in order to be a responsible, active member of this global community is a critical skill. As diversity increases, the future leaders of our country need to broaden their perspectives and understandings of other people and their cultures. Understanding other cultures and how people use language to communicate their views is fundamental to this mind-set.

What is the Vision of Wisconsin's Standards for Learning World Languages?

In the 1990s the National Standards in Foreign Language Education Project brought together a wide array of educators, organizations, and interested individuals to develop standards for language learning in the United States. The resulting document, *Standards for Foreign Language Learning: Preparing*

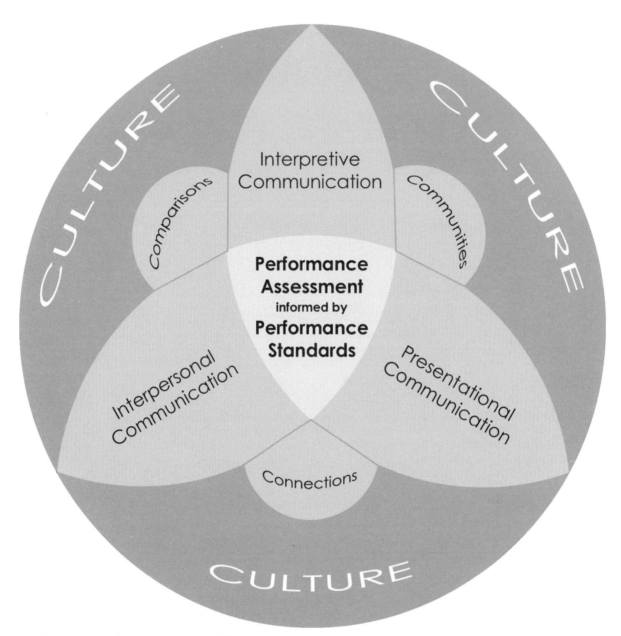

Curriculum Design for Learning World Languages
In a world language classroom, standards influence the curriculum, assessment, and instruction. The three purposes of Communication (interpersonal, interpretive, and presentational) form the heart. Culture is always embedded in the instruction. Connections, Comparisons, and Communities enrich the learning activities. The performance standards inform the assessments that show students their progress toward higher levels of proficiency in using the target language. The focus is on what students can do with the language they are learning.

for the 21st Century, provides a bold vision and clear framework for language learning. Specifically, the standards identify and describe 11 content standards based on the organizing theme of five interconnected C's: *Communication, Culture, Connections, Comparisons,* and *Communities.*

Following the publication of this national document, a state task force developed *Wisconsin's Model Academic Standards for Foreign Languages.* The Wisconsin content standards were adopted from the national standards and define what students should know and be able to do. The Wisconsin Standards include performance standards to describe how students will show achievement of the content standards and Performance Guidelines to assess how well students are able to do what is described in the performance standards.

Since their publication, these national and state standards have had a powerful impact on the teaching profession, creating a new vision for learning languages. They have challenged educators to reconsider what it means to know and use a language, resulting in the development of new approaches to curriculum, classroom instruction, and student assessment. The major shift is to look at language learning not as an abstract study of vocabulary, grammar, and linguistics, but as a useful tool to meet the demands of contemporary life. Standards give us the purposes for learning languages and direct teaching toward those purposes. The standards show that communication has natural connections to cultural awareness and understanding, other academic disciplines, and the world in which we live.

The world language standards describe the pathway that develops skills for using a language and understanding a culture, skills that have multiple benefits (see chapter 8). The world language standards describe what students can expect to accomplish in a continuous sequence of instruction from kindergarten through Grade 12. Even though today few districts have sequential programs that begin in elementary grades, the standards represent what the public desires from Wisconsin's language programs: *a high level of language proficiency.* To achieve such high standards, students must begin to study the second language in elementary grades. Beginning later means that students will not reach the highest levels of proficiency described in the standards.

The world language standards provide a common vision across program lines, a vision to connect goals for language learning at the elementary school, middle school, and senior high levels. Since language programs in Wisconsin begin in so many different grades, the standards do not have grade level targets; rather, they have proficiency targets, described for four levels of language learning: beginning, developing, transitioning, and refining. These titles characterize the student's development of language skills. These levels provide a common vision for preparing students to make the transition from high school to technical colleges, two-year colleges, or four-year institutions.

The key shift in using standards to guide language programs is moving from an emphasis on teaching to a focus on learning. Standards tell us what the student does, not what the teacher does; the targeted performance for students is described, not what the teacher does to create that performance.

The major shift is to look at language learning not as an abstract study of vocabulary, grammar, and linguistics, but as a useful tool to meet the demands of contemporary life.

The key shift in using standards to guide language programs is moving from an emphasis on teaching to a focus on learning.

What Do We Expect Students to Know and Be Able to Do as a Result of Instruction in Another Language?

The standards for learning world languages are summarized by five words all beginning with the letter *C*. These standards capture the purposes for learning a language and thus direct the content choices, the learning activities, and the means of assessment in the classroom. The purposes are described in terms of what students will know and be able to do as a result of instruction. These five C's are

- Communication
- Cultures
- Connections
- Comparisons
- Communities

Overview of Wisconsin's Standards for Learning World Languages

Five C's—Four Language Levels

Our national standards gave us the words of the five C's and the specific standards that describe each *C*. A major contribution to teaching world languages was the description of communication as three modes: interpersonal, interpretive, and presentational. Wisconsin's content standards are identified by the letters A through K. (See Table 1.1.) Under the C's of Communication and Culture, performance standards describe what the *C* looks like in the language learning classroom across four levels of language development. The four language levels illustrate students' increasing proficiency as they move from *beginning* language skills, to *developing* their ability to use the target language, to *transitioning* into more creative application of the target language, and finally reaching a stage of *refining* their language proficiency. The performance standards under the three C's of Connections, Comparisons, and Communities are not divided into language levels as the specific performances are differentiated only by a student's sophistication in using the target language, already described under the *C* of Communication.

TABLE 1.1 **Wisconsin's Standards for Learning World Languages: The Five C's**

Language Levels	Communication Three Modes			Culture	
	Interpersonal	Interpretive	Presentational	Practices	Products
Beginning	A	B	C	D	E
Developing	A	B	C	D	E
Transitioning	A	B	C	D	E
Refining	A	B	C	D	E

Language Levels	Connections		Comparisons		Communities	
	Across Disciplines	Added Perspective	Language	Culture	Practical Applications	Personal Enrichment
Same for all four levels	F	G	H	I	J	K

Communication: A—Interpersonal

Students in Wisconsin will engage in conversations, provide and obtain information, express feelings and emotions, and exchange opinions in a language other than their own.

Rationale: Students must know how to use the language effectively in order to exchange ideas and information with other people in a culturally appropriate manner. This standard focuses on the goal of learning to engage in conversations.

Interpersonal: Communicating successfully with another person or persons in an unrehearsed situation. This mode is characterized by spontaneous conversation where participants must actively negotiate meaning. Rehearsal or memorized dialogues represent a practice or training phase for interpersonal communication, but not the end in itself. They help students get comfortable with situations requiring spontaneous, unrehearsed communication. The interpersonal mode may employ speaking and listening (face-to-face or over the phone) or may employ reading and writing (E-mail exchanges, written telephone messages).

Communication: B—Interpretive

Students in Wisconsin will understand and interpret a language other than their own in its written and spoken form on a variety of topics.

Rationale: Students must develop strong listening and reading skills to interpret the concepts, ideas, and opinions expressed by members of other cultures through their media and their literatures. This standard focuses on increasing the level of understanding as students listen to, read, or view materials in their new language.

Interpretive: Understanding spoken and written language. As students advance in their language learning, they move from understanding the gist to picking up details, using context clues rather than just translating. Students learn to predict, guess, and use structures to aid meaning. Students need to interpret a wide variety of materials: brochures, magazine articles, Web sites, instructions, advertisements, and literature—all with a specific purpose in mind. The interpretive mode also includes listening and viewing. Students learn to understand spoken language, including radio and TV broadcasts, movies, speeches, and plays.

Communication: C—Presentational

Students in Wisconsin will present information, concepts, and ideas to an audience of listeners or readers on a variety of topics in a language other than their own.

Unique to the world language classroom is the focus on communication in another language. This is not talking about the second language or another culture in English; rather, it is using the second language to learn, to communicate, and to enter another culture.

Introduction to Wisconsin's Standards for Learning World Languages

> *Rationale:* Students must develop strong speaking and writing skills in order to communicate their thoughts, concepts, and opinions effectively to members of other cultures. This standard focuses on presenting information in a way that is appropriate for the audience.
>
> Presentational: A polished, practiced, and rehearsed presentation for an audience of listeners, readers, or viewers. With this mode, students become increasingly aware of the audience and how to communicate in a culturally appropriate way, including use of more formal, more stylized language as appropriate.

Communication does not occur in a vacuum, nor is it merely a process of translation.

Unique to the world language classroom is the focus on communication in another language. This is not talking *about* the second language or another culture in English; rather, it is *using* the second language to learn, to communicate, and to enter another culture.

Communication is not four separate skills of listening, speaking, reading, and writing to be taught and tested in isolation. Communication is defined as three modes that represent different purposes for using language:

- to engage in conversation, exchange ideas, or negotiate meaning with another person (interpersonal mode),
- to understand information that may be read, heard, or viewed (interpretive mode), and
- to express ideas or deliver information through speaking, writing, or showing (presentational mode)

The language learning standards constantly link to these three purposes and describe the pathway for developing increasing proficiency in using language in the interpersonal, interpretive, and presentational modes. Teachers design instruction based on the language purpose needed. The goal is to help students acquire the knowledge and skills necessary to use language for conversation (interpersonal), understanding (interpretive), or presentation of information (presentational). Learning vocabulary and grammar are no longer sufficient by themselves; rather, students learn the vocabulary and grammar they need in order to successfully communicate. The purpose behind the communication must drive all instructional decisions.

To study another language and culture gives one the powerful key to successful communication: knowing how, when, and why, to say what to whom.

National Standards 1996, 11

Each skill must be taught and tested in relation to its communicative purpose. For example, all writing cannot be evaluated in the same way. Writing an E-mail exchange with a friend is different from writing a short story, which is different from writing a business letter. In the first example, the meaning exchanged is paramount; lack of adherence to punctuation and spelling rules may not interfere with the communication as the receiver is more interested in what is being said. This is interpersonal communication. In writing a short story, negotiation of the meaning between the author and the reader is not possible so the accuracy of how the story is written becomes very important. In a business letter, the impression made by adhering to a culturally appropriate letter format and style is critical, and spelling errors would reflect poorly on the writer. These last two examples are presentational communication. In the classroom, when the purpose and intent of the communication differs, so too the expectation for accuracy and style of the writing must be different.

Looking at communication through the lens of these three modes helps teachers to answer many instructional questions. Since the communication modes represent the purposes of language use, each purpose can provide guidance on dictionary usage, reasonable expectations of accuracy, and the amount of spontaneity or rehearsal to build into an assessment.

Should Students Be Allowed to Use a Bilingual Dictionary?

During the preparation phase for a presentational task native speakers would use a dictionary to help make sure that the word choices and spellings are correct, but during an interpersonal conversation a native speaker would rarely use a dictionary since it would only slow down the conversation. In an interpretive task, particularly reading, students may be asked to use context clues or prediction to guess the meaning of words, or the teacher may decide to have students use a dictionary or may provide a glossary, depending on the instructional goal.

Should Accuracy Be One of the Criteria for Evaluation?

Accuracy is most important in presentational tasks, since the reader, listener, or viewer does not have the chance to clarify meaning with the author. With interpersonal communication, the negotiation of meaning is the most important factor and accuracy is important to ensure that the right message is transferred. In an interpretive task, accuracy focuses on how completely the student understood the message.

Should Students Practice the Assessment Task?

Presentational tasks call for prior preparation and access to resources to guarantee that the speaker or writer will be understood. Rough drafts and rehearsals are very appropriate for success. In interpersonal tasks, spontaneity is required, so students begin to build confidence in "thinking on their feet" to accomplish the task. In interpretive tasks, students should practice similar tasks in preparation for the assessment.

Communication does not occur in a vacuum, nor is it merely a process of translation. Successful communication is sensitive to cultural nuances and differences. For example, when someone in Guatemala uses the word *casa*, the image expressed does not equal the same thing that is expressed when a resident of Wisconsin says *house*. The object itself looks different and different objects may be found in various rooms within that home, while the basic purposes of a home are the same across cultures.

As stated in the national standards, to study another language and culture is "knowing how, when, and why, to say what to whom." (National Standards 1996, 11). This underlies the unbreakable link of communication to the next *C:* Cultures.

> ### Culture: D—Practices
>
> Students in Wisconsin will demonstrate an understanding of the relationship between the practices and perspectives of the cultures studied.
>
> *Rationale:* To fully understand another culture, students need to develop an awareness of another people's way of life, of the patterns of behavior that order their world, and of the traditional ideas, attitudes, and perspectives that guide their behaviors.

> ### Culture: E—Products
>
> Students in Wisconsin will demonstrate an understanding of the relationship between the products and perspectives of the cultures studied.
>
> *Rationale:* To respect and appreciate the diversity of their world, students need to learn about the contributions of other cultures to the world and the solutions they offer to problems confronting them. Awareness of these contributions helps students understand how their views and other people's views of the world have been influenced.

The standards for learning world languages go beyond mere collections of cultural facts. The culture standards stress the importance of learning the perspectives behind the products and practices of the cultures of people who speak the language being studied. The goal is to understand why the similarities or differences exist and how they help students understand another culture's perspective or view of the world.

In a curriculum, the communication standards are overarching, with the culture providing the underpinning of all communication. Communication and culture cannot be learned in isolation from each other. Learning becomes enduring, meaningful, and valuable when communication and culture are linked in each instructional unit.

Communication and culture find their definition in today's world through the last three C's of the standards. Communication and culture are made meaningful when learned in a real context. Both need a real purpose for using this knowledge and skill. That purpose is provided in the three C's of Connections, Comparisons, and Communities:

Culture provides the underpinning of all communication.

Learning a language is far more than an intellectual, cognitive challenge. It is a means to grow and mature through the experience of other cultures. It gives breadth and depth to our personalities. It allows us to approach problems differently because we have experienced different worlds; it allows us, as Proust says, to see with new eyes.

—Veronica Lacey

- Connections with other disciplines (providing content and insights)
- Comparisons (comparing and contrasting languages and cultures)
- Communities (real-life applications and lifelong learning)

These three goals provide the necessary context and enrich the learning activities.

Connections: F—Across Disciplines

Students in Wisconsin will reinforce and further their knowledge of other disciplines through a language other than English.

Rationale: The conscious effort to connect the study of languages with other disciplines opens doors to information and experiences that enrich students' entire lives. Students can use information and skills learned in other classes to practice their new language. Conversely, language classes provide additional information to enhance what students learn in other disciplines.

Connections: G—Added Perspective

Students in Wisconsin will acquire information and recognize the distinctive viewpoints that are available only through a language and its cultures.

Rationale: Being able to access information in more than one language gives students a much richer base of knowledge. Not only is there a greater choice of resources but there is also the opportunity to analyze a topic from another culture's perspective, providing students with unique insights.

This standard creates a context that brings the curriculum of other disciplines into the classroom. Likewise, students take insights from the language classroom out into the classrooms of other disciplines.

The *C* of Connections provides a broader concept of the content within the language classroom. A context needs to be established for communication. The pool of potential content in a language classroom is virtually limitless. This standard creates a context that brings the curriculum of other disciplines into the language classroom. For example, a language teacher in an elementary school may use the life cycle of the butterfly as the context for learning Japanese. Students act out the various phases from caterpillar to butterfly, describe how they feel at different points of the butterfly's life, describe what the insect looks like in each phase, make comparisons with other animals' lives, trace migration routes of butterflies found in Wisconsin, fill in charts to capture the information learned, and make butterfly kites. All of this practices language at the learner's beginning level, using very simple phrases and descriptions to talk about butterflies, learning to describe things, make comparisons, and tell simple stories. At the same time, the learner is using language to gain knowledge in science. The content is interesting and important. The students are engaged both in the content and the use of language. The goals of language learning do not suffer; the content choice is made from a broader base brought into the language classroom.

Likewise, as a result of the knowledge gained about another culture or about how to communicate in another language, students take insights from the language classroom out into the classrooms of other disciplines. Students often report how they shared some information, perspective, or insight in another class that their non-foreign-language peers did not know. This may be sharing information about the relationships of families and the elderly in another culture during a discussion in their family and consumer education class, telling important details about the French Revolution in a world history course, or explaining to their English class how language is constantly changing through examples from their German course.

Learning a second language has tremendous impact on one's first language.

Comparisons: H—Language

Students in Wisconsin will demonstrate understanding of the nature of language through comparisons of the language studied and their own.

Rationale: Students who study more than one language gain insight into the nature of their own language and can analyze the power of word choice. They can compare how different language systems express meaning and reflect culture.

Comparisons: I—Culture

Students in Wisconsin will demonstrate understanding of the concept of culture through comparisons of the cultures studied and their own.

Rationale: Students who study more than one language continuously compare and contrast the practices of people in different cultures. This helps students understand themselves better and builds understanding of different responses to similar situations.

Comparisons lead us to see common concepts about language and about culture. The comparisons help students understand that as many similarities exist as differences. Furthermore, students gain a greater understanding of their own language and culture through these comparisons.

Learning a second language has tremendous impact on one's first language. Students are looking at language from a new perspective and are more attentive to how language is formed and what is necessary to get across one's meaning than when they are using their native language. In their native language, students are able to express meaning and may not be very observant as to how that meaning is created. When trying to express meaning or understand in another language, students do learn to pay attention to how this happens, which has the effect of being attentive to the same elements of language in their native language. Students in French, German, and Spanish immersion schools in Milwaukee earn higher scores in reading and language on Wisconsin's state assessments than their counterparts in regular elementary schools, even though they learned how to read and write and express themselves in a world language and were tested in English.

In bringing cultural comparisons to the language classroom, the teacher can broaden the learning context to include cultures in countries that speak languages other than the one being studied. When learning about families in French class, information about families in Nigeria, Japan, and India is just as valuable as information about families from Quebec. The discussion will be in French, but the cultural knowledge will extend to include a broader view. The goal is for students to learn universal concepts of culture: What do people have in common? What are common differences? What makes a group unique? What are the factors that create and impact a culture? An important goal is for students to begin to look at their own culture with a new lens, asking the same questions about the components of culture in their own country. Comparisons lead to insights.

Communities: J—Practical Applications

Students in Wisconsin will use the language both within and beyond the school setting.

Rationale: As businesses expand domestic and international markets, and as people of the world meet each other more often through face-to-face encounters and/or the use of technology, the need for students to be proficient in other languages becomes critical in order for the United States to maintain international respect and economic competitiveness.

Communities: K—Personal Enrichment

Students in Wisconsin will show evidence of becoming lifelong learners by using the language for personal enjoyment and enrichment.

Rationale: Students who study another language are better prepared to be responsible members of their communities because of their global perspective. They have expanded their employment opportunities both at home and abroad and have access to a wider variety of resources where they can pursue topics of personal interest.

The Communities standards ask students to connect with people who use the language in their school, work, or daily life.

This *C* reminds teachers to look beyond the four walls of the classroom in their instruction, to make sure that students see how to apply the skills and knowledge gained in that classroom. The standards under Communities ask the teacher to design lessons that help students make practical applications of their new language and use it for personal enrichment. Communities impacts what goes on in the classroom by extending the reach for resources beyond the textbook to include authentic materials, Internet sites, and current realia from the cultures of people who speak the language being studied. These standards ask students to seek out ways to connect with people who use the language in their school, work, or daily life. If native speakers of the language cannot be found in the local community, technology allows students to exchange information via E-mail or videoconferences with sister schools around the world or to search the Web literally worldwide for voices from other cultures.

Students also need to use their new language for personal enrichment. This is what provides ongoing motivation to improve their level of proficiency in using the language. Such enrichment through the target language may include reading literature, viewing plays or movies, exploring careers that involve knowledge of a second language, and expanding interests in areas influenced by other cultures, such as the arts.

This standards vision takes world languages far beyond a purely intellectual discipline, to essential knowledge, skills, attitudes, and understandings. World language instruction has a critical role in educating today's students, who truly are citizens in a connected world.

What Is the Bridge from Standards to the Classroom?

Linking Standards-Based Assessment to Curriculum and Instruction

In November 1995, world language teachers across the United States cheered a document that represented major professional consensus around what we teach: *Standards for Foreign Language Learning: Preparing for the 21st Century*. We quickly became familiar with and excited by the focus on five C's: Communication, Culture, Connections, Comparisons, and Communities. We found both comfort and challenge in the document as we began to implement the standards in our language programs in elementary schools, middle schools, and high schools. In November 1999, we received the next level of specificity: *Standards for Foreign Language Learning in the 21st Century*. This follow-up document gave us a language-specific version of the standards and extended the five C's into the postsecondary level, showing us standards for instruction K–16.

The 1999 document itself describes best the effects on the profession that national standards were already having:

> Standards preparation is forcing attention to the broader view of second language study and competence: what should students know and be able to do—and how well? Clearly, the foreign language standards provide the broader, more complete rationale for foreign language education that we have sought for decades but never managed to capture in words or in concept until now.
>
> *National Standards 1999, 15*

In our day-to-day teaching, however, we soon realized that this broad view was not sufficient by itself to focus student learning. A bridge from the standards to the classroom was necessary. That bridge is the triangular interrelationship of curriculum, instruction, and standards-based assessment. This is the shift: Language teachers now begin by generating their assessment from the standards, focus their curriculum on the standards-based assessments, and plan their instruction in order to prepare students for the assessments, which then provide evidence that the students have achieved the language learning goals as described in the standards.

This switch in the unit and lesson planning cycle is the basis of this new guide to planning curriculum for learning world languages. The process of designing units beginning from the mind-set of the standards and working backward to the level of grammatical structures and vocabulary was confirmed by participants in various summer workshops. What might an example look like? Think of most beginning language experiences, whether it's teaching seventh graders French, first graders Japanese, or ninth graders German, Latin, or Spanish. Instead of beginning with a list of numbers, colors, the alphabet, and the days of the week, the first step in planning a unit of instruction is to identify a logical beginning context. Language at the beginning level centers around answering the questions "Who am I? Who are you?" As students begin to learn a new language they will want to introduce and describe themselves and to talk about others. With such a context in mind, and reading the communication standards, teachers will now select vocabulary to teach that helps students describe people (physical and personality traits). Colors might enter *as needed* to describe clothing, or one's house, or one's hair. Numbers might enter *as needed* to talk about how many siblings or pets someone has, or how old family members are, or an address. The context is now driving the decision about what to teach. Teachers will develop the unit in order to accomplish the standards: "Ask and answer questions, including biographical information," "Write and present a short narrative about themselves," and "Observe and imitate appropriate patterns of behavior (such as greetings or gestures) used with friends and family in the cultures studied." This is not a unit to teach and complete one standard, but is a unit driven by multiple standards, designed to motivate students as they learn to use a new language for meaningful communication.

Do we still need to teach some vocabulary and some structures? Of course. Students need and want some language pieces to pull together for a communicative purpose. So, what has changed? It's the beginning point. It's identifying the communicative goal first, rather than teaching the vocabulary and structures and then trying to find a purpose for using these isolated lists and concepts.

[Adapted and reprinted with permission from Sandrock, 2001.]

This switch in the unit and lesson planning cycle is the basis of this new guide to planning curriculum for learning world languages. The process of designing units begins from the mind-set of the standards and works backward to the level of grammatical structures and vocabulary.

References

National Standards in Foreign Language Education Project. 1996. *Standards for Foreign Language Learning: Preparing for the 21st Century.* Lawrence, Kans.: Allen Press.
———. 1999. *Standards for Foreign Language Learning in the 21st Century.* Lawrence, Kans.: Allen Press.
Sandrock, Paul. 2001. Bringing Our Standards into Our Classrooms. *Voice of WAFLT* 29:1, pp. 7–8.
Wisconsin Department of Public Instruction. 1997. *Wisconsin's Model Academic Standards for Foreign Languages.* Madison, Wis.: Wisconsin Department of Public Instruction.

Implications of Standards for Curriculum and Assessment

> A Standards-Based Curriculum: How Can It Help?
> A Mind-Set for Curriculum
>   How Does a Standards-Based Curriculum Differ from a Traditional Curriculum?
>   How Do Standards Change Our View of Curriculum and Assessment?
> A Mind-Set for Assessment
>   The Role of Standards in Assessment
>   Performance Assessments: Linking the Three Modes of Communication
>   Designing Assessment Units Incorporating All Three Communication Modes
>   Using the Performance Guidelines as a Mind-Set to Set Realistic Expectations
> Performance Guidelines Linked to Key Questions: Context
> Characteristics of Interpersonal, Interpretive, and Presentational Communication: Implications for Assessment
> Characteristics of a Standards-Based Curriculum: A New Basis for Articulation
> References

A Standards-Based Curriculum: How Can It Help?

I keep hearing about these standards, but I have to know what to teach. The standards tell me what students are supposed to be able to do, but they don't tell me what to teach.

These are common sentiments expressed as teachers discuss how to bring the standards into their classroom. While these thoughts may be expressed as a problem, these ideas really provide a framework for understanding the solution.

The standards tell me what students are supposed to be able to do.

The broad standards written as our national professional consensus say that students should learn to use their new language for three purposes: to communicate interpersonally, to interpret, or to present information and ideas. In Wisconsin, our standards are further defined as learning goals for students in terms of what a student's performance looks like at four different levels of language development. These performance standards describe what students should be learning to do, such as "ask and answer questions, including biographical information" or "tell a story incorporating some description and detail."

The standards don't tell me what to teach.

The standards are written as learning targets, what students should be able to do. They cannot be seen as a list to be taught one at a time and then checked off. It doesn't work to say that I will teach one unit on one standard and then be done with it, moving on to conquer another standard. We know that students learn a new language in a spiral, coming back over and over again to the same skills, grammatical structures, and vocabulary, and using them in a variety of ways, increasing the complexity and accuracy over time. Standards are a mind-set: think of the standards as the goals that are driving every instructional decision in our classrooms. Use the standards to help plan units of instruction and to create the assessments that show student progress toward these goals.

> *When I first started teaching Spanish, I would look at my curriculum's list of grammar concepts and vocabulary and then try to figure out how to make them interesting and easy to learn. I would create a context for learning commands or -AR verbs or the imperfect subjunctive. What my textbook and my curriculum didn't make clear were the bottom-line objectives of what the student was supposed to be able to do. I never knew how much of the grammar concept to teach. How many of the irregular forms did students need? How much of the philosophical background of the concept was important or useful to know? When could I consider my teaching done?*

Standards turn around this planning cycle so that we begin with what we want students to be able to do. Once we know what success looks like, once we have in mind the goals we are working on and the way that students will show their achievement, we can decide what grammar and vocabulary they need in order to be successful. We can decide what grammar and vocabulary are needed in order to reach the goal.

[Adapted and reprinted with permission from Sandrock 2001.]

During the development of standards in Wisconsin, colleagues across disciplines shared several metaphors to help understand what standards really are. One metaphor clearly described the relationship linking standards and curriculum: standards are like the food pyramid. The chart showing the six basic food groups is a guide to good eating. A daily balance of the basic food groups will lead to better health. The description of the food groups does not lead to standardization of eating habits or minimal choices at grocery stores or restaurants. We have a variety of menus available to us, just as curriculum can vary. The food groups are interpreted through the specific context of the population being served. Specific purposes may lead to creative presentation of the food groups in a wide variety of ethnic menus. The food groups guide the choices in the daily, monthly, or yearlong menus we create and implement.

The same applies to language learning, where standards guide our choices, but the curriculum needs to fit the context of the age of the learners, their interests and motivations, and any special focus such as a career or travel need. Even two teachers teaching the same course in the same school don't need to offer identical lessons if over time they are focused on the same overarching goals and work to prepare students to be able to do the same kinds of tasks in the target language.

A standards-based curriculum provides key markers for teachers, students, and parents to know that the instruction is on the right path. Rather than providing only one specific path, a standards-based curriculum makes multiple journeys possible. The goals are the same, even though students might follow somewhat different routes to get there.

A Mind-Set for Curriculum

How Does a Standards-Based Curriculum Differ from a Traditional Curriculum?

> While this document suggests the types of content and curricular experiences needed to enable students to achieve the standards, and supports the ideal of extended sequences of study, it does not describe specific course content, nor a recommended scope and sequence.
>
> *National Standards 1999, 28*

Standards have broadened our sense of what it is we teach and why. Instead of just focusing on what facts and information we should teach our students, standards force us to state the essence of our discipline, that is, not just what students should know but also what they should be able to do in order to show that they have learned a language. Since standards serve as the pathway for developing higher and higher levels of proficiency in using a language and entering a culture, we need to organize our instruction differently. What we need is a clear target for the instruction: assessment focused on capturing real evidence of achieving the standards.

The concept of curriculum and assessment has changed in this standards era. What used to be linear and sequential now becomes more like a jigsaw puzzle, with a variety of pieces forming a picture of a competent speaker. Curriculum used to be a list of grammar and vocabulary, each assigned to a specific course where it was taught, or at least "covered." Testing followed this curriculum, providing evidence of the students' ability to memorize lists of vocabulary and to manipulate grammatical rules, but the degree to which students could *use* this grammar and vocabulary in a real-life situation caused frustration in both the students and their teachers. When standards-based performance assessment becomes the heart of the curriculum, however, the focus is switched to how students can show their use of the language. These assessment targets, captured in the curriculum, truly direct instruction in the classroom. Each instructional decision is made by asking, "What do my students need in order to be successful in the assessment?"

The logic of learning how to do things is also different from the logic of an explanation. Attempts to perform begin with a specific goal in mind, an end that shapes how the content is introduced and unfolds. People don't need the whole subject laid out to master a challenge; rather, they need specific knowledge tools to accomplish a specific task. The requirements of the task, not an outline of topics, supply the logic of instructional design.

Wiggins and McTighe 1998, 137

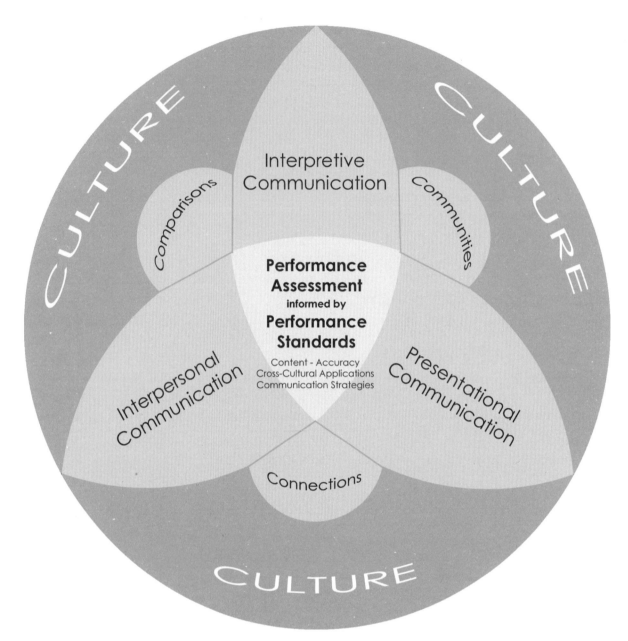

In a world language program, curriculum centers on performance assessment tasks that bring the Wisconsin performance standards into a classroom focus. Communication is embedded in Culture and enriched by Connections, Comparisons, and Communities. The Wisconsin Performance Guidelines add the criteria for evaluation, criteria that mark progress through four levels of language learning. Students' language performances can be judged on the basis of the content, accuracy, communication strategies, and cross-cultural applications.

Curriculum, assessment, and instruction are inseparable. Today's language curriculum describes what students need to do to demonstrate that they have reached the standards. Based on this target performance, what students need to know in order to accomplish this performance is delineated. Assessment now drives curriculum choices and instruction.

How Do Standards Change Our View of Curriculum and Assessment?

The *Standards for Classical Language Learning* explains what a standards document is *not*:

> It is not a curriculum for a Latin or Greek course; it is not a guide for daily lesson planning. *Standards for Classical Language Learning* does not mandate methodology; it is not textbook bound. It does not tell how to teach. It provides a destination, not a road map.
>
> *National Standards 1999, 159*

Creating curriculum, then, is no small task; it is a journey. Curriculum should capture and communicate our beliefs about the essence of what we teach. The essential components that will guide our instructional decisions need to be captured for ourselves, for our teaching colleagues, for the teachers of the levels/grades that follow, for our administrators, (to understand our focus, so that they can provide helpful feedback from classroom observations and in performance evaluations), for parents, and for students.

Creating curriculum, then, is no small task; it is a journey.

**A Standards-Based Curriculum:
What Does It Provide for Us?**

For the classroom teacher—guides lesson planning, focusing on broad goals, allowing teachers to make choices to meet the needs and interests of the students

For the teacher of the next level—outlines evidence of students' real achievement

For administrators—provides focus for classroom observations

For the community—provides a basis for accountability

For students—gives a real-world purpose for learning a new language

---

In designing a day's lesson, what goes through a teacher's mind? On what basis are the many decisions made? If you can turn to a curriculum that embodies the major goals for a course, and that clearly places those goals in the flow of an entire program's goals, then you will make sure that you are aimed at the correct target as you decide what students will need in the context of the current unit in order to show achievement of the year's goals. Without such a target, classroom decisions might be made on the basis of an activity that looks good, an exercise that worked last year, or an isolated piece of knowledge that needs to be checked off. Testing would focus on isolated pieces of the puzzle, checking off vocabulary and grammatical structures

Curriculum should capture and communicate our beliefs about the essence of what we teach.

taken out of context. Without clear communication standards, testing rarely gives students the opportunity to put the pieces together into a real situation, one in which students need to use multiple skills and various components of language to accomplish their communicative purpose.

This does not mean that vocabulary and grammatical structures have no place in a standards-based curriculum; rather, they are placed in their proper role of supporting students' achievement of the performances described in the standards. They are not, however, the goals of instruction; vocabulary and grammatical structures are tools that students manipulate with increasing accuracy, both linguistic and cultural, to achieve the purpose of communication as described in the standards. In my first years of teaching, if asked what I was teaching in a given week, I would have replied with a grammatical term such as object pronouns or the irregular forms of the preterite tense. Today, I would say I'm helping students learn to ask questions, questions that require their conversational partners to provide details and description. I would teach some vocabulary and some question formation, but my focus would be on how students were able to use them in order to better communicate. Assessment would then provide evidence of how well students were able to use the tools they had learned in real and purposeful communication.

Performance standards answer the question of what students should know and be able to do, providing the first key component of a standards-based curriculum. Wisconsin's performance standards are based on national standards. The state performance standards capture the goal for instruction and for assessment by describing the expected student performance more explicitly than in the broader national document. Wisconsin's performance standards combine the functional use and purpose of language with the targeted level of proficiency.

National Standards to State Standards: From Broad Goals to Specific Skills

National Standards:

Interpersonal: engage in conversations, provide and obtain information, express feelings and emotions, and exchange opinions

Interpretive: understand and interpret a language other than their own in its written and spoken form on a variety of topics

Presentational: present information, concepts, and ideas to an audience of listeners or readers on a variety of topics

State Performance Standards: Beginning Level

Interpersonal: ask and answer questions

Interpretive: understand spoken and written language that has strong visual support

Presentational: write and present a short narrative about their personal lives

Curriculum, then, describes the path for learning a language. Curriculum provides clear markers that lay out the route to follow as students progress in their use of a new language and their understanding of another culture. A standards-driven model of curriculum and assessment gives the teacher the indicators and topics that will help students chart their progress as language learners, indicators that are not just lists of vocabulary or grammar, but functional goals that are both within reach and motivating in their challenge.

[Adapted with permission from Sandrock 2000.]

A Mind-Set for Assessment

"Learning is what you do for Friday's quiz and then you forget by Tuesday."
Rosie, age 14

"Acquisition is when you soak stuff up like a sponge and it sticks with you."
Tom, age 14

Shorewood (WI) Intermediate School
(Provided by Pablo Muirhead, Spanish Teacher, Shorewood School District)

Imagine a typical test in school:
Okay, class, it's time for today's test. Take out a piece of lined paper. Listen carefully and follow all of the instructions. Remember, no talking!
First, at the top of the paper, write the name of your elementary school.
Next, write the word kindergarten and then the numbers one through six down the left side of your paper.
Next to each grade, write the name of the teacher you had for that grade.
Next to each teacher's name, write the room number where you went each day in that grade.
Next to the room number, list one field trip taken that year.
Finally, list how many students were in your class in each grade.

Imagine a different approach to finding out what the student knows and can do:
You've just received a letter from your elementary school announcing that you are to be honored as the alumnus of the year. You will give a short speech at your elementary school about the education you received there and what it meant to you. To get ready to write your speech, you need to remember what it was like in your elementary school.

First, close your eyes and think about your elementary school. Can you picture the building? Walk through the front door. What do you see, hear, smell, feel? Think of as many associations as you can as you walk around your elementary building. Think of what went on in each room, in different years, with different teachers. What special events or field trips shaped your experience?

Let us imagine an educative assessment system that is designed to improve, not just audit, student performance.

Grant Wiggins 1998, 1

On a piece of paper, list the words that came to mind as you did your mental tour of your elementary school.

All done? Okay, now share your list with a partner. Find out what words you both wrote down. Ask questions to find out more about words you have that are different. Feel free to add any new ideas to your list.

Did you have a good conversation? Now look at your list of words and images from your elementary school and pull out three words that seem to capture what your elementary school education really meant to you. You may want to link several ideas together and give the cluster a new word title that sums up the idea you have in mind. Are there other words you want to link to the three you have chosen as a summary? Connect words, phrases, and images to the three key words you selected.

Now you are ready to write your acceptance speech. Take each of your three words and write several sentences explaining how that word represents what your elementary school education meant to you. When you have your three paragraphs, think of an interesting way to begin and end your speech.

Okay, how did you feel about the two assessments?

Conversation following the first test:
"From the minute I heard the word 'test,' I panicked! I couldn't think straight. I know I knew the answers, but I couldn't remember them."

"Yeah, I started out fine with the grades and the teachers. But when she said 'room numbers' I knew I was doomed!"

"I have a knack for numbers, and I actually got most of the rooms right, but the number of students, I just never thought she'd ask something like that."

"The only time I had any fun was thinking about the field trips. But even then, did it really matter which year they went with? They just kind of blended together in my mind and made elementary school what it was for me. What was the point of listing each trip by a grade level? I just made it up and hoped the teacher wouldn't really care to check it for accuracy anyway."

Conversation following the second test:
"Wow, I've never had a test like that before. It didn't even feel like a test. I felt like I would be evaluated on what was really important, not on the facts I was lucky enough to memorize."

"Can you imagine being able to talk to other kids during a test? And yet, it really helped me to remember some things that I just hadn't thought of on my list of what elementary school meant to me. I mean, the ideas came from me, but they came out of me because I was having a conversation with a peer."

"Yeah, and I really freaked when I first heard that we had to write a speech. But then we were led through a process that made me forget about the writing of a speech and simply helped me to work through a way to plan it. I actually learned something from this process that I can use again, namely how to go about organizing my thoughts before starting to write a paper."

"This was an assessment in which I could show what I could do. I think my students wouldn't mind this kind of assessment."

[Adapted from Sandrock 1998.]

While both tests elicit what students remember about their elementary schooling, only one simulates what people do in real life and helps students learn and practice. The first test is perfect for finding out specific facts that a student remembers, but cannot predict how well students will be able to use those facts. If we are trying to gather evidence of achieving our learning goals, our standards, we would probably share the teachers' reaction that this first test did not really gather the most important information. We need to look at how useful the information we learn from any test really is. Are we able to set future instructional goals based on the first test? Does the student find out what he or she needs to work on in the next unit of instruction? Can we make the assumption that the recall of facts indicates achievement of the performance standards?

Standards capture what students should know and be able to do with what they know. Assessment must evolve to provide evidence of achieving these goals. It is not a question of whether teaching to the test is good or bad; rather, the issue is whether it's the best way to assess. Standards-based assessment provides the vision of what the standards look like in terms of actual student performance.

The Role of Standards in Assessment

> The aim of assessment is primarily to *educate* and *improve* student performance, not merely to *audit* it.
>
> Wiggins 1998, 7

Through classroom assessment, teachers consciously or unconsciously tell students exactly what matters for learning the subject in that classroom. If classroom testing only focuses on the components of language, grammatical structures, and vocabulary, students will quickly put their energy into these elements and downplay all of the communicative activities the teacher may be doing. The match between goals and assessment must be clear not only to the teacher, but also to the students. If the communication standards are to truly count in the classroom, the teacher must make them the core of the classroom assessment.

Classroom assessment answers the question of how students will show achievement of the performance standards and captures how well students achieve these goals. The assessment needs to be specific enough to describe what students will do, but not so specific as to dictate only one possible per-

> *Assessment must capture the essence of the curriculum, the key elements of the instruction, embodying what we truly believe is the most important component of what is taught.*

We need to constantly ask ourselves if our assessment is gathering the right kind of evidence.

formance. Rather than asking students to translate a paragraph or fill in blanks with specific vocabulary, they are asked to do something like describe their family. Different students will describe their family by using different words and structures; some may present their description in written form, others orally, some via video, with the key criteria on which the students will be evaluated presented ahead of time through a descriptive rubric. Regardless of the mode used by the student, the teacher will be able to gauge each student's progress toward the goal. While there may be times that the teacher needs specific evidence of written versus oral presentation, the more summative the assessment, that is at the quarter, semester, or year level, the more open ended it needs to be. Assessment must capture the essence of the curriculum, the key elements of the instruction, embodying what we truly believe is the most important component of what is taught. We need to constantly ask ourselves if our assessment is gathering the right kind of evidence of students' achievement of the curriculum goals.

> ### How Are the Communication Standards Translated into Assessments?
>
> Interpersonal—To prepare for the first night at their host family's home, students pair up and practice what the conversation might be like. They share photographs to describe themselves and their home and community. They ask each other questions about their lives (home, school, family, likes and dislikes). This is videotaped.
>
> Interpretive—To check their success, the students watch three of the videotaped conversations and write down all that they learned about the students in the videotape.
>
> Presentational—Students present a description of themselves for the host family where they will be staying in Spain (oral, written, and/or video).

Performance Assessments: Linking the Three Modes of Communication

In designing assessment, teachers need to focus on what students will be expected to do as a result of the unit of instruction. This is a focus far beyond the list of what is to be covered; it is justifying what will be taught on the basis of what is necessary to achieve the end goal of the instruction. This changes the interplay between assessment and instruction. Traditionally, a teacher would teach the list of vocabulary and grammar and when those items in a textbook chapter had been covered, students would have a test. Designing with the end goal in mind requires that the teacher identify up front what the unit assessment will be, designing an application of the knowledge gained and the skills practiced during the unit. Students should be clear on what the hallmarks of a quality performance are, perhaps given in the form of a rubric, listing the criteria for evaluating the expected performance and describing these criteria in easy-to-understand terminology.

When we know where we are going, we can ensure that each day's lesson is focused on getting students to that destination. Designing with the end in mind helps drive the development of the daily lessons that come together to achieve the goals of a curriculum unit. Instead of doing three exercises out of the textbook because they are on sequential pages, the teacher will select those that are best targeted to moving students toward the assessment. The teacher will also adapt exercises in order to provide the necessary practice, such as turning a fill-in-the-blanks exercise into a question-and-answer activity for pairs.

The performance assessment can check progress over a relatively short period of time or at a quarter, semester, or year level. At all levels the performance assessment should incorporate all three modes of communication: interpersonal, interpretive, and presentational. In effect, the three performance modes form a unit of assessment, where one mode leads to the next.

In one scenario, beginning students would start by reading letters from pen pals describing their families and would fill in the information that could be understood from the letter to describe the family members. The next phase of the assessment unit would be presentational; the beginning students would write or present orally the description of their own family, prompted by a photograph. In the final phase of the assessment unit, an interpersonal task would have students ask each other questions about their families, trying to find out what they have in common and what is different. While this assessment is within a single context, that is, family, the skills and knowledge that students will use come from practice in a variety of contexts, including how to describe people (physically, clothing, character), vocabulary for family members, age, making simple comparisons, or even professions. While these language components may have been learned and even tested via quizzes in isolation, the performance assessment requires students to pull these pieces together and use them in a meaningful and motivating way.

When developing such a unit of assessment, there is no perfect order in which to arrange the modes of communication. Teachers have shared from their experiences with such assessment units that often beginning students need more preparation before doing the interpersonal task. Beginning students might benefit from having interpretive and presentational tasks as preparation prior to doing the interpersonal task. This supplies the student with more practice on the vocabulary and language structures from which to pull the memorized chunks of language that beginning students need and use to be successful in interpersonal tasks. By building up their repertoire, beginning students will be able to accomplish the interpersonal task.

At the unit level, all three modes should be assessed in every unit so students realize that all three modes are part of learning a language. K–12 students are developing literacy skills in their first language. Building literacy skills as they learn their second (or third) language coincides with what students are learning in their native language. At the beginning, students benefit from an extended listening phase. When care is taken to make this input comprehensible, students are able to understand more than they can produce in

While these language components may have been learned and even tested via quizzes in isolation, the performance assessment requires students to pull these pieces together and use them in a meaningful and motivating way.

the first years of learning a language. However, focusing only on listening and speaking in the beginning stage cannot prevent students from attempting to write down words and phrases in their own way. They should simultaneously be learning reading and writing skills to support listening and speaking when developmentally appropriate. All of these skills, rather than being taught in isolation or without a language purpose, should be taught within a context leading to meaningful and purposeful communication: interpersonal, interpretive, or presentational.

Designing Assessment Units Incorporating All Three Communication Modes

How does one design performance assessments? Chapter 3 provides a step-by-step guide to the development of an assessment unit that serves as the centerpiece of curriculum. This section focuses on designing assessment for the three modes of communication. The development of a unit often begins with brainstorming what students could do under the thematic context of the unit. Teachers generate a lot of activity ideas, sharing what students could do. Some of these activity ideas lead to end goals described as performance assessments. Others remain as ideas for learning various components of language, for practicing a thematic cluster of vocabulary, or for putting these together in some communicative whole. Students need to be led to constantly put together the pieces they are learning in order to work closer and closer to the approximation of the final goal. That goal is captured in the final assessments for a unit of instruction.

After identifying the specific performance standards for interpersonal, interpretive, and presentational modes as well as a thematic context, the curriculum must provide focus through performance assessment tasks that capture the target of what students will do at the end of a unit of instruction. The performance assessments allow students to show what they know and can do, through an application of their language learning. The performance assessment tasks clarify what the student is expected to do as a result of instruction. The assessment task brings the language learning into a real-life application, reinforcing that the student learned something worthwhile. If the unit's instructional goal is a test that merely involves filling in blanks, reproducing a memorized dialogue, or writing five sentences in past tense, the teacher has no real evidence that her students can apply what they have learned. Instead of relying on such substitute evidence, the unit assessment should provide evidence of achievement of the identified communication standards. To check if the assessment tasks accomplish this, ask the following questions:

1. Is there a sense of connectedness among the three modes?
   —Does one mode lead logically to the next?

> *The logic of application derives its sequence from specific performance goals. In coaching, we organize a sequence backward from specific tasks and standards: Lessons are derived from desired results. Here Whitehead's maxim of "get your knowledge and use it quickly" always applies: We head right to the desired performance, even if it has to be in simplified or scaffolded form (e.g., T-ball for six-year-olds); we build up performance progressively; and we revisit the fundamentals as we do so.*
>
> Wiggins and McTighe 1998, 144

—Are all three modes necessary in order to complete the picture?
—Is the picture complete when the three modes are completed?
2. Are the communication standards targeted in the performance appropriate for the task?
   —Are the most important standards identified?
   —Are the standards that were selected really critical to the performance?
   —Is the activity a real example of the performance standard?
3. Are students engaged in learning while they are doing the assessment?
   —Does the assessment blend with the instruction rather than stand out as a separate, unrelated item?
   —Will students receive meaningful feedback in order to improve their performance?
4. Are the expected performances set at the appropriate level? (Refer to the Performance Guidelines.)
   —Not too easy (just cosmetic).
   —Not too hard (input + 1, the idea that students are challenged to use language slightly above their current level of proficiency).
   —Do students have the opportunity to show that their language proficiency is increasing?
5. Is the unit worth doing?
   —Does the unit address the standards beyond the *C* of Communication in a significant way?
   —Is the task meaningful to the student?

Using the Performance Guidelines as a Mind-Set to Set Realistic Expectations

Performance Guidelines: An Overview

When designing standards-based performance assessment, the teacher must make sure each task is targeted at the appropriate level of language development. Performance guidelines provide realistic expectations for student performance. The Wisconsin Performance Guidelines are based on the Oral Proficiency Guidelines and the K–12 Performance Guidelines of the American Council on the Teaching of Foreign Languages (ACTFL). Experience suggests that students in K–12 programs are likely to achieve oral proficiency up to the level of intermediate-high. Based on this, the Wisconsin Performance Guidelines are divided into four broad levels, roughly covering the range of the novice and intermediate levels. The titles capture the nature of a student's progress: *beginning, developing, transitioning,* and *refining.* For each level, the Wisconsin Performance Guidelines break down broad descriptions into the specific components of language used in all three modes of communication.

TABLE 2.1 **Wisconsin's Standards for Learning World Languages: The Five C's**

Four Language Levels	Communication Three Modes			Culture	
	Interpersonal	Interpretive	Presentational	Practices	Products
Beginning	A	B	C	D	E
Developing	A	B	C	D	E
Transitioning	A	B	C	D	E
Refining	A	B	C	D	E

Language Levels Same for all four levels	Connections		Comparisons		Communities	
	Across Disciplines	Added Perspective	Language	Culture	Practical Applications	Personal Enrichment
	F	G	H	I	J	K

Wisconsin Performance Guidelines

Four Language Levels: Beginning, Developing, Transitioning, Refining

Content	Accuracy	Communication Strategies	Cross-Cultural Applications
• Complexity/ sophistication • Vocabulary • Spontaneity • Situation	• Time/tense • Ease • Pronunciation • Spelling/ orthography	• Comprehension • Comprehensibility • Monitoring • Clarification • Impact	• Verbal • Nonverbal • Awareness

Performance Standards and Performance Guidelines

The performance standards describe the broad content standards (A–K) in terms of what students will be able to do as they progress through four levels of language learning. For assessment and instruction, the Performance Guidelines answer the question of how good is good enough. The Performance Guidelines describe the expected performance at each of the four language levels. The Guidelines contain four major categories (content, accuracy, communication strategies, and cross-cultural applications) that are divided into a total of 16 subcategories to help describe specific aspects of interpersonal, interpretive, and presentational communication.

Performance Guidelines: Four Levels

One cannot look at these four levels of the performance guidelines and attach years to them, as level I, II, III, and IV. Each level is defined by what the student can do, not seat time. In addition, students do not learn in lockstep nor move all at once from one level to the next. Students are not limited to the descriptors under a single level to describe their abilities. Evaluation will reveal individual profiles in a student's performance, with some language components rated at a lower level and other components rated at a higher level than the majority of the student's ratings. At different stages in their language development, students will be stronger in different skills, for example, listening skills will be stronger than any language production at the beginning level; also, younger learners will be stronger in speaking than writing, since writing is not yet a strong skill in their native language.

Each performance level includes elements from the previous one, in increasingly strong and sustained ways. This is not linked to grade level or age. Beginners may be in any grade: kindergarten, seventh grade, ninth grade, or adults. Depending on the student's age or grade and program model when beginning to learn a language, the speed and style of learning will vary.

Since proficiency is a function of time and experience, students will not reach the refining level without an early beginning, early in the elementary grades. High school students will barely enter the transitioning level if they have only four years of instruction.

Proficiency is a function of time and experience.

Descriptions of Four Levels

Beginning: This level is more receptive in nature, with the student taking in sounds and patterns and then beginning to imitate language heard. The situation is controlled; the speaker is parroting. In other words, a beginner can successfully participate in memorized dialogues and can respond with memorized answers to memorized questions. Thus, accuracy is high.

Developing: This level is characterized by language behavior that moves from imitative to reflective (that is, a more thoughtful rather than automatic response to a situation or a question). Students now begin to move out of the controlled box, recombining memorized or learned pieces. They begin to respond in more complete and purposeful ways to meet their practical needs. As students begin to create with language, their accuracy decreases.

Transitioning: This level is characterized by movement from reflective to interactive language behavior. Students are struggling to act more independently in their language, successfully creating with language to express their own thoughts instead of recombining other people's words.

Refining: This level is characterized by language behavior moving from interactive to initiative, where the speaker takes on full responsibility for engaging, maintaining, and furthering the conversation. Students can successfully act independently in the new language, initiating with language to meet a wide variety of purposes.

Accuracy changes over these levels as well. At the beginning level, accuracy is high because language is basically memorized and the context is so controlled. At the following levels, learners have to be comfortable struggling with using language more creatively and independently. Teachers, too, need to both encourage this stretching and be comfortable with the resulting drop in accuracy, especially during spontaneous interpersonal communication. Allowing students to work in this way is essential for them to reach the higher levels, with accuracy serving as a lifelong destination.

Performance Guidelines Linked to Key Questions: Context

Language must be taught within a context. Teaching language in isolation is to remove the motivation and the purpose for using it. Key questions (Table 2.2) provide just such a context, an arena within which the language learning and practice can occur. The key questions coincide with the type of language students can use comfortably at a given level of language learning. The key questions fit the level of sophistication and complexity that the student can handle. Derived from the mind-set of the performance standards and performance guidelines, the key questions provide a broad thematic context for applying the language skills students are learning. The key questions capture the general characteristics of how to approach a specific unit context or topic for a specific level.

TABLE 2.2 **Key Questions: Thematic Topics**

Beginning	**Developing**
Who am I?	**What is my life like?**
Who are you?	**What is your life like?**
Identify similarities and differences	*Investigate similarities and differences*

Self and Community

• Biographical facts	• Geography, climate, political divisions
• Interests/hobbies	• Urban, suburban, rural
• Family	• Community, housing
• School/studies	• Stores/shopping/restaurants
• Friends/peers	• Travel, transportation

Transitioning	**Refining**
How do I look at the world?	**What do I think and feel?**
How do you look at the world?	**What do you think and feel?**
Share and compare perspectives	*Discuss and defend opinions*

Personal, Local, and Global Issues

• Intellectual and aesthetic pursuits	• Politics
• Religion, philosophy	• History
• Cultural heritage, traditions, practices, celebrations	• Current events
	• Ecology, environment
	• Work/career

Beginning Level: Who Am I? Who Are You?

Students at the *beginning level* are able to list, identify, name, and provide concrete information. Beginning language students typically can identify similarities and differences. The context of "Who am I/Who are you?" provides an arena within which students can use their limited language ability to discuss important issues related to self and community. Under this thematic topic, students could explore biographical facts, family, friends and peers, interests and hobbies, and school and studies. They might also begin to identify items of geography, climate, political divisions; differences among urban, suburban, and rural living; types of housing and communities; specifics of stores, shopping, and restaurants; and travel and transportation. They are most successful asking and answering questions for which they personally know the answer.

Developing Level:
What Is My Life Like? What Is Your Life Like?

Students in the *developing level* of language learning are able to investigate similarities and differences. The overarching question is "What is my life like?" and "What is your life like?" Students are now better able to describe and provide more details, rather than just name and identify. This leads to a deeper exploration of the same context-forming topics under the broad categories of self and community. Instead of providing memorized lists and phrases, students begin to recombine known language to create new meaning, extending their expression to phrases and sentences. Students will be able to extend their descriptions, but will be limited in their ability to connect ideas and narrate.

Transitioning Level:
How Do I Look at the World?
How Do You Look at the World?

At the *transitioning level* of language learning, students are able to examine perspectives behind the surface appearances. The key question that matches their language ability is "How do I look at the world?" and "How do you look at the world?" Students at this level can explain with a deeper understanding, sharing and comparing perspectives on larger issues. They are able to talk about personal, local, and global issues on a concrete level, taking advantage of prompts from authentic materials. The issues that students can now explore with discussions in the second language include religion and philosophy; cultural heritage, traditions, practices, and celebrations; intellectual and aesthetic pursuits; politics, history, and current events; ecology and the environment; and work and career.

Refining Level:
What Do I Think and Feel?
What Do You Think and Feel?

After students have acquired a basic understanding and use of the major components of the language, they move into a period of refining their language skills. With knowledge of a broad range of language components, these students need to refine their skill at using the language they know. At the *refining level,* the key questions are "What do I think and feel?" and "What do you think and feel?" Students now can delve into how they think and feel about issues, digging deeper into the personal, local, and global issues that were explored for an understanding of different cultural perspectives during the transitioning level. Now students work on extended use of language, discussing and defending their opinions as well as analyzing issues from various perspectives.

How Would a Topic Such as "Where We Live" Play Out Across the Four Language Learning Levels?

Example: Beginning Level
Key Question: Who am I? Who are you?
Students at the beginning level of language learning might do the following:

- name rooms in their home and identify different rooms in a home in the target country
- name furnishings commonly found in each room in their homes and identify differences in where things might be found in a home in the target culture (such as where is a TV likely to be found, how many TVs are common, where is the phone located and how many are available in a home, is the toilet in a separate room from the bathtub, where do students study in the United States and in the target countries)
- on hearing a sentence about the home, check off whether that is common in the United States, in the target culture, or in both

Example: Developing Level
Key Question: What is my life like? What is your life like?
Students at the developing level of language learning might do the following:

- describe their local community by describing their neighborhood or downtown, walking distance versus driving distance to stores and schools, variety of individual stores versus one-stop shopping, and kinds of services provided by the local government versus privately
- compare the description of their local community with a typical community in the target culture, noting commonalities and differences
- outline a description of a typical day in their life identifying each form of transportation used and each destination in the community throughout the day

Example: Transitioning Level
Key Question: How do I look at the world? How do you look at the world?
Students at the transitioning level of language learning might do the following:

- write a letter to an exchange student from the target culture, describing a typical day in a teenager's life in the local community and activities available for young people, noting activities that are typical of their community or region of the United States
- discuss why they would like to live in a certain community (either in the United States or in the target culture), sharing advantages and disadvantages; ask questions of each other to explore other potential advantages and disadvantages
- create an introduction to their community for foreign visitors, noting places and services that a visitor from another country would find useful

Example: Refining Level
Key Question: What do I think and feel? What do you think and feel?
Students at the refining level of language learning might do the following:

- describe historical, political, environmental, and other factors that have shaped the nature of their community; examine a community in the target culture with a focus on identifying the same factors at work to influence its design
- watch a travelogue in the target language, and discuss cultural similarities and differences in the appeal made to the audience compared to a travelogue for a U.S. audience
- debate how prepared they feel U.S. students are to live abroad for 4–12 months and how well they will be able to participate in the other culture

Characteristics of Interpersonal, Interpretive, and Presentational Communication: Implications for Assessment

TABLE 2.3 Characteristics of Interpersonal, Interpretive, and Presentational Communication: Implications for Assessment

	Interpersonal	Interpretive	Presentational
Characteristics	■ Message is most important ■ Spontaneous ■ Staying on topic ■ Follow through on ideas ■ Attentive to partner ■ Authentic reactions ■ Negotiation of meaning (two-way communication)	■ Begin with the gist ■ Move to deeper levels of details ■ Use context clues ■ Predict, guess, use structures to aid meaning ■ Authentic materials	■ Delivery of the message is most important ■ Awareness of audience ■ Maintain audience's attention ■ Nonnegotiated (one-way communication) ■ Rehearsed, practiced ■ Edited, polished
Sample Beginning Level Assessments	■ Meet a friend at a café and talk about what you did today ■ Talk to a friend about a prepared illustration (family photograph, postcard from a trip)	■ Tell the main idea or purpose of a news article ■ Identify from a list of key ideas those actually found in a short story	■ Role-play a scene such as ordering in a restaurant, going to the post office, or buying clothes ■ Write a letter of introduction
Sample Developing Level Assessments	■ Identify what you and your partner have in common on a given topic (school, relatives)	■ Make a list of the key ideas, and highlight where they are found in a reading ■ Give details that support the main idea of a short story ■ Use context clues to predict the meaning of words or phrases in a reading	■ Retell a story or personal anecdote ■ Present a public service announcement
Sample Transitioning Level Assessments	■ Come to an agreement on a topic that has various points of view	■ From a list of statements, identify logical and illogical inferences, explaining the choice made	■ Give a short speech about living in another culture ■ Stage an authentic piece of literature or drama
Sample Refining Level Assessments	■ Convince your partner or small group to adopt your stand on an issue	■ Explain the author's (speaker's, director's) perspective on the subject matter, drawing on what is known about the target culture	■ Write an essay comparing and contrasting U.S. culture and the target culture, analyzing how the similarities and differences impact each country's view of the world

Interpersonal Communication

Characteristics

Interpersonal communication is two-way communication, not just talking at the other person, nor waiting to ask a predetermined question or series of questions regardless of the answers given; rather, the participants are truly trying to understand each other and pay attention to each other. Interpersonal communication has the following characteristics:

- the message communicated is the most important element.
- spontaneity (may be a familiar context, but the exact performance is not memorized or practiced; beginning students may use memorized chunks of language, but the exact flow of the conversation is not memorized; rehearsal or memorized dialogues are a means, not the end in itself).
- staying on topic rather than turn taking (interpersonal conversation would not follow one pattern such as I ask a question, then you ask a question, then I ask another question, and so on, nor I ask five questions and then you ask five questions).
- follow through on ideas, maintaining and furthering the conversation (rather than a random series of questions; pursuing the direction taken by a partner's information or comment; actively trying to involve the partner).
- attention to one's communication partner (shown by eye contact, nodding in agreement, even helping out one's partner by supplying words and/or clarifying meaning).
- authentic reactions (expressing surprise, support, encouragement, sympathy).
- meaning is negotiated through the means of strategies to seek clarification when necessary (from simply saying "What?" to offering substitutions for words or phrases not understood to paraphrasing what one thought was said to verify one's perception).

Implications for Assessment

We must help students get comfortable with situations requiring spontaneous, unrehearsed communication. Interpersonal may employ speaking and listening (face-to-face or over the phone) and may employ reading and writing (E-mail exchanges, telephone messages). The interpersonal task needs to be one to which each student can personally relate, involving and engaging students in the task. For an interpersonal assessment, students should not be asked to take on roles with which they are not familiar, such as pretending they are a famous person.

Sample Performance Assessment Ideas

The key to interpersonal performance tasks is to ensure that the performance is spontaneous. Obviously, especially at earlier stages of language learning, the context needs to be familiar. Otherwise, students will not understand anything and will have hardly anything to say. In addition, beginning level students need to be personally familiar with the task and situation. Beginning students can play themselves, but will have difficulty in role plays where they have to be someone else, since besides the challenge of using the second language they also are challenged to think of how to respond to a prompt that is beyond their realm of experience.

However, providing students with a repertoire of language and ideas and giving students a wide variety of practice using that repertoire to communicate does not mean that the actual performance is to be practiced or memorized. Students in elementary grades may be evaluated purely on the scale of whether they can do it or not. Students in middle school grades may be offered some personal choices within a limited menu, practicing the larger topic prior to the assessment but then choosing a more specific focus in their spontaneous conversational assessment.

The interpersonal performance task might ask students to have conversations prompted as follows:

- Beginning level: Meet your friend at a café and talk about what you did today.
- Beginning level: Talk to a friend about a prepared illustration (family photograph, postcard from a trip).
- Developing level: Identify what you and your partner have in common on a given topic (school, relatives).
- Transitioning level: Come to an agreement on a topic that has various points of view.
- Refining level: Convince your partner or small group to adopt your stand on an issue.

Interpretive Communication

Characteristics

Interpretive communication is characterized by

- moving from understanding the gist to comprehending deeper and deeper levels of details
- using context clues rather than just translating
- helping students to predict, guess, and use structures to aid meaning
- building comfort with authentic materials

Implications for Assessment

Students need to interpret a wide variety of materials: literature, flyers, brochures, Web sites, instructions, advertisements, magazine and newspaper articles—all with a specific and purposeful motive. "Interpret" also includes listening, reading, and viewing. Students listen to radio and TV broadcasts, songs, movies, lectures, and plays. A variety of checks will help students show that they understand. The interpretive communication mode is by nature tied to interpersonal and presentational tasks, but it also has to be addressed on its own.

Sample Performance Assessment Ideas

The prompt for the assessment of the interpretive mode should be from authentic materials; that is, something to read, hear, or view that comes from the target culture and that was designed for native speakers of the language, not for language learners. The prompt should not be glossed with words translated on the side. The prompt should look like the original context from which it was taken, not cleaned up. Therefore it will look like a newspaper or magazine article with its telltale formatting, or it will have background sounds from having been recorded on the street or in a restaurant or at school in the target culture, or it will be a video produced in the target culture with specific images and allusions.

After reading, hearing, or viewing the authentic prompt, the performance assessment might require students to do the following:

- Beginning level: Tell the main idea or purpose of a news article.
- Beginning level: Identify from a list of key ideas the ones that are actually found in the prompt and where.
- Developing level: If a reading, make a list of the key ideas and then highlight where they are found.
- Developing level: Tell the details that support the main idea of a short story.
- Developing level: Use context clues to predict the meaning of words or phrases that are likely to be unknown in a reading.
- Transitioning: From a list of statements about the article, identify logical and illogical inferences, explaining the choice made.
- Refining level: Explain the author's (speaker's, director's) perspective on the subject matter, drawing on what is known about the target culture.

Presentational Communication

Characteristics

Presentational communication is characterized by

- emphasis on the delivery of a message
- awareness of the characteristics and expectations of the audience
- efforts to maintain the audience's attention
- nonnegotiated communication (one way)
- more rehearsed, practiced than "interpersonal"
- may be written, rewritten, and edited before the final "presentation"
- may be rehearsed, critiqued, and rerehearsed before performance

Implications for Assessment

Students exhibit an increasing awareness of the audience and how to be culturally appropriate, and an awareness of the more formal, more stylized language that may be required. Demonstrations may be presented through writing, speaking, or even a video presentation.

Sample Performance Assessment Ideas

Presentational communication may take many forms. At the formal end of the spectrum, it may be a speech, a dramatization, a reading of a story or poem, or a written composition. At the informal end students tell personal stories, give explanations, provide directions, send a postcard, or write in a diary. All of these examples can also move along a continuum from simple to extensive, from descriptive to reflective or analytical. Presentational communication is sharing information, concepts, and ideas to a specific audience.

The key difference between presentational and interpersonal communication is the preparation and rehearsal that precedes the presentational assessment task. In presentational, students are able to write, submit, and revise a composition; they script an oral presentation and rehearse it; they create a video through editing until it is precisely as they want it to be. Presentational can showcase a higher quality of language usage than interpersonal because of the opportunity to draft, practice, and improve the presentation before the task is evaluated.

Students need to learn how to tailor their message to the audience receiving it, by using visuals or gestures to underscore their points, or at more sophisticated levels by making choices of a phrase or image in order to maintain the audience's attention. At even higher levels of language skill, students are able to personalize their message, sharing real stories or providing comparisons and contrasts in order to reinforce the message. Ultimately, students will learn to present convincing arguments by providing multiple examples and by varying their style to match the nature of the presentation. They will be able to function in a range of styles from informal to formal, from lighthearted to serious.

The presentational performance task might require students to do the following:

- Beginning level: Role-play a scene such as ordering in a restaurant, going to the post office, or buying clothes.
- Beginning level: Write a letter of introduction.
- Developing level: Retell a story or personal anecdote.
- Developing level: Present a public service announcement.
- Transitioning level: Give a short speech about living in another culture in order to win a trip abroad.
- Transitioning level: Stage an authentic piece of literature or drama.
- Refining level: Write an essay comparing and contrasting U.S. culture and the target culture, analyzing how these similarities and differences impact each country's view of the world.

Characteristics of a Standards-Based Curriculum: A New Basis for Articulation

This state guide provides content standards, performance standards, and performance guidelines as the broad ends to which our teaching of languages will lead. By providing these at the state level, a consistency is possible across the state. Such consistency is not a top-down prescription of what must be taught in every language course in every grade level, but rather provides a common set of goals for the wide variety of language programs in Wisconsin. These performance standards and performance guidelines are written to accommodate differences in the years of language instruction available (e.g., K–12, 4–12, or 7–12), the frequency of instruction (e.g., daily or three times per week), and the length of instruction (20, 45, or 60 minutes per lesson). If the goals are the same, students will be making progress down the same path, toward the same ends. This is preferable to seeing our students who began to study a language in elementary or middle school start back at level one in high school because the student couldn't produce the exact same vocabulary or

What does curriculum for understanding look like? How do we make student understanding more likely (as opposed to resorting to the hit-or-miss "teach, test, hope for the best" approach seen in coverage-driven teaching)?

Wiggins and McTighe 1998, 98

grammar on demand compared to those students who began in high school. These common goals will serve Wisconsin well by providing the appropriate basis for articulation: a focus on our common destination.

> **Characteristics of a Standards-Based Curriculum**
>
> - Guide to the process of learning a language, continually leading to higher levels of proficiency
> - Guide to how to use the textbook effectively and efficiently
> - Guide to choosing wisely from the lists that formerly defined our curricula
> - Guide to a realistic definition of what students can achieve in a 2-, 4-, 6-, 8-, or 12-year sequence of language study
> - Guide to help new teachers understand the goals for each level of instruction
> - Guide to achieving the standards through performance-based assessments created within a thematic unit

A standards-based curriculum, then, is not a tightly prescribed series of topics to teach; rather, it focuses on the end goals of the instruction, the actual student performances that will truly represent what it is to know another language. Assessment provides feedback as to each student's progress toward the standards. How these standards are manifested at a certain language level is the curriculum. Table 2.4 summarizes the nature of the shift required when moving to a standards-based curriculum. Knowing another language is not being able to fill in blanks on a worksheet; it is not identifying a series of dates. Knowing another language is having the knowledge *and* skills to communicate, involving understanding and being understood, applying knowledge of the culture and the ways of functioning in a culture, and employing various strategies for effective communication. These performances and evaluation of these characteristics of knowing a language need to be captured in the curriculum and assessment, both for an entire program of instruction across many grade levels and also for each specific course.

TABLE 2.4 **Designing a Standards-Based Curriculum: A Shift in Focus**

LESS…	MORE…
• Teacher-centered	• Student-centered
• Talking about language	• Using the language
• Coverage	• Developing proficiency
• Testing	• Assessment
• One right answer	• Multiple ways to show learning
• Sequential curriculum design	• Spiraling curriculum design

Source: Karen Fowdy and Lisa Hendrickson, Monroe High School, 2002

References

American Council on the Teaching of Foreign Languages. 1986. *ACTFL Proficiency Guidelines*. Yonkers, N.Y.: ACTFL.

———. 1999. *ACTFL Performance Guidelines for K–12 Learners*. Yonkers, N.Y.: ACTFL.

National Standards in Foreign Language Education Project. 1999. *Standards for Foreign Language Learning in the 21st Century.* Lawrence, Kans.: Allen Press.

Sandrock, Paul. 1998. *TEKS for LOTE Teacher Training Module III—Assessment.* Austin, Tex.: Southwest Educational Development Laboratory.

———. 2000. Creating a Standards-Based Curriculum. In *Teaching Spanish with the Five C's: A Blueprint for Success,* ed. Gail Guntermann, 9–13. AATSP Professional Development Handbook Series for Teachers K–16, Volume 2. Orlando, Fla.: Harcourt, Inc.

———. 2001. Bringing Our Standards into Our Classrooms. *Voice of WAFLT* 29: 1, pp. 7–8.

Wiggins, Grant. 1998. *Educative Assessment: Designing Assessments to Inform and Improve Student Performance.* San Francisco: Jossey-Bass.

Wiggins, Grant, and Jay McTighe. 1998. *Understanding by Design.* Alexandria, Va.: Association for Supervision and Curriculum Development.

Wisconsin Department of Public Instruction. 1997. *Wisconsin's Model Academic Standards for Foreign Languages.* Madison, Wis.: Wisconsin Department of Public Instruction.

Creating a Standards-Based Curriculum

3

Introduction: The Curriculum Design Process
Implications of a Standards-Based Design in Curriculum Planning: The Mind-Set
The Process for Developing Units in a Standards-Based Curriculum
    Step One: Mind-Set
    Step Two: Key Question/Theme
    Step Three: Brainstorming
    Step Four: Performance Assessment
    Step Five: Wisconsin Standards: Communication
    Step Six: Wisconsin Performance Guidelines
    Step Seven: Links to Culture and the Other Wisconsin Standards: Connections, Comparisons, Communities
    Step Eight: Structures and Vocabulary
    Step Nine: Check the Unit—Reflection
Planning for Instruction
References

Listen in on this imaginary conversation as members of the curriculum guide writing team discuss what they might have looked for in a new curriculum guide from the Department of Public Instruction (DPI) before standards became part of their mind-set for curriculum, assessment, and instruction.

Karen: Oh, my gosh, I am *so* excited—the DPI's new world language curriculum guide. I have been waiting and waiting for this!

Pat: Oh I know—I don't think I could have stalled any longer—my principal was really getting upset that I hadn't finished revising my curriculum yet. Now I can just go home and copy this and hand it to him on Monday morning—this is just great!

Jody: I know—we've been trying to write curriculum at our school too. When I say "we," I really mean "me"—I am a department of one you know.

Karen: Well, at least you don't have to argue with anyone about what to put in the curriculum. I tell you, we have been "discussing" our curriculum for over a year now and we just can't agree on what to teach when. I am *so* glad we have the DPI guide now…no more after-school meetings that go from 4:00 to forever with nothing accomplished!

Pat: Oh I know what you mean! Here, let me find the section that tells when to teach each verb tense. It's got to be here somewhere. I just know it is. I can't wait to show my colleagues that teaching grammar is still okay! It's got to be in here somewhere. I want to see when the DPI says to introduce past tense. You know that some teachers are actually having their first-year students learn to talk in the past! Can you believe it? They say that it really helps conversation when the kids want to talk about what they did on the weekend or over vacations. I'm willing to give it a shot but I just want to see if I should just do regular past tense verbs or if I should introduce some irregular past tense verbs. I have got to find that list in here. *And* I want to see if the DPI recommends that our advanced level students study the pluperfect subjunctive. You know they really should. It gives my seniors such a sense of pride when they complete that unit. I've had students come back from college and tell me that they are the only ones in their Spanish class who know that tense. Isn't that great?

Jody: (has been leafing through the guide while Pat is talking) You know Pat, if I am reading this introduction correctly, I don't think you're going to find that list of grammar points and verbs you're looking for.

Pat: (continues paging through the draft copy) What are you talking about? Of course there is a list of grammar points in here. How else would you organize your curriculum? My gosh, Jody, think about it!

Jody: I *am* thinking about it. Maybe the DPI is getting smart finally and is starting to listen to those of us in the elementary schools. Obviously, I haven't had time to really read all this stuff that they put in the beginning of the guide, but I did see something about teaching thematically.

Pat: (stops paging through the draft copy) *What* is *that* all about?!!

Jody: Well, instead of telling the kids that they are going to learn about adjectives, now I come up with a theme for each unit.

Karen: A theme like what?

Jody: Oh you know, a theme like *colors.* After all, learning colors is a pretty basic part of beginning language classes, *especially* in the elementary school. It is a really rich theme. The kids can point to different colors in the room when I call them out. They can color a picture according to the color I tell them to use. I can hold up a colored piece of paper and they can tell me what color it is. And you know, I sing a lot with my students. We made up a song using the names of the colors to the tune of "Three Blind Mice." It goes: bleu, bleu, bleu, bleu, bleu, bleu, rouge, rouge, rouge, rouge, rouge, rouge, violet, violet, violet, violet, violet, violet, violet, violet, bleu, bleu, bleu. The kids love it and they really know their colors now.

Pat: (rolling her eyes) I bet they do.

Jody: They sure do. Let's see if we can find a list of themes. It would be so nice if everyone could agree to teach the same things in the same order so that the students wouldn't have to repeat anything when they change teachers or schools. I told you I was trying to write the curriculum for my school. Even though I am a department of one, I am really having a hard time. The first year is really easy: colors, numbers, weather, family. After that it gets really complicated. I don't know if it is better to do clothing in second year or the house. And then there is the food unit. Once I do that, it's the only unit the kids want to do! If the DPI would just tell us when these themes should be taught, it would really help everyone.

Karen: You know Jody, you might think that a list of what themes to teach each year is a good idea. You sort of do your own thing in the elementary school. When those kids hit middle school, we use a textbook so that they can really study the language. What would I do if my textbook didn't teach those themes in the same order as the DPI recommended? I would have a real mess.

Jody: Couldn't you just find the chapter that had the right theme?

Pat: Oh sure, and what if it is the second month of school and the theme is at the end of the book? Do you know how much grammar there is between the beginning and end of a textbook? The kids wouldn't understand a thing.

Karen: Plus, you can't jump around with middle school kids. They jump around enough without my help! They need lots of structure, page by page, one step at a time. You have to take things nice and slow. If the DPI were smart, they would look at a few textbooks and see how they are set up. Then they could map out a curriculum that followed the general pattern of most of the textbooks.

Pat: Or maybe they could recommend a textbook for everyone to use. Isn't that what Texas and California do?

Jody: How would they ever find one textbook that everyone likes? And besides, there just aren't really any textbooks that fit my elementary school program.

Karen: You know, the more we talk, the more I wonder what the DPI came up with. This is no easy task. There is so much to think about. I don't think I want the DPI to tell me that I have to teach clothing in second year. I might want to teach it in third year or first year or maybe I don't want to teach it at all.

Jody: (shocked) Not teach clothing???? That is one of my favorite units. I have tons of flashcards for it.

Karen: Well, maybe clothing, like colors, will come up in a variety of units. Maybe clothing and colors are just vocabulary. Let's think about it, what do we really want kids to do with colors or clothing anyway? Maybe a lot of our "themes" are really just vocabulary lists. Maybe this guide isn't going to have any lists at all.

Jody: There *have* to be *some* lists. It *is* a curriculum *guide.* They *have* to tell us what to teach.

Karen: It doesn't seem like the curriculum gurus are being so prescriptive anymore. Maybe it's because of that multiplying factor of what there is to learn today. I can't remember the exact formula but I *know* that my children have a lot more to learn than I did when I was their age.

Pat: No kidding!

Karen: I have been doing a lot of reading about how children learn their first language. And I was thinking of my own children. I didn't use flashcards to teach them to speak English.

Pat: You're right...and I really didn't speak only in the present tense with my children so that they wouldn't get confused. They understood me. When you think about it, there really isn't a sacred order for teaching language structures. And there certainly isn't a special order to learn vocabulary, I mean "themes" as you call them. I learned English by speaking it every day and listening to it every day, and making mistakes every day.

Karen: I suppose we really have to keep that practice piece in mind if we want our students to be able to use the language successfully. And the only way they are going to practice using the language is if we find something that they want to talk about.

Pat: ...or if *they* find something that they want to talk about.

Karen: Right...it's probably a little of both.

Pat: I agree.

Jody: So...what you two are saying now is that this new curriculum guide is probably not organized by grammatical points. And it probably isn't organized by themes. It can't be organized according to a textbook because we don't do state adoptions here. So...what does that leave?

Pat: I don't know...

Karen: You got me...but aren't you all glad you didn't have to be on *that* committee!

[Adapted from Clementi, 2000.]

Introduction: The Curriculum Design Process

A curriculum in the past was meant to guide teachers in answering one question: What am I supposed to teach in this class? A curriculum today must guide teachers in responding to multiple questions: What will the students know and be able to do when they have completed this class? How will I know they have learned? How do I evaluate the quality of the students' performance? With these questions in mind, we have to determine an organizing principle to help answer these questions and therefore create our curriculum.

Is the Textbook the Organizing Principle?

A standards-based curriculum places textbooks, grammar, and functions in their appropriate support roles in reaching our goals of instruction.

If so, we simply write down the table of contents from our textbooks and save hours of curriculum development time. The teacher's task then is to cover the material in the predetermined order established by the publisher. However, the textbook may or may not address what we, as professional language educators, believe to be the most important concepts for our students to know. The text may or may not create real-life situations of interest to our students. The text may or may not provide the kinds of meaningful practice that our students need in order to learn. The text may or may not emphasize the interconnectedness of the three modes of communication in the standards. Therefore, the textbook cannot be the organizing principle. It can, however, be an important resource in the planning of our curriculum. Using a standards-based approach to curriculum design helps teachers make informed, thoughtful decisions in determining which portions of a chapter in a textbook to use and which ones to discard. A standards-based curriculum uses the textbook as a resource, not as the definition of the course.

Is Grammar the Organizing Principle?

If so, what is the magical sequence that will lead students to increased proficiency in using the language? The *ACTFL Performance Guidelines for K–12 Learners* describes the sequence of language performance from novice to intermediate to preadvanced levels of proficiency. Those guidelines talk about increasing the ability of the student to communicate in a variety of situations. They do not talk about mastering present tense, then future, then past, and finally subjunctive. In the guidelines, novice learners are expected to use memorized words and phrases to communicate in real-life situations. Therefore, grammar cannot be the organizing principle. It can, however, be a tool *as needed* to help students successfully communicate meaning. Using a standards-based approach to curriculum design places grammar in its appropriate role, as a tool and not as the goal of instruction. To meet a communicative goal, some grammar may help students better understand how to express their thoughts. In a standards-based curriculum grammar is introduced on an *as needed* basis.

Are Language Functions the Organizing Principle?

Wisconsin's 1986 *Guide to Curriculum Planning in Foreign Language* was designed around language functions. The functions pushed us to make our drills meaningful, help our students apply their knowledge in simulated situations, and work toward real communication among students, not just fill-in-the-blank exercises. A focus on language functions placed grammar and vocabulary in a supportive role. Teaching didn't stop with these components of the language; we sought to engage students to use language in meaningful ways. Fifteen years after the last curriculum guide, we understand more about how students learn languages. While functions don't fully organize our curriculum, they can help us identify the kinds of language patterns that students will need in order to successfully communicate in a given situation. In a standards-based curriculum, functions are tools that students use to accomplish a multifaceted communication task.

To study another language and culture gives one the powerful key to successful communication: knowing how, when, and why, to say what to whom.

National Standards 1996, 11

Why Are Standards the Organizing Principle?

Throughout the curriculum planning guide, standards have been characterized as learning goals: what students will know and be able to do as a result of instruction. Standards are broad descriptors of desired performances that teachers can personalize in the actual performance assessments they design for their students. A standards-based curriculum allows the teacher to choose themes or topics that are interesting and motivating to students. The teacher can then design assessments that relate to the chosen theme or topic and give evidence that the students have also met the performance standards. For example, if a teacher wants students to meet the standard of retelling a story about an event from the past, the teacher could design lessons so that the students are ultimately able to talk about a favorite summer vacation or perhaps retell their favorite legend or retell the life story of a historic figure. All of these performances do meet the standard. All students in Wisconsin do not have to be able to retell a legend, but all students in Wisconsin *do* need to be able to retell a story about an event from the past. The emphasis is on the communication goal, not on the content. In a standards-based curriculum the goal is meaningful communication.

A standards-based curriculum places textbooks, grammar, and functions in their appropriate support roles in reaching our goals of instruction, summed up in the national *Standards for Foreign Language Learning:* learning a world language is knowing how, when, and why to say what to whom. If we are to help our students use a second language effectively we must keep the standards front and center as goals of instruction, and the vocabulary, grammar, functions, and textbooks as tools to help us achieve these goals. "In the classroom, we need to focus on the actual performance, in its wholeness, rather than teaching all of the components in isolation hoping that students will be able to remember all of them when needed in a real-life situation." (Wiggins and McTighe 1998, 136)

Implications of a Standards-Based Design in Curriculum Planning: The Mind-Set

A curriculum that is based on standards requires a teacher to "plan backward." In other words, the teacher must ask: How will I know if my students have achieved the standards? The students must demonstrate what they know and are able to do through a performance assessment. The performance assessment can be developed for any topic or theme that the teacher chooses, understanding that students are more successful when they are learning something that they find interesting and useful. What is critical is that the performance assessment reflect the goals expressed in the standards.

The Performance Standards for Communication and Culture and the Performance Guidelines each contain four levels: beginning, developing, transitioning, and refining. These levels reflect the development of increasing depth and complexity of communication over time. Teachers cannot look at these levels in isolation but must consider them as a framework to support choices in curriculum and instruction within a classroom, within a certain course, and across courses within a language department or program. When planning instruction, teachers cannot focus exclusively on one level to the exclusion of the preceding or following level. Language development is not rigid but fluid. An individual student's profile of language proficiency may reflect some skills at a beginning level, some at a developing level, and some at a transitioning level. A classroom of students will certainly represent this diversity. The curriculum must, therefore, reenter concepts and ideas continuously throughout the program to address the needs of all students, allowing all students to make continuous progress on the proficiency path.

Given this requirement, the teacher must have a "standards mind-set" before starting to plan curriculum. A standards mind-set has two components: performance standards and Performance Guidelines. The performance standards reflect what students should know and be able to do for each of the five C's. The Performance Guidelines reflect how well students are expected to perform, setting a target for evaluation of that performance. From this mind-set, the standards will continue to influence the development and design of curriculum, assessment, and instruction.

A Teacher's Reflection: Designing a Curriculum Unit

When I consider themes and performance assessments that will become my curriculum, I am guided by the goals of the five C's. To illustrate this point, consider a unit on teenagers. As I start brainstorming this unit, I think of what I want my students to know and be able to do at the end of the unit. This list of activity ideas will help me generate the performance assessment for the three modes of communication. And as I think of the components I need in order to teach this unit, the choice and focus of the unit will be guided by the other four C's. Language in real use is a complex interaction of several skills, requiring the user to employ various modes of communication, aware of the cultural requirements and influences in the background of the communicative situation. The standards need to be considered as a whole, not as isolated skills and content to be checked off one by one. I cannot successfully plan my curriculum if I don't have the standards front and center in my mind.

The second part of my mind-set before the actual detailed planning begins is the Performance Guidelines. The Performance Guidelines ground my performance assessment in reasonable, realistic expectations for what the students can do. These guidelines describe the key components of how students at each level use the target language in a sustained way in a spontaneous performance. The words "sustained" and "spontaneous" help me think differently about the end goals for a unit, compared to what I might expect from students in controlled practice activities. In the planning process, I will consider these performance guidelines in more detail when I develop my assessment. But I must keep them in mind so that my performance assessment is designed at an appropriate level for my students. Besides setting reasonable expectations, these guidelines also help me think about the kinds of activities that will move my students to increased proficiency. I know that opportunity to practice is key in this development. I can optimize this practice by targeting certain skills that will help my students improve their communication ability. The performance guidelines help me assess my students appropriately. The guidelines lay out what is good for a beginner, and then show the key changes that students and the teacher want to focus on in order to move to the next level. With these guidelines in mind, I can say, "This student is demonstrating excellent skills for a beginner," instead of "This student can't say very much and is still making mistakes."

When I consider themes and performance assessments that will become my curriculum, I am guided by the goals of the five C's.

The standards mind-set gives teachers the fundamental belief system about how language is taught and learned. It allows teachers to choose topics and themes that are interesting and important for the students to learn. It allows teachers to have a personal teaching style in instructing their students. It provides consistency and unity in what the students should know and be able to do. The proverb that all roads lead to Rome is most definitely true in a standards-based curriculum. If we know that Rome is where we want our students to end up, we can then begin "mapping" our route to provide an interesting, useful, and learning-filled journey.

The Process for Developing Units in a Standards-Based Curriculum

Keeping the Performance Standards and the Performance Guidelines as a mind-set, teachers can now develop a curriculum that helps students move along the continuum toward greater proficiency in a second language. The

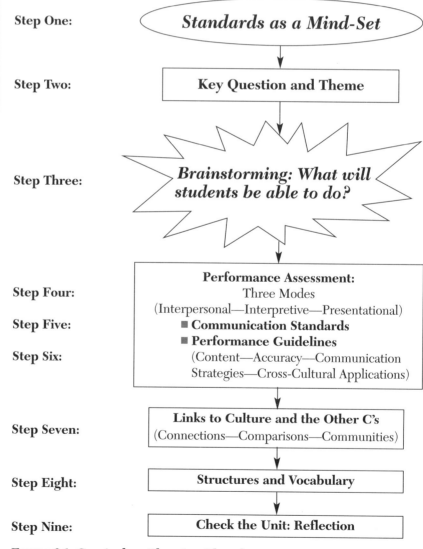

FIGURE 3.1 **Curriculum Planning Flowchart**

step-by-step process is outlined here and illustrated in the flowchart (Figure 3.1). In the curriculum development process, teachers think through each step and then fill in the appropriate section of the curriculum planning template. Table 3.1 links each step to the related section of the curriculum template. A blank template for teachers to copy and use for curriculum unit development and a summary of the steps for curriculum development on an annotated template are provided in Part IV: Resources.

TABLE 3.1 **Unit of Instruction—Curriculum Planning Template**

Step Two:	**Key Question:**		**Theme:**	**Topic:**
	Communication Mode:	Interpersonal Interpretive Presentational	Interpersonal Interpretive Presentational	Interpersonal Interpretive Presentational
Step Four:	**Performance Assessment**			
Step Five:	Wisconsin Standards: **Communication**			
Step Six:	*Target Performance (Key elements from the Performance Guidelines to consider in rubric development)*	Content:	Content:	Content:
		Accuracy:	Accuracy:	Accuracy:
		Communication Strategies:	Communication Strategies:	Communication Strategies:
		Cross-Cultural Applications:	Cross-Cultural Applications:	Cross-Cultural Applications:
Step Seven:	Links to **Culture** and the other Wisconsin Standards ✓ **Connections** ✓ **Comparisons** ✓ **Communities** *Evidence (How these standards are incorporated in the instruction)*			
Step Eight:	**Structures and Vocabulary:** *What needs to be taught for students to be successful in the performance assessment*			

Step One: Mind-Set

Until the Performance Standards and the Performance Guidelines become a permanent part of the teacher's thinking, a copy of the documents should be kept in the teacher's planning book. The teacher should take time to look over the two documents before beginning the development of a unit. With those broad goals for performance in mind, the teacher is ready to begin planning.

Step Two: Key Question/Theme

A sound curriculum helps students define themselves and their role as responsible members of their school, community, state, country, and world. To help with this definition, this guide has targeted four key questions (see Table 3.2) that reflect the four levels of development in the performance standards. The four key questions and their corresponding levels are

- **Who am I? Who are you?**
  Beginning level: Students will identify similarities and differences between their culture and other cultures.
- **What is my life like? What is your life like?**
  Developing level: Students will investigate similarities and differences between their culture and other cultures.
- **How do I look at the world? How do you look at the world?**
  Transitioning level: Students will share and compare perspectives concerning their culture and other cultures.
- **What do I think and feel? What do you think and feel?**
  Refining level: Students will discuss and defend opinions concerning their culture and other cultures.

The teacher selects the key question based on the proficiency level of the students. Once the question is selected, the teacher must choose a theme. This guide suggests two broad areas for theme development. For beginning and developing levels, the theme should relate to self and community. For transitioning and refining levels, the theme should relate to personal, local, and global issues. In Table 3.2 is a list of suggested themes. These are suggestions and are not dictated at the state level. Broad themes will likely be recycled in different courses, with each level's unit focusing on specific topics within the given theme. For example, under the theme of family, beginning level students might focus on the topic of basic description, such as name, age, physical description, and descriptive adjectives. At higher levels, students may have another unit on family, but the topic choices might be roles for doing household chores or cultural influences on attitudes toward elders. It is the local decision of each language department to determine how to answer the key questions in order to meet the needs and interests of their students.

The Performance Standards and the Performance Guidelines are a mind-set to guide all lesson planning.

TABLE 3.2 **Key Questions: Thematic Topics**

Beginning	**Developing**
Who am I? Who are you? *Identify similarities and differences*	What is my life like? What is your life like? *Investigate similarities and differences*
**Self and Community**	
• Biographical facts • Interests/hobbies • Family • School/studies • Friends/peers	• Geography, climate, political divisions • Urban, suburban, rural • Community, housing • Stores/shopping/restaurants • Travel, transportation
Transitioning	**Refining**
How do I look at the world? How do you look at the world? *Share and compare perspectives*	What do I think and feel? What do you think and feel? *Discuss and defend opinions*
**Personal, Local, and Global Issues**	
• Intellectual and aesthetic pursuits • Religion, philosophy • Cultural heritage, traditions, practices, celebrations	• Politics • History • Current events • Ecology, environment • Work/career

Step Three: Brainstorming

After determining a theme, the teacher must decide what students will know and be able to do in relation to that theme. In other words, if the theme is family, what exactly are the students to know about families and what will the students be able to do (communicate) about families? At this point, the teacher begins by listing skills and knowledge related to this theme in a brainstorming activity. As part of the brainstorming, the teacher might refer to a textbook or other resources to generate ideas. A brainstorm list might include the following:

- Name the members of your immediate family and their relationships to each other.
- Give the ages of the family members.
- Give the professions of the family members.
- Describe each family member's personality.
- Learn about a family from the target culture.

Step Four: Performance Assessment

With the brainstorm list as a reference, the teacher can now design the performance assessment. The performance assessment has three components to reflect the three modes of communication: interpretive, interpersonal, and presentational. By designing a performance assessment that reflects the three

By designing a performance assessment that reflects the three modes, the teacher is guaranteeing that the three modes are valued in instruction.

modes, the teacher is guaranteeing that the three modes are valued in instruction. Here again, it is critical that the teacher keep the Performance Standards and the Performance Guidelines as a mind-set. Teachers should ask themselves: What standards will my students demonstrate through this performance assessment, and are my students capable of performing this task? Next the teacher must consider in what order to assess students. Keep in mind the interconnectedness of the three modes and how one mode can help the students complete another mode. There is no magic to the order in which the three modes are assessed; assessing all three modes is critical. Each assessment task should connect to the next in a logical flow. Based on the sample brainstorming list for family, here are the three components of the performance assessment in the order that they will be completed:

	Beginning	Developing	Transitioning	Refining
	Key Question: Who am I? Who are you?			
	Theme: Family		Topic: Basic description	
Communication Mode:	**Interpretive**	Interpersonal Interpretive Presentational	Interpersonal Interpretive **Presentational**	**Interpersonal** Interpretive Presentational
Performance Assessment	Listen to a video where a (French) student is describing his or her family. In English list the members of his or her family and what you learned about each person.	Create a picture book about your family, writing a short description of each family member under each picture.	Share a picture book about your family with your classmates and look at your classmates' picture books. Find out additional information about the people pictured on each page.	

Step Five: Wisconsin Standards: Communication

After designing the assessment, the teacher must check the Wisconsin standards for Communication to verify that the assessment reflects these standards. These can be found in Part IV at the end of this guide. For this unit on family, the following standards are being assessed:

Wisconsin Standards: Communication	Interpretive B1: Listening:	Presentational C5: Forms of writing:	Interpersonal A2: Questions:
	Students will understand spoken language on familiar topics that has strong visual support.	Students will write personal journals, and/or brief messages to friends (postcard, letter, E-mail).	Students will ask and answer questions, including biographical information.

Step Six: Wisconsin Performance Guidelines

In order to complete the assessment, the teacher has to know the criteria to use to evaluate student performance. The Wisconsin Performance Guidelines are an invaluable tool in helping to determine these criteria. The descriptors for these guidelines are written to reflect increasing proficiency from beginning to developing to transitioning to refining levels of proficiency. The descriptors address four major characteristics for performance: *content, accuracy, communication strategies,* and *cross-cultural applications.* (The complete set of Performance Guidelines can be found in Part IV at the back of this guide.) For this unit, the criteria shown in this chart are selected to help evaluate students' performances. Notice that sometimes a characteristic is left blank. In those cases, the characteristic didn't apply to this particular performance. When developing the evaluation tool, some specific criteria that do not appear as part of the performance guidelines may be included.

	Interpretive	Presentational	Interpersonal
Target Performance (Key elements from the Performance Guidelines to consider in rubric development and other forms of evaluation)	**Content:** *Complexity/sophistication* Relies primarily on memorized phrases and short sentences on very familiar topics in both oral and written presentations.	**Content:** *Situation* Accomplishes a task directed by the teacher; can meet limited writing needs such as a short message or note.	**Content:** *Spontaneity* Responds automatically to high frequency cues such as "hello," "how are you," "what's your name"; can ask memorized questions such as "What's your name?" "How are you?"
	Accuracy:—	**Accuracy:** *Spelling* Can copy with accuracy memorized language.	**Accuracy:** *Ease* Expresses memorized phrases with ease and with few errors; may show evidence of false starts and pauses as topics expand beyond memorized dialogues.
	Communication Strategies: *Comprehension* Understands short, simple conversations and narration with highly predictable and familiar contexts.	**Communication Strategies:**—	**Communication Strategies:** *Impact* Focuses on successful task completion; uses gestures or visuals to maintain audience's attention and/or interest as appropriate to purpose.
	Cross-Cultural Applications: *Awareness* Understands a story line or event when it reflects a cultural background similar to their own.	**Cross-Cultural Applications:**—	**Cross-Cultural Applications:** *Verbal* Imitates appropriate linguistic patterns (formal vs. informal address, intonation) when modeled by the teacher.

Creating a Standards-Based Curriculum

Step Seven: Links to Culture and the Other Wisconsin Standards: Connections, Comparisons, Communities

Wisconsin's Model Academic Standards for Foreign Languages includes four other C's beyond Communication. These standards also need to be addressed in the development of units of instruction within a curriculum. Culture is set apart from the other C's because of its unbreakable tie to language. You cannot fully understand and appreciate another language unless you understand the culture where the language is spoken. Likewise, you cannot fully understand and appreciate another culture unless you understand its language. Just as there is a continuum in the development of language proficiency, there is a continuum in the development of cultural understanding in the Wisconsin standards. If the curricular unit is solid, it will reflect all five of the C's of the standards. Some of these may appear as part of the assessment, some will appear in the activities that lead up to the assessment. Some will receive more attention than others, but they will all be represented. Considering this unit on family, the following standards are targeted in addition to the Communication Standards. The teacher needs to plan specific classroom activities based on these standards, so students will know that these standards are truly being addressed. That is the "evidence" that we are teaching to the standards and not just superficially including them.

The teacher needs to plan specific classroom activities based on these standards. . . . That is the "evidence" that we are teaching to the standards and not just superficially including them.

Links to Culture and the other Wisconsin Standards: ✓ Connections ✓ Comparisons ✓ Communities Evidence (How these standards are incorporated in the instruction of the unit)	**Culture: D3: Beliefs and Attitudes** Identify some common beliefs and attitudes within the cultures studied, such as social etiquette or the role of the family. **Evidence:** Introduce a reading about a (French) family. **Connections: G1: Popular Media** Students will read, view, listen to, and talk about subjects contained in popular media from other countries in order to gain a perspective on other cultures. **Evidence:** Students will look at magazine ads to see how families are represented. **Comparisons: I2: Comparisons** Students will compare the form, meaning, and importance of certain perspectives, products, and practices in different cultures. **Evidence:** Students will compare their family to the (French) family presented in the video. **Communities: J2: Communication** Students will exchange information with people locally and around the world through avenues such as pen pals, E-mail, video, speeches, and publications. **Evidence:** Students will send E-mails to students in (France) asking for information about their families.

Step Eight: Structures and Vocabulary

The final step in this process is to look at the structures and vocabulary that will help the students succeed in the performance assessment. It is important to note that this is the last step in the process and not the first step, as it used to be. By setting up a curriculum unit based on the standards, by building the unit based on the assessment, the teacher now has a strong sense of what structures and vocabulary will be important for students to know. Structures and vocabulary now serve a purpose. They are not the goal of instruction; they are the pieces that help students communicate with confidence. To help select specific structures and vocabulary, a listing of language functions is included in Part IV at the end of this guide. The chart of language functions provides specific structures for students to learn and use at the four language levels: beginning, developing, transitioning, and refining. This helps teachers make the choice of structures and vocabulary based on the language functions needed for the performance assessment, rather than based on a sequential list of grammar topics.

The items needed for this unit on family are listed here:

Structures and Vocabulary: What needs to be taught for students to be successful in the performance assessment	■ names of family members ■ how to state age ■ adjectives of personality, physical description ■ question words: Who? Where? What? When?

Step Nine: Check the Unit—Reflection

After creating a curriculum unit of instruction, the teacher needs to reflect on the decisions. On one level, the teacher checks to make sure that the performance assessments are appropriate for the desired language level, not just allowing students to plateau, but encouraging and pushing students to stretch to higher levels of proficiency and competence in using the target language. On another level, the teacher reflects on how motivated students will be to engage in the unit's tasks and assessments.

The chart of language functions is one tool to help check the level of language targeted in a unit. The following questions from chapter 2 also help teachers to reflect on the curriculum designed:

(1) Is there a sense of connectedness among the three modes?
 —Does one mode lead logically to the next?
 —Are all three modes necessary in order to complete the picture?
 —Is the picture complete when the three modes are completed?
(2) Are the communication standards targeted in the performance appropriate for the task?
 —Are the most important standards identified?
 —Are the standards that were selected really critical to the performance?
 —Is the activity a real example of the performance standard?
(3) Are students engaged in learning while they are doing the assessment?
 —Does the assessment blend with the instruction rather than stand out as a separate, unrelated item?
 —Will students receive meaningful feedback in order to improve their performance?

Creating a Standards-Based Curriculum

(4) Are the expected performances set at the appropriate level? (Refer to the Performance Guidelines.)
—Not too easy (just cosmetic).
—Not too hard (input + 1, i + 1, the idea that students are challenged to use language slightly above their current level. See Chapter 6).
—Do students have the opportunity to show that their language proficiency is increasing?

(5) Is the unit worth doing?
—Does the unit address the standards beyond the *C* of Communication in a significant way?
—Is the task meaningful to the student?

Planning for Instruction

Now the teacher is ready to answer the question "What do I teach?" Before designing the instruction, the teacher has already done the following:

- set clear language targets (standards) and expectations (performance guidelines)
- developed a context for the unit by identifying the overarching question that fits the stage of language learning (beginning, developing, transitioning, or refining) and that has been focused by a thematic topic that provides a richness of content to explore
- described the end-of-unit performance assessment that will provide solid evidence of achievement, assessment that incorporates all three modes of communication (interpersonal, interpretive, and presentational)
- identified the key structures and elements of vocabulary that students will need to know in order to be successful in the performance assessment

    The instructional unit focused on what students needed to know and to practice in order to successfully complete the performance assessment tasks. The teacher broke the performance assessment into its component language functions. From the content standard of "Students will ask and answer questions, including biographical information," the teacher developed the assessment task of having students share picture books about their family with classmates, finding out additional information about the people pictured on each page. The teacher determined which structures and vocabulary the students needed. The list included certain question words, question formation, how to say "my" and "your," and a list of descriptive adjectives. Rather than teaching everything there is to know about possessive adjectives or how to ask questions, the instruction focused on what was needed for success in this unit. Grammatical structures and vocabulary were included as needed for the unit assessment.

    In order to make sure students were able to perform the assessment task, the teacher designed classroom activities in which students practiced asking questions about people. Students read questions to a partner and wrote down the information learned; they asked memorized questions in rotating pairs, alternating asking and answering; they took a bingo sheet filled with questions about people around the room, asking questions of each other, trying to fill their sheet with positive responses; and they practiced looking at family photographs, asking and answering questions.

Planning for instruction involves making very conscious choices about what students need to learn. Instead of teaching too much of a grammatical structure because the curriculum simply lists the item under the course syllabus or teaching a random series of vocabulary words because they will be seen in a text reading, the teacher consciously chooses what students need based on the end goal. The teacher is highly selective in choosing how much of any grammatical topic to introduce, practice, or review as well as which vocabulary categories and words need to be taught—all selected by the criteria of what is necessary to be successful in the already envisioned performance assessment for this unit of instruction. With the standards as a mind-set the teacher has a solid basis for making critical instructional decisions.

References

American Council on the Teaching of Foreign Languages. 1999. *ACTFL Performance Guidelines for K–12 Learners.* Yonkers, N.Y.: ACTFL.

Clementi, Donna. 2000. *Framework for Success: A New Guide for Creating Your Language Curriculum.* Wisconsin Association of Foreign Language Teachers Annual Conference, Focus Session. Appleton, Wisconsin, November 4, 2000.

National Standards in Foreign Language Education Project. 1996. *Standards for Foreign Language Learning: Preparing for the 21st Century.* Lawrence, Kans.: Allen Press.

Wiggins, Grant, and Jay McTighe. 1998. *Understanding by Design.* Alexandria, Va.: Association for Supervision and Curriculum Development.

Wisconsin Department of Public Instruction. 1986. *A Guide to Curriculum Planning in Foreign Language.* Madison, Wis.: Wisconsin Department of Public Instruction.

———. 1997. *Wisconsin's Model Academic Standards for Foreign Languages.* Madison, Wis.: Wisconsin Department of Public Instruction.

Standards-Based Curriculum Units

4

What's Different?
Sample Templates for Designing Curriculum
Benchmark Examples of Thematic Content across Language Levels, K–12: Work and Career Units
    Beginning Level: Grade 3: When I Grow Up
    Developing Level: Grade 5: Community Worker
    Transitioning Level: Grade 8: Interests and Careers
    Transitioning Level: Grade 10: Future Careers/Goals
    Refining Level: Grade 12: Preparing for International Careers
Sample Thematic Curriculum Units: Grouped by Level
    Beginning Level: 6 Sample Units
    Developing Level: 4 Sample Units
    Transitioning Level: 3 Sample Units
    Refining Level: 3 Sample Units

What's Different?

Good language instruction is based on what we know about language learning. Good curriculum design is based on what is needed to guarantee good language instruction. The curriculum should provide that set of targets so that all assessment and instruction produces the desired results, described as the curricular goals.

Standards-based curriculum units need to be based on progress toward the key element of our standards: the three communication modes (interpersonal, interpretive, presentational). Units that are thematically and linguistically rich should include all three modes. Some units are more developmental in nature, without big projects or presentations. Some units may be more summative in nature, where skills and knowledge are pulled together from previous units. In all units, however, the emphasis should be on the targeted performance that will provide students and teachers with clear evidence of progress toward stronger and more independent use of the language.

Sample Templates for Designing Curriculum

The examples provided here are not a complete curriculum. Curriculum needs to be based on the unique program in your school or district. Not all world language programs begin in elementary grades, nor do all districts have middle school programs that provide sufficient time to develop any degree of proficiency in using the language. With the variety of program designs in Wisconsin, this guide can not dictate a curriculum for each grade level nor for all classes identified as Level I, Level II, and so on. That must be a local decision.

These curriculum examples do provide

- a vision of a standards-based curriculum
- a guide to creating your own curriculum
- assessment targets against which you can check your own curriculum, asking if you have selected assessments that match your performance goals and are the appropriate challenge for your students' stage of language development
- a yardstick for expanding curricula that have traditionally only focused on a grammatical sequence or units organized by vocabulary topics such as school and food; this expansion is provided by the template's connection to all five major goal areas for language learning, emphasizing the improvement of students' communication skills

TABLE 4.1 **Sample Curriculum Units**
Benchmark Examples of Thematic Content Across Language Levels, K–12: Work/Career Units

Level	Beginning	Developing	Transitioning	Refining
Starting in Kindergarten	Gr. 3	Gr. 5	Gr. 8	Gr. 10
				Gr. 12

Sample Units by Language Levels

Level	Beginning	Developing	Transitioning	Refining
Starting in Kindergarten/ Gr. 1	Gr. 1 Art-Colors	Gr. 3 Food Pyramid	Gr. 5 Art-Artists	
			Gr. 8 Geography	Gr. 11 Cultural Celeb.
				Gr. 12 Lit.
Starting in Gr. 3/4			Gr. 8 Cultural Celeb.	Gr. 10 Legends/Folk Tales
				Gr. 12 Immigration
Starting in Gr. 6/7	Gr. 6 City Directions	Gr. 8 Introducing Myself	Gr. 10 Teen Life	Gr. 12 Famous People-Fame
Starting in Gr. 8/9	Gr. 9 Free Time	Gr. 10 Geography	Gr. 12 Music	

The curriculum units presented in this chapter provide examples for each of the four language levels in different grades. The grade level at which students begin their study of the target language, the amount of time per class, the frequency of class sessions, and the continuity of classes scheduled over the course of a school year directly impact students' progress across the continuum of language proficiency. For each sample unit, the grade at which instruction began is indicated to help illustrate reasonable progress to expect from students who continue their study of the language each year. For each sample unit provided in this guide, a bar graph in Table 4.1 indicates the progress toward reaching the standards of each language level. This is repeated at the top of each sample unit. The first 5 sample units (pages 68–91) focus on the same theme: work and careers. The 16 remaining sample units (pages 100–137) are grouped by language level: beginning, developing, transitioning, and refining. The descriptive titles to the right of each bar graph show the wide variety of thematic content.

Benchmark Examples of Thematic Content Across Language Levels, K–12: Work and Career Units

Beginning Level	—Grade 3	These sample units can be adapted to any grade level with appropriate modification for the age of the student. The beginning level may occur in any of grades K–12. These examples demonstrate the rising expectation of what students can do within the same thematic focus as they move to higher levels of language proficiency. An early elementary start is necessary for students to reach the refining level by the end of senior high school.
Developing Level	—Grade 5	
Transitioning Level	—Grade 8	
	—Grade 10	
Refining Level	—Grade 12	

These benchmark examples provide sample curriculum units for the four levels of language development spread across a K–12 program. The targeted point of progress along the proficiency continuum is shown at the top of each curriculum unit. Each example highlights the characteristics of a quality performance at the given level. Placing the unit at the beginning point of a particular language level shows how a unit can work toward the level's language goals while not holding students accountable for fully achieving them. Placing the unit near the end point of a language level indicates that the expectations for student performance meet the descriptors of that level's performance guidelines.

These five units have the same theme of work and careers. As you read these examples, focus on the growth in language across the K–12 program; that is, what students are able to do differently with the same topic at different levels of language proficiency.

While more than one standard may be involved in a performance task, the teacher needs to focus on the primary standard to be emphasized within each unit.

The performance assessment is not designed to find out what students know about *the language, rather it is designed to find out what students can do* using *the language.*

The performance assessment tasks that are the core of each curriculum unit will be conducted entirely in the target language. The exception is assessment of the interpretive mode (reading and listening comprehension), which may require use of English to demonstrate understanding of the texts. Everything that students see, hear, and read and everything that they show, say, and write will be done in the target language. The performance assessment is not designed to find out what students know *about* the language, rather it is designed to find out what students can do *using* the language.

Work and Career Units

Benchmark Example
Beginning Level—Grade 3

Students who begin instruction in a second language in kindergarten will be secure in the skills of the beginning level of language development by Grade 3. This assumes a program of continuous instruction that meets for a minimum of three times a week for 30 minutes each day. The performance assessments are matched to the cognitive and developmental characteristics of students at that age. The assessments are targeted to show achievement of the beginning level Standards and Performance Guidelines. The key overarching question is "Who am I? Who are you?" Students are able to state similarities and differences between themselves and others in simple statements such as "I eat cereal for breakfast; he eats bread and butter for breakfast."

Benchmark Example
Developing Level—Grade 5

Students who begin instruction in a second language in kindergarten will demonstrate skills in the developing level of language development by Grade 5. They will still need more practice in order to be secure in the skills associated with this level. The performance assessments are matched to the cognitive and developmental characteristics of students at that age. The rubrics for these assessments show that the expected performance is not securely at the end point of the developing level. The key overarching question is "What is my life like? What is your life like?" Students are able to investigate similarities and differences between themselves and others, giving reasons for the differences and some description of these differences and similarities.

Benchmark Example
Transitioning Level—Grade 8

Students who begin instruction in a second language in kindergarten will demonstrate skills in the transitioning level of language development by Grade 8. Their language proficiency will securely demonstrate the profile of the developing level, so the target for this unit of instruction needs to begin to pull from the Performance Standards of the transitioning level. The rubric likewise pulls from the transitioning level Performance Guidelines. Students are asked to try tasks geared at the transitioning level; however, the expectation for their performance takes into consideration that they are only beginning to show the characteristics of this level. The key overarching question to target students' language performance is "How do I look at the world? How do you look at the world?" Students begin to share and compare perspectives as they learn more about their world and the variety of viewpoints and opinions that exist within it.

Benchmark Example
Transitioning Level—Grade 10

Students who begin instruction in a second language in kindergarten will demonstrate skills in the transitioning level of language development with confidence by Grade 10. Their language proficiency will securely demonstrate the profile of the transitioning level. The key overarching question to target students' language performance is "How do I look at the world? How do you look at the world?" Students share and compare perspectives as they learn more about their world and the variety of viewpoints and opinions that exist within it.

Benchmark Example
Refining Level—Grade 12

Students with continuous instruction from kindergarten through Grade 12 are refining their language skills as stated in the characteristics of the refining level. They will not yet be exhibiting the full expectation of the Performance Guidelines at this level; however, their performance will be solidly within the refining level. The key overarching question to target students' language performance is "What do I think and feel? What do you think and feel?" Students will discuss and defend opinions on issues of national and international importance.

The curriculum unit and the rubrics for the performance assessments directly guide each instructional decision, completing the vital link of curriculum, assessment, and instruction.

Concerning Sample Rubrics

Each benchmark example in this section is followed by a rubric to help anchor the performance assessment along the continuum of proficiency. These are provided as examples to make clear the distinctions between the three modes of communication: Interpersonal, Interpretive, and Presentational. Specific criteria are given for evaluating the performances within each assessment unit. These criteria are taken from the Wisconsin Performance Guidelines and focus the practice and assessment throughout the unit of instruction. The benchmark curriculum unit and the rubrics for the performance assessments will directly guide each instructional decision, completing the vital link of curriculum, assessment, and instruction.

These sample rubrics are based on the following definition of a rubric: criteria by which student work is evaluated. In several of the examples the rubric provides the characteristics of excellent work. The teacher can then evaluate the student work in terms of how closely it matches the definition of excellence.

In both cases the goal is the same: provide students with criteria that will help them achieve excellence in their performance.

In other cases, descriptors are provided for "excellent," "good," and "needs work." In both cases the goal is the same: provide students with criteria that will help them achieve excellence in their performance. The rubric not only guides the students; it guides the teacher in giving the students appropriate instructions in how to complete the task. Furthermore, it guides the teacher in the kind of practice that is needed in order for the students to perform the task.

Another feature of some of the rubrics presented is a checklist of nonnegotiables. The rubric focuses the student on characteristics that lead to an excellent performance, but some criteria are merely basic requirements for completing the assessment. For example, if the document is supposed to be word processed, that can be listed as a nonnegotiable. Then if the document is not word processed, it is simply not ready to be evaluated. This approach demands a certain level of quality in the product before students turn it in for the teacher's evaluation. In other words, the rubric highlights qualities of a product worthy of evaluation; it does not allow for incomplete or unacceptable work.

As you look at the rubrics, you will see that not all the target performance indicators in the unit appear in all the rubrics. Again, these indicators are meant to guide teacher reflection concerning the expectations for a particular level of proficiency. They may serve as a reminder to focus practice in a certain way. They may not be pertinent in the actual performance assessment but serve to guide practice for the performance. There may be other characteristics that are important to include as part of the rubric even though they don't appear in the Performance Guidelines. These may deal with the actual content of the performance or the style, length, or variety of the performance. Again, the teacher must continuously reflect on the characteristics of a high-quality performance and focus the students' attention on those criteria.

Note on Rubric for the Presentational Mode: One of the characteristics of the presentational mode is that it is a practiced, polished performance. This implies that the student has worked on making the final product perfect, which requires rough drafts, practice sessions, or rehearsals. How does a teacher evaluate this work? Each teacher will have to make decisions concerning the role of drafts, rehearsals, and final products. A rough draft may be graded according to criteria over which the student has control. For example, students can proofread for spelling, gender, and agreement. They can look up unknown words in a dictionary. In other words, the draft shouldn't be viewed as a way for the teacher to do all the editing work for her students. After several rehearsals or drafts, students submit their final product. This is akin to a final recital or concert. Now the criteria for evaluation are not in the details, but in the overall quality of the presentation.

As rubrics are developed, Grant Wiggins provides an excellent rule for determining the quality of the rubric:

> One simple test of criteria is negative: can you imagine someone meeting all your proposed criteria but not being able to perform well at the task? Then you have the wrong criteria.
>
> *Wiggins 1998, 167–68*

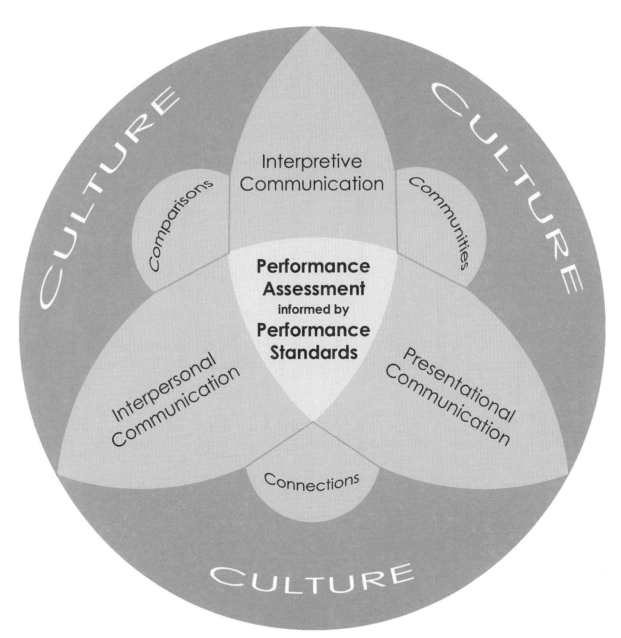

Curriculum Design for Learning World Languages

In a world language classroom, standards influence the curriculum, assessment, and instruction. The three purposes of Communication (interpersonal, interpretive, and presentational) form the heart. Culture is always embedded in the instruction. Connections, Comparisons, and Communities enrich the learning activities. The performance standards inform the assessments that show students their progress toward higher levels of proficiency in using the target language. The focus is on what students can do with the language they are learning.

Thematic Curriculum Unit—Performance Assessment and Planning Guide
Elementary School, Grade 3

Key Question: Who am I? Who are you? **Theme: Work/careers** **Topic: When I grow up**

Beginning	Developing	Transitioning	Refining

Students who begin instruction in a second language in kindergarten will be secure in the skills of the beginning level of language development by Grade 3. This assumes a program of continuous instruction that meets for a minimum of three times a week for 30 minutes each day. The performance assessments are matched to the cognitive and developmental characteristics of students at that age. The assessments are targeted to show achievement of the beginning level Standards and Performance Guidelines. The key overarching question is "Who am I? Who are you?" Students are able to state similarities and differences between themselves and others in simple statements such as "I eat cereal for breakfast; he eats bread and butter for breakfast."

The intention is that all instruction and assessments are completed in the target language, with the exception of reading and listening comprehension assessments, which may require use of English to demonstrate understanding of the texts.

Communication Mode:	Interpretive	Presentational	Interpersonal
Performance Assessment	Listen to a story about someone in a profession in the community; on a paper with pictures of different scenes from the story; place #1 by the first scene, #2 by the second scene, etc.	Make a picture book showing members of a family and what they do for a living; include yourself and what you want to do some day. Label the pictures with the person's family role and profession. (Here is my mother. She is a dentist.) Place a star by anyone who uses/could use more than one language on the job. Share your picture book with other classmates.	After sharing your picture book with other classmates, answer questions about the people in your picture book. Ask classmates questions about the people in their picture books. (Who is that? What does he do?)
Wisconsin Standards: **Communication**	**B1: Listening:** Students will understand spoken language on familiar topics that has strong visual support.	**C2: Speeches:** Students will write and present a short narrative about themselves.	**A2: Questions:** Students will ask and answer questions, including biographical information.
Target Performance (Key elements from the Performance Guidelines to consider in rubric development)	**Content:** *Complexity/sophistication:* Relies primarily on memorized phrases and short sentences on very familiar topics in both oral and written presentations.	**Content:** *Complexity/sophistication:* Relies primarily on memorized phrases and short sentences on very familiar topics in both oral and written presentations.	**Content:** *Spontaneity:* Responds automatically to high frequency cues (i.e., hello, how are you, what's your name); can ask memorized questions (i.e., what's your name, how are you).

	Accuracy: — **Communication Strategies:** *Comprehension*: Understands short, simple conversations and narration with highly predictable and familiar contexts; relies heavily on visuals, gestures, facial expressions in order to understand; generally needs repetition, restatement, and contextual clues in order to understand; relies heavily on background information. **Cross-Cultural Applications:** *Awareness*: Understands a story line or event when it reflects a cultural background similar to own; begins to associate symbols, famous people, places, songs, etc. with a certain culture.	**Accuracy:** *Ease*: Expresses memorized phrases with ease and with few errors; may show evidence of false starts and pauses as topics expand beyond memorized dialogues. **Communication Strategies:** *Impact*: Focuses on successful task completion; uses gestures or visuals to maintain audience's attention and/or interest as appropriate to purpose. **Cross-Cultural Applications:** *Awareness*: Understands a story line or event when it reflects a cultural background similar to own; begins to associate symbols, famous people, places, songs, etc. with a certain culture.	**Accuracy:** *Ease*: Expresses memorized phrases with ease and with few errors; may show evidence of false starts and pauses as topics expand beyond memorized dialogues. **Communication Strategies:** *Monitoring*: May self-correct on high-frequency items. **Cross-Cultural Applications:** *Verbal*: Imitates appropriate linguistic patterns (i.e., register, formal vs. informal address, intonation) when modeled by the teacher.

Links to Culture and the other Wisconsin Standards:

✓ **Connections**
✓ **Comparisons**
✓ **Communities**

Evidence (How these standards are incorporated in the instruction)

Culture: E1: Objects and Symbols: Identify objects and symbols, such as flags or currency, that are used day-to-day and represent other cultures. (Identify uniforms associated with certain professions.)

Connections: F1: Speaking and Writing: Students will use topics and skills from other school subjects to discuss and/or write in the language studied. (Discuss professions: social studies.)

Comparisons: H1: Structures: Students will identify cognates (words similar to English), word roots, prefixes, suffixes, and sentence structure to derive meaning. (Compare names for professions in English and the target language.)

Communities: K2: Students will investigate careers where skills in another language and/or cross-cultural understanding are needed. (Discuss professions where knowing another language could be helpful.)

Structures and Vocabulary:
What needs to be taught for students to be successful in the performance assessment

Structures:
- He is/she is (profession)
- He is/she is my (mother, father, sister, brother, etc.)
- Questions (Who is that? What does he/she do?)

Vocabulary:
- Professions
- Family members

Benchmark—Grade 3—Rubrics

Interpretive Task: No rubric is needed; students are sequencing the pictures to reflect the story they heard.

Presentational Task: Students will submit a draft of their booklet before they put together their final product. This rubric is in the form of a checklist that the students can use to help them prepare the draft and final copies. A rubric for the final copy is also included.

My Family Picture Book

1. I followed directions:

    __I have pictures of five different people.

    __I have a picture of myself.

    __For each person, I wrote a sentence saying who the person is. (Example: This is my mother.)

    __For each person, I wrote a sentence saying what they do. (Example: He is a teacher.)

    __I put a ☆ next to the people who could use another language where they work.

2. Spelling:

    __I checked the spelling of words in my personal dictionary.

3. Sentences:

    __I have two complete sentences for each picture. (Example: This is my brother. He is a student.)

Final Product:
Exceeds Expectations: You followed all the directions on the checklist. Your booklet is neat and attractive. You provided more information than required.

Meets Expectations: You followed all the directions on the checklist. Your booklet is neat and attractive.

Needs Work: Your final product may be missing some of the items on the checklist or the booklet may have words crossed out or misspelled. The pictures and/or sentences may be presented in a sloppy way.

Interpersonal Task: Students share their picture books with each other in pairs or small groups. The teacher may have students switch partners several times and monitor the class to see that everyone is engaged in the activity and using the target language. The teacher can also randomly sample pairs of students to hear how well they can accomplish the task. If there is a parent volunteer available, the volunteer could audio- or videotape the pairs of students in the hall while the teacher is teaching the class. The following evaluation tool is meant to be used for one student.

Sharing Family Picture Books

1. The student is able to ask "Who is that?" and "What does he or she do?" about the people in partner's picture book.

    ___ Yes   ___ With help   ___ Needs practice

2. The student can answer "Who is that?" and "What does he or she do?" about the people in own picture book.

    ___ Yes   ___ With help   ___ Needs practice

3. The student asks additional questions about the people in partner's picture book.

    ___ Yes   ___ With help   ___ Needs practice

4. The student responds to partner's answers with a comment. (Example: That's interesting. He is handsome, etc.)

    ___ Yes   ___ With help   ___ Needs practice

5. The student uses correct pronunciation and intonation.

    ___ Yes   ___ With help   ___ Needs practice

Standards-Based Curriculum Units

Thematic Curriculum Unit—Performance Assessment and Planning Guide
Elementary School, Grade 5

Key Question: What is my life like? What is your life like? **Theme:** Work/careers **Topic:** Community workers

Beginning	Developing	Transitioning	Refining

Students who begin instruction in a second language in kindergarten will demonstrate skills in the developing level of language development by Grade 5. They will still need more practice in order to be secure in the skills associated with this level. The performance assessments are matched to the cognitive and developmental characteristics of students at that age. The rubrics for these assessments show that the expected performance is not securely at the end point of the developing level. The key overarching question is "What is my life like? What is your life like?" Students are able to investigate similarities and differences between themselves and others, giving reasons for the differences and some description of these differences and similarities.

The intention is that all instruction and assessments are completed in the target language, with the exception of reading and listening comprehension assessments, which may require use of English to demonstrate understanding of the texts.

Communication Mode:	Interpretive	Interpersonal	Presentational
Performance Assessment	Watch a video or a slide presentation of a city in a country where the target language is spoken showing the various businesses and city services. Match on a paper the names of the various businesses and a short description of what happens at each business.	With a group of two or three classmates, discuss how to make a decorative tourist map for an imaginary city in a country where the target language is spoken. Plan a tourist map with streets, businesses, and city services labeled.	Work with a group of two or three classmates to prepare and present a commercial for job opportunities in your imaginary city. The commercial should include a variety of jobs, where they are located in the city, and a reason to choose each job.
Wisconsin Standards: Communication	**B2: Listening:** Students will comprehend the main idea and some supporting ideas of selected authentic materials including recordings, broadcasts, videos.	**A2: Questions:** Students will ask and answer a variety of questions, giving reasons for their answers.	**C2: Speeches:** Students will write and deliver a short presentation about their school or community.
Target Performance (Key elements from the Performance Guidelines to consider in rubric development)	**Content:** *Situation:* Meets basic communication needs in a controlled setting; can meet practical writing needs such as short letters and notes.	**Content:** *Spontaneity:* Responds with short answers to questions that have been rehearsed; asks simple yes/no questions, informational questions (i.e., who, when, where, what); begins to express reactions to responses (i.e., really, that's great, that's too bad).	**Content:** *Complexity/sophistication:* Begins combining and recombining phrases into short strings of sentences on familiar topics in both oral and written presentations.

	Accuracy: *Ease:* Restates and recombines memorized language with frequent pauses, hesitations, and false starts; many errors may occur as creativity increases. **Communication Strategies:** *Monitoring:* Self-corrects on well-learned items.	**Accuracy:** *Pronunciation:* May mispronounce words in a new context or words being read for the first time; understandable to a sympathetic native speaker, though this may require special efforts by the native speaker at times. **Communication Strategies:** *Impact:* Asks follow-up questions; provides continuity to a presentation; begins to make choices of a phrase, image, or content to maintain the attention of the audience.
	Communication Strategies: *Comprehension:* Understands general concepts and some supporting ideas of short conversations and narration on familiar topics; relies on visuals, gestures, facial expressions; may need repetition, restatement, and contextual clues in order to understand; uses background experience to help anticipate meaning. **Cross-Cultural Applications:** *Awareness:* Begins to use knowledge of own culture and the target culture(s) to help interpret oral and written texts.	**Cross-Cultural Applications:** *Awareness:* Begins to use knowledge of own culture and the target culture(s) to help interpret oral and written texts.
Links to **Culture** and the other Wisconsin Standards:	**Culture: E1:** Objects and Symbols: Students will compare objects and symbols, such as flags or currency, from other cultures to those found in their own culture. (Identify symbols that represent various business and city services and compare them to the symbols used in their community.)	
✓ *Connections* ✓ *Comparisons* ✓ *Communities*	**Connections: F1:** Speaking and Writing: Students will use topics and skills from other school subjects to discuss and/or write in the language studied. (Use skills of perspective, design, visual appeal to create tourist map.)	
Evidence (How these standards are incorporated in the instruction)	**Comparisons: I1:** Cultural Variations: Students will discuss the meaning of perspectives, products, and practices in different cultures. (Compare stores, services in a town in the target culture to those found in local community.)	
	Communities: K3: Understanding: Students will deepen their understanding of other cultures through various avenues such as cuisine, sports, theatre, dance, and art. (Create a tourist map; create a commercial.)	
Structures and Vocabulary: *What needs to be taught for students to be successful in the performance assessment*	**Structures:** ■ Prepositions of location ■ Questions ■ Descriptive adjectives and agreement	**Vocabulary:** ■ Businesses and services in a town ■ Prepositions of location ■ Professions ■ Items on a city map (corner, street, square, sidewalk, etc.)

Benchmark—Grade 5—Rubrics

Interpretive Task: No rubric is needed; students are matching the names of businesses with descriptions of the services provided at each business.

Interpersonal Task: This task has two portions: one is the conversation about making a tourist map (interpersonal); the other portion is the actual map itself (the product of the interpersonal conversation).

The teacher determines how to assess student participation in this task. A group grade or individual grades may be given by the teacher and/or by the students based on observation of the groups in action. It should be noted that this grade would reflect effort to accomplish the task and stay in the target language, rather than a grade that reflects the quality and accuracy of the language used.

Discussion: Making a Tourist Map

1. Students speak the target language to accomplish the task.

    ___ 90%–100% of the time
    ___ 70%–89% of the time
    ___ 50%–69% of the time
    ___ less than 50% of the time

2. There is equal participation in speaking the target language from all group members.

    ___ Yes ___ No

    If you responded "no," please describe the participation of the group members.

3. Students ask simple, informational questions and yes/no questions.

    ___ Frequently ___ Sometimes ___ Rarely

4. Students respond to questions appropriately.

    ___ Frequently ___ Sometimes ___ Rarely

5. Students react to responses with follow-ups such as: "really," "I agree," "Good idea."

    ___ Frequently ___ Sometimes ___ Rarely

6. There is equal participation in creating the tourist map.

    ___ Yes ___ No

    If you responded "no," please describe the participation of the group members.

7. The cooperation among the group members was:

    ___ Excellent ___ Good ___ Needs work

Standards-Based Curriculum Units

Interpersonal Product: *Tourist Map:* The teacher determines the requirements for the product. These requirements can be given to the students as part of the directions. They can be put in the form of a checklist so that students can verify that they have all the necessary components of the project. The components of the checklist can be considered nonnegotiable; in other words, all of the components must be present before the product can be graded. If the teacher desires, quantities can be part of the requirements (number of streets, number of businesses, and so on). Or the teacher could provide a list and have the students choose a certain number of items.

Tourist Map

Requirements:

1. The tourist map contains the following elements:

   __City name that reflects the target language/culture.

   __Street names that reflect the target language/culture.

   __Businesses that reflect the target language/culture.

   __City services that reflect the target language/culture.

2. The tourist map must be:

   __at least 8½ × 14 inches in size.

   __drawn in colored marker or ink.

   __checked for spelling accuracy with the teacher before the final map is labeled.

The final tourist map will be evaluated according to this scale:

Exceeds expectations: The layout of the city reflects the target culture: There is a wide variety of businesses, city services, and locations that are typically found in a city in the target culture. The layout of the city streets reflects the target culture. There are additional details such as parks, cars, pedestrians, public transportation, decorations, map key that reflect the target culture/language. The spelling of place names is accurate. The map is neatly done.

Meets expectations: The layout of the city reflects the target culture: Several businesses, city services, and locations that are typically found in a city in the target culture are included. The spelling of place names is accurate. The map is neatly done.

Needs work: The layout of the city reflects the target culture. The map may lack businesses, city services, and locations that are typically found in a city from the target culture. The layout of the city streets may or may not reflect the target culture. There may be spelling mistakes of place names. The map is neatly done.

Presentational Task: The teacher determines how to assess student participation in this task. A group grade or individual grades may be given by the teacher or by the students for all or some of the categories listed. The teacher may wish to give the students some nonnegotiables to ensure a baseline level of quality for this task. The teacher may also elect to grade the script for the commercial for correctness of structures that are targeted in this unit (example: correct use of prepositions, adjective agreement).

Job Opportunities Commercial

Requirements:

The commercial you prepare must include the following:

__Each member of your group must speak in the commercial.

__There must be at least three jobs featured in the commercial.

__The location of each job in the city must be included.

__There must be a reason to choose each job.

__The commercial must be memorized.

__The script must be checked by the teacher before rehearsing for the videotaping.

__The commercial must be videotaped.

The commercial will be evaluated according to the following criteria:

	Excellent	Good	Needs work
Pronunciation: Speakers imitate pronunciation and intonation of the target language.			
Impact: Speakers maintain the attention of the audience.			
Impact: Gestures or visuals help audience understand message.			
Impact: Speakers have practiced their roles and can recite their lines with confidence.			
Comprehensibility: The spoken language is structurally correct.			

Thematic Curriculum Unit—Performance Assessment and Planning Guide
Middle School, Grade 8

Key Question: How do I look at the world? How do you look at the world?   **Theme:** Work/careers   **Topic:** Interests and careers

Beginning	Developing	Transitioning	Refining

Students who begin instruction in a second language in kindergarten will demonstrate skills in the transitioning level of language development by Grade 8. Their language proficiency will securely demonstrate the profile of the developing level, so the target for this unit of instruction needs to begin to pull from the Performance Standards of the transitioning level. The rubric likewise pulls from the transitioning level Performance Guidelines. Students are asked to try tasks geared at the transitioning level; however, the expectation for their performance takes into consideration that they are only beginning to show the characteristics of this level. The key overarching question to target students' language performance is "How do I look at the world? How do you look at the world?" Students begin to share and compare perspectives as they learn more about their world and the variety of viewpoints and opinions that exist within it.

The intention is that all instruction and assessments are completed in the target language, with the exception of reading and listening comprehension assessments, which may require use of English to demonstrate understanding of the texts.

Communication Mode: *Performance Assessment*	**Interpretive**	**Presentational**	**Interpersonal**
	Read about a student from the target culture who describes his/her daily schedule including interests, part-time jobs, school coursework, weekend activities, social life, future plans. Summarize similarities and differences between the student's life and your own; draw some conclusions about how compatible you would be with this student, giving reasons for your conclusions.	Give a presentation about your life and interests. Indicate how these activities reflect your personality. Include some possibilities for your future in terms of career, study, travel, pursuing personal interests.	Discuss with a group of classmates plans for high school. Indicate what kinds of courses you will take and how they will prepare you for your future plans. Discuss career options and which ones interest or don't interest you and why.
Wisconsin Standards: **Communication**	**B4: Reading:** Students will comprehend the main idea and key supporting ideas and begin to make inferences in selected authentic written materials.	**C2: Speeches:** Students will write and deliver a short speech on a topic of personal interest.	**A3: Opinions:** Students will defend personal preferences, feelings, opinions with more complete explanation.
Target Performance (Key elements from the Performance Guidelines to consider in rubric development)	**Content:** *Situation:* Meets communication needs in a variety of settings; can meet writing needs including letters, articles, short essays.	**Content:** *Complexity/sophistication:* Expresses own thoughts to describe and narrate using sentences and strings of sentences on familiar and some unfamiliar topics in both oral and written presentations.	**Content:** *Vocabulary:* Uses vocabulary from a variety of topics; if precise vocabulary is lacking, can often find another way to express an idea/term; uses a dictionary as needed and selects correct translation most of the time; shows some understanding and use of idiomatic expressions; may invent a word or phrase in order to stay in the target language.

	Accuracy: — **Communication Strategies:** *Comprehension*: Understands the main idea and some supporting ideas of conversations, lectures, and narration on familiar and some unfamiliar topics; uses contextual clues, inferences, key words and ideas, and text types to aid understanding; uses background knowledge to help understand the discourse. **Cross-Cultural Applications:** *Awareness*: Recognizes differences and similarities in the perspectives of the target culture(s) and their own as they are expressed in oral and written texts.	**Accuracy:** *Time/tense*: Expresses own thoughts in present time with accuracy; with preparation can use present, past, and simple future times—some errors may be present. **Communication Strategies:** *Impact*: Personalizes to maintain or reengage audience; able to provide comparisons and/or contrasts to reinforce message. **Cross-Cultural Applications:** *Verbal*. Recognizes and produces linguistic patterns appropriate to the target language.	**Accuracy:** *Ease*: Creates with both familiar and new language; presents thoughts and ideas with some pauses and hesitations; errors may occur but do not interfere with communication. **Communication Strategies:** *Clarification*: May use paraphrasing, question asking, circumlocution. **Cross-Cultural Applications:** *Verbal*. Recognizes and produces linguistic patterns appropriate to the target language.
Links to Culture and the other Wisconsin Standards: ✓ **Connections** ✓ **Comparisons** ✓ **Communities** *Evidence (How these standards are incorporated in the instruction)*	**Culture: D3:** Beliefs and Attitudes: Students will discuss and compare beliefs and attitudes within the cultures studied and their own in relation to home, school, community, and nation. (Compare lifestyles of someone your age in the target culture to your own.) **Connections: G1:** Popular Media: Students will read, view, listen to, and talk about subjects contained in popular media from other countries in order to gain a perspective on other cultures. (Read articles, interviews about young people in teen magazines from target culture.) **Comparisons: I2:** Comparisons: Students will compare the form, meaning, and importance of certain perspectives, products, and practices in different cultures. (Compare lifestyles of teenagers in the target cultures with your own.) **Communities: J1:** Service: Students will provide service to their school and community through such activities as tutoring, teaching, translating, interpreting, and assisting speakers of other languages. (Identify outside activities or community service activities in which to participate to investigate or prepare for future careers.) **Communities: K2:** Careers: Students will investigate careers where skills in another language and/or cross-cultural understanding are needed. (Discuss future plans and career options.)	
Structures and Vocabulary: *What needs to be taught for students to be successful in the performance assessment*	**Structures:** ■ Subjunctive to express opinions ■ Adjective comparison	**Vocabulary:** ■ Careers ■ Daily activities, hobbies, interests ■ Courses of study

Standards-Based Curriculum Units

Benchmark—Grade 8—Rubrics

Interpretive Task: This task has two components. First, the students must demonstrate that they understand the main idea and some supporting ideas of the article. Then they must use this information as a point of comparison in discussing their own lifestyle. The second requirement of the task, to discuss compatibility, is a strategy to help students start making inferences from a text. The teacher may decide to keep the grading for the two components separate.

Magazine Article: Lifestyle of a Teenager

1. Comprehension of information provided in the article:

    Exceeds expectations: The student can summarize the main idea and all supporting ideas presented in the article. Any inaccuracies are minor and do not detract from the meaning of the article.

    Meets expectations: The student can summarize the main idea and most of the supporting ideas presented in the article. Any inaccuracies are minor and do not significantly detract from the meaning of the article.

    Needs work: The student can summarize the main idea of the article. Several supporting ideas are missing or inaccurate.

2. Making inferences about the compatibility of the person in the article with the student:

    Exceeds expectations: The student can synthesize information from the article and logically defend reasons concerning why he or she would or would not be compatible with the person in the article, citing details from the article and the implications of these details.

    Meets expectations: The student can synthesize information from the article into broad characteristics. The student can then use these broad characteristics to state how compatible he or she would be with the student in the article, based on examples from the article.

    Needs work: The student is not able to synthesize the information in the article in order to determine compatibility.

Presentational Task: For this presentation, students might make a PowerPoint presentation showing their interests, hobbies, favorite classes, and other activities in which they are involved. The presentation should also include some career possibilities that reflect their personal interests. At the end of the presentation, there could be an opportunity for students to ask questions of the presenter. The teacher may wish to include some nonnegotiables in the directions for the project to ensure that certain components are part of all projects. The teacher may also elect to grade a script before the final product is prepared. This is where accuracy of certain structures can be evaluated (example: correct use of the subjunctive mood; adjective comparison).

PowerPoint Presentation: Personal Lifestyle

Requirements:

The PowerPoint presentation you prepare must include the following:

- __ The presentation must last 4–5 minutes.
- __ The student provides the narration for the PowerPoint (it is not prerecorded).
- __ In providing narration for the presentation, the student may use notecards that contain an outline of key points; the entire script cannot be written on the notecards.
- __ The presentation must include the student's special interests and some career possibilities related to these interests.
- __ The script must be written and checked by the teacher before the final project is completed.
- __ Any language used in the PowerPoint slides must be checked by the teacher before the final project is completed.

The script for the PowerPoint presentation will be evaluated according to the following criteria:

	Excellent	Good	Needs work
A wide variety of interests, hobbies, and activities is presented in the script including details about these topics.			
Potential career choices are presented with reasons why these choices would be appropriate.			
There are at least five correct examples of the subjunctive mood.			
The sentences are varied in structure and length.			
The overall style includes appropriate use of formal language and idiomatic expressions.			
Comparison structures are used appropriately.			

The PowerPoint presentation will be evaluated according to the following criteria:

	Excellent	Good	Needs work
Pacing: The PowerPoint slides and the narration are delivered at a comfortable rate of speed so that the audience can absorb what is being said.			
Pronunciation: The student imitates pronunciation and intonation of the target language.			
Impact: The PowerPoint visuals are used effectively to enhance comprehension.			
Impact: The PowerPoint visuals are used effectively to maintain the interest of the audience.			
Spontaneity: The student responds to unrehearsed comments and questions appropriately.			

Interpersonal Task: The teacher determines how to assess student participation in this task. A group grade or individual grades may be given by the teacher or by the students based on observation of the groups in action. These discussions could be audio- or videotaped so that the teacher can review them at a later time for a more accurate assessment. Again, it should be noted that if this task is done without taping, the grade would reflect effort to accomplish the task and stay in the target language, rather than a grade reflecting the accuracy and sophistication of the language used.

Discussion: Future Plans

1. Students speak the target language to accomplish the task.
   ___ 90%–100% of the time
   ___ 70%–89% of the time
   ___ 50%–69% of the time
   ___ less than 50% of the time
2. There is equal participation in speaking the target language from all group members.
   ___ Yes ___ No
   If you responded "no," please describe the participation of the group members.
3. Individual students can be evaluated during the group discussion according to these criteria:

	Frequently	Sometimes	Rarely
Responds to unrehearsed comments, questions appropriately.			
Asks a variety of questions to encourage discussion.			
Uses expressive reactions and follow-up questions to elicit more information from participants			
Uses paraphrasing, question asking, or circumlocution to stay in the target language			

Thematic Curriculum Unit—Performance Assessment and Planning Guide
High School, Grade 10

Key Question: How do I look at the world? How do you look at the world? **Theme:** Work/careers **Topic:** Future careers/goals

	Beginning	Developing	Transitioning	Refining

Students who begin instruction in a second language in kindergarten will demonstrate skills in the transitioning level of language development with confidence by Grade 10. Their language proficiency will securely demonstrate the profile of the transitioning level. The key overarching question to target students' language performance is "How do I look at the world? How do you look at the world?" Students share and compare perspectives as they learn more about their world and the variety of viewpoints and opinions that exist within it.

The intention is that all instruction and assessments are completed in the target language, with the exception of reading and listening comprehension assessments, which may require use of English to demonstrate understanding of the texts.

Communication Mode: *Performance Assessment*	**Interpretive** Read interviews of workers in the target culture describing their career selection and preparation. Summarize their education, training, and career path. Note positive or negative implications about their career choice.	**Interpersonal** Using questions adapted from career preference surveys, students interview each other about what is important in a chosen profession including talents, interests, skills, education, preparation, opportunities.	**Presentational** Complete a curriculum vitae (CV) or resume with biographical data, education, and work history. Create a cover letter in which career and workplace desires are described, highlighting personal characteristics that make one well suited for a particular career.
Wisconsin Standards: Communication	**B4: Reading:** Students will comprehend the main idea and key supporting ideas and begin to make inferences in selected authentic written materials.	**A2: Questions:** Students will ask and answer a variety of questions that require follow-up questions and responses for more information.	**C5: Forms of Writing:** Students will write formal compositions and letters for a variety of purposes.
Target Performance (Key elements from the Performance Guidelines to consider in rubric development)	**Content:** *Vocabulary:* Uses vocabulary from a variety of topics; if precise vocabulary is lacking, can often find another way to express an idea/term; uses a dictionary as needed and selects correct translation most of the time; shows some understanding and use of idiomatic expressions; may invent a word or phrase in order to stay in the target language. **Accuracy:** —	**Content:** *Spontaneity:* Responds to unrehearsed comments, questions on familiar topics; asks a variety of questions and uses some expressive reactions and questions to elicit more information. **Accuracy:** *Ease:* Creates with both familiar and new language; presents thoughts and ideas with some pauses and hesitations; errors may occur but do not interfere with communication.	**Content:** *Vocabulary:* Uses vocabulary from a variety of topics; if precise vocabulary is lacking, can often find another way to express an idea/term; uses a dictionary as needed and selects correct translation most of the time; shows some understanding and use of idiomatic expressions; may invent a word or phrase in order to stay in the target language. **Accuracy:** *Spelling/orthography:* Pays more attention to correct orthography.

	Communication Strategies: *Comprehension:* Understands the main idea and some supporting ideas of conversations, lectures, and narration on familiar and some unfamiliar topics; uses contextual clues, inferences, key words and ideas and text types to aid understanding; uses background knowledge to help understand the discourse. **Cross-Cultural Applications:** *Awareness:* Recognizes differences and similarities in the perspectives of the target culture(s) and own as they are expressed in oral and written texts.	**Communication Strategies:** *Clarification:* May use paraphrasing, question asking, circumlocution. **Cross-Cultural Applications:** *Verbal.* Recognizes and produces linguistic patterns appropriate to the target language.	**Communication Strategies:** *Monitoring:* Begins to notice incorrect language structure and/or need for idioms but may not know how to correct the structure. **Cross-Cultural Applications:** *Verbal.* Recognizes and produces linguistic patterns appropriate to the target language.

Links to Culture and the other Wisconsin Standards:

Culture: D1: Patterns of Interaction: Students will interact with respect according to the social and cultural requirements of most social and some formal contexts. (Formal letter-writing protocol.)

✓ *Connections*
✓ *Comparisons*
✓ *Communities*

Connections: G1: Popular Media
Students will read, view, listen to, and talk about subjects contained in popular media from other countries in order to gain a perspective on other cultures. (Read articles, interviews in magazines, and newspapers from target culture.)

Comparisons: H4: Cultural Characteristics: Students will identify cultural characteristics of language such as formalities, levels of politeness, informal and formal language. (Formal letter-writing protocol.)

Evidence (How these standards are incorporated in the instruction)

Communities: K2: Careers: Students will investigate careers where skills in another language and/or cross-cultural understanding are needed. (Discuss future plans and career options.)

Structures and Vocabulary:
What needs to be taught for students to be successful in the performance assessment

Structures:
- Subjunctive to express opinions
- Hypothesizing

Vocabulary:
- Careers
- Letter-writing formalities
- CV terminology

Standards-Based Curriculum Units

Benchmark—Grade 10—Rubrics

Interpretive Task: This task has two components. First, the students need to demonstrate that they understand the main idea and key supporting ideas of the article they read. Then they must draw conclusions from the information in the article about the positive and negative implications of the career choices of the people interviewed in the article. This second component allows students to make inferences from an authentic text. The teacher may decide to keep the grading for the two components separate.

> **Magazine Article:**
> **Interviews with People Representing Various Careers**
>
> 1. Comprehension of information provided in the article:
>
> **Exceeds expectations:** The student is able to summarize the education, training, and career path for all people interviewed in the article. The summary includes a complete listing of both general and specific information for each person interviewed. The information is accurate according to the article.
>
> **Meets expectations:** The student is able to summarize the education, training, and career path for all people interviewed in the article. The summary includes general information for each person interviewed and some key supporting ideas. The information provided is accurate. Any inaccuracy is minor.
>
> **Needs work:** The student is able to summarize the education or training or career path for most or all of the people interviewed in the article. The summary lacks key details for one or more of the people interviewed. There may be inaccuracies in the information that is provided.
>
> 2. Drawing conclusions about the positive and negative implications of the career choices of the people interviewed.
>
> **Exceeds expectations:** The student draws appropriate conclusions with detailed explanations for the conclusions about the career choices of the people interviewed. These conclusions are based on the information in the article combined with prior knowledge and information about the careers in question and the target culture.
>
> **Meets expectations:** The student draws appropriate conclusions with some explanation for these conclusions about the career choices of the people interviewed. These conclusions are based on the information in the article combined with some prior knowledge and information about the careers in question and the target culture.
>
> **Needs work:** The student is unable to draw appropriate conclusions with explanation for these conclusions about the career choices of the people interviewed.

Interpersonal Task: The teacher determines how to assess students in this task. Since it is an interview situation, it is possible to audio- or videotape the interview so that each pair of students can be evaluated by the teacher. The teacher can also choose to have other students evaluate pairs of students. Because this task asks that students draw from career preference surveys in order to interview their partners, the teacher may choose to review some of the questions or categories of questions that the interviewers plan to use. The teacher would decide if the interview framework would receive a separate evaluation or just feedback to help students plan a successful interview. In the effort to make this task authentic, it is normal for an interviewer to prepare questions in advance. The spontaneity enters in how the interviewer follows the responses.

Interview: Career Preferences

1. The students will submit their list of questions for the interview in advance. These questions will be graded using the following rubric:

	Excellent	**Good**	**Needs work**
The questions include a variety of topics including talents, interests, skills, education preparation of the person being interviewed.			
Many of the questions are open ended to allow the person being interviewed to provide detailed information.			
Several questions include hypothetical situations (what would you do if…).			
The questions are structurally correct.			

2. The interviewer will be evaluated according to the following criteria concerning his or her questioning technique:

Exceeds expectations: The interviewer is able to follow the prepared questions with requests for more detail, explanation, more information when appropriate. The interviewer listens carefully to the answers being given and uses expressive reactions and follow-up questions to elicit more information consistently throughout the interview. The interviewer is in control of the interview, keeping the person interviewed focused on the topic to be discussed.

Meets expectations: The interviewer is able to follow the prepared questions with requests for more detail, explanation, more information. The interviewer listens to the answers being given, using expressive reactions and follow-up questions from time to time. The interviewer is generally in control of the interview, keeping the person interviewed focused on the topic to be discussed.

Needs work: The interviewer is not consistently able to ask follow-up questions for more detail, explanation, more information. The interviewer seems tied to the scripted questions, seldom reacting to the statements of the person interviewed.

3. The interviewer will be evaluated according to the following criteria concerning the accuracy of the communication:

Exceeds expectations: The interviewer is able to conduct the interview entirely in the target language with few pauses and hesitations. Structural or vocabulary errors are minor and infrequent and do not interfere with communication.

Meets expectations: The interviewer is able to conduct the interview entirely in the target language with few pauses and hesitations. Structural or vocabulary errors do not interfere with communication.

Needs work: The interviewer conducts the interview with several pauses or hesitations. Structural or vocabulary errors interfere with communication.

Presentational Task: This task has two distinct parts. First, the students need to create a curriculum vitae. Then they need to create a cover letter to accompany the CV. The teacher determines how to evaluate these two final products and the rough drafts. The use of nonnegotiables helps students prepare a rough draft of quality.

Curriculum Vitae and Cover Letter

Requirements:

1. The CV you prepare must include the following:

   __The CV must be typed.

   __The CV must include the following categories:
   - Personal information: name, address, telephone, fax, E-mail
   - Position applied for
   - Your objectives
   - Employment history
   - Education
   - Other related experiences
   - References

2. The cover letter you prepare must include the following:

   __Formal letter format according to target culture.

   __The letter must be typed.

   __The letter must be limited to one page.

   __The letter must include the following elements:
   - The job for which you are applying
   - Special qualifications that make you a lead candidate
   - Availability to begin work

The draft of the CV and cover letter will be evaluated according to the following criteria:

	Exceeds Expectations	**Meets Expectations**	**Needs Work**
Vocabulary	Precise and appropriate; idioms are used appropriately to demonstrate an advanced command of the language.	Appropriate; idioms are used appropriately to enhance communication.	May be inappropriate or inaccurate for this formal task.
Accuracy: Orthography	There are no spelling errors.	Spelling errors are infrequent.	Several spelling errors.
Accuracy: Structures	Structural errors are minor and infrequent.	Structural errors are due to idiomatic usage or structures that the student does not know.	There are several structural errors concerning basic mechanics.
Format	All protocols for CV and formal letter writing within the target culture are followed accurately.	Protocols for CV and formal letter writing within the target culture are generally followed.	Protocols for CV and formal letter writing are not consistently respected.
Content	The CV and cover letter provide a thorough and accurate portrait of the job candidate, including compelling reasons why the person should be considered for the job.	The CV and cover letter provide an accurate portrait of the job candidate, including reasons why the person should be considered for the job.	The CV and cover letter provide information about the job candidate; the information may be incomplete, inaccurate, or without details. There may not be good reasons why the person should be considered for the job.

The final copy of the CV and cover letter will be judged according to the following criteria:

Exceeds expectations: The CV and cover letter are error free in language and format. The presentation of both products is professional and attractive.

Meets expectations: The CV and cover letter are error free in language. The format is generally correct. The presentation of both products is neat and attractive.

Needs work: The CV and cover letter are not error free in language. The format may or may not be correct. The presentation of both products is neat.

Standards-Based Curriculum Units

Thematic Curriculum Unit—Performance Assessment and Planning Guide
High School, Grade 12

Key Question: What do I think and feel? **What do you think and feel?** **Theme: Work/careers Topic: Preparing for international careers**

Beginning	Developing	Transitioning	Refining

Students with continuous instruction from kindergarten through Grade 12 are refining their language skills as stated in the characteristics of the refining level. They will not yet be exhibiting the full expectation of the Performance Guidelines at this level; however, their performance will be solidly within the refining level. The key overarching question to target students' language performance is "What do I think and feel? What do you think and feel?" Students will discuss and defend opinions on issues of national and international importance.

The intention is that all instruction and assessments are completed in the target language, with the exception of reading and listening comprehension assessments, which may require use of English to demonstrate understanding of the texts.

Communication Mode: *Performance Assessment*	**Interpretive** Listen to a presentation by a guest speaker concerning how he/she uses languages on the job. Summarize the presentation. Discuss how important knowledge of another language and cross-cultural understanding are to success in this career. Include any questions that the speaker may not have directly answered, hypothesizing why he/she may have avoided a direct answer.	**Interpersonal** Discuss in a group of four to five people your options for career choices based on a variety of criteria including: availability of jobs, competition for jobs, salary, security, opportunity for travel, opportunity to use another language, opportunity for advancement, personal satisfaction, service to humanity, etc. Discuss the pros and cons of each career possibility.	**Presentational** Write a letter applying for an internship with a foreign company where you would like to work. State your qualifications, your career goals, and your knowledge of languages and cross-cultural understanding, which could enhance your candidacy.
Wisconsin Standards: Communication	**B2: Listening:** Students will comprehend the main idea and supporting ideas of oral presentations and authentic spoken materials.	**A3: Opinions:** Students will defend personal preferences, feelings, and opinions with substantive arguments.	**C5: Forms of Writing:** Students will write formal compositions, research papers, letters for a variety of purposes.
Target Performance (Key elements from the Performance Guidelines to consider in rubric development)	**Content:** — **Accuracy:** —	**Content:** *Spontaneity:* Initiates and maintains conversations using a variety of questions and rejoinders. **Accuracy:** *Ease:* Expresses a wide variety of topics with few pauses and hesitations; errors may occur but do not interfere with communication.	**Content:** *Situation:* Meets communication needs in a variety of settings; can meet a variety of writing needs including compositions, reports. **Accuracy:** *Spelling/orthography:* Can proofread to write the target language with few errors.

Links to **Culture** and the other Wisconsin Standards: ✓ *Connections* ✓ *Comparisons* ✓ *Communities* Evidence (*How these standards are incorporated in the instruction*)	**Communication Strategies:** *Comprehension:* Understands the main idea and most supporting ideas of conversations, lectures, and narration on a wide variety of topics; uses organizing principles, inferences, contexts, background knowledge to aid understanding. **Cross-Cultural Applications:** *Verbal:* Recognizes and produces linguistic patterns appropriate to the target language; begins to show an awareness of the underlying meaning and importance of these patterns. **Culture: D1:** Patterns of Interaction: Students will interact in a variety of cultural contexts (formal/informal, social/work) with sensitivity and respect. (Protocols for job search in another country.) **Connections: F1:** Speaking and Writing: Students will use topics and skills from other school subjects to discuss and and/or write in the language studied. (Writing letter applying for a job.) **Comparisons: H4:** Cultural Characteristics: Students will identify cultural characteristics of language such as formalities, levels of politeness, informal and formal language. (Formalities in asking questions of a guest speaker, in writing a letter of application.) **Communities: K2:** Careers: Students will investigate careers where skills in another language and/or cross-cultural understanding are needed. (Exploring career options via guest speakers, discussions, Internet search for internships.)	**Communication Strategies:** *Clarification:* Uses a variety of strategies to maintain communication. **Cross-Cultural Applications:** — **Communication Strategies:** *Monitoring:* Can proofread to correct errors in structures and/or idioms when they are part of the student's prior learning. **Cross-Cultural Applications:** *Awareness:* Applies understanding of the target culture(s) and its unique perspectives to enhance comprehension of oral and written texts.
Structures and Vocabulary: *What needs to be taught for students to be successful in the performance assessment*	**Structures:** ■ Subjunctive ■ Comparisons/superlatives	**Vocabulary:** ■ Formal language for letter writing ■ Job-related qualifications

Benchmark—Grade 12—Rubrics

Interpretive Task: This task has two components: The students must summarize an oral presentation, and they must judge how important knowledge of other languages and cross-cultural understanding are to the job presented. As part of the inference section of the task, students must also note if the speaker avoided answering any questions and why this might have happened. The second portion of the task asks the students to be critical listeners, making judgments about the information presented. The teacher may decide to grade the two components separately.

Oral Presentation: International Career

1. Comprehension of information provided by the speaker:

Exceeds expectations: The student is able to give a detailed summary of the speaker's presentation. The information is accurate and complete.

Meets expectations: The student is able to give a summary of the key ideas and many supporting ideas presented by the speaker. The information is accurate.

Needs work: The student is able to summarize the main ideas of the speech. Details are lacking and there may be some inaccuracies.

2. Making judgments about the speaker's career and responses to questions:

Exceeds expectations: The student is able to make astute observations about the candid responses of the speaker to questions and the importance of language and cross-cultural understanding in the career presented, because of background knowledge about the goals of the company and its role in the target culture.

Meets expectations: The student is able to make some observations about the candid responses of the speaker to questions and the importance of language and cross-cultural understanding in the career presented, because of background knowledge about the company and knowledge of the target culture.

Needs work: The student is able to make some observations about the candid responses of the speaker to questions and the importance of language and cross-cultural understanding in the career presented. These observations are not justified by background knowledge about the company or the target culture.

Interpersonal Task: The teacher determines how to assess students in this task, choosing to monitor groups as they discuss the topic, audio- or videotape each group, or have the students evaluate the success of the group. The teacher may choose any of these options or a combination. Because the students are at the refining level of language development, the emphasis should be on the quality of discussion.

Discussion: Career Options

1. Students speak the target language exclusively to accomplish the task.
 ___ Yes ___ No

2. There is equal participation in speaking the target language from all group members.
 ___ Yes ___ No

If you responded "no," please describe the participation of the group members.

	Consistently	Sometimes	Rarely
Defends personal preferences, feelings, and opinions with substantive arguments.			
Initiates or maintains the discussion using a variety of questions and rejoinders.			
Includes all group members in the discussion.			
Listens respectfully to other opinions.			
Provides excellent, factual information on the topic being discussed.			

Presentational Task: This task implies that the student will research on the Internet companies where internships are available before completing the task. The teacher may decide to evaluate this work as part of the unit. The task is a letter of application. In order to judge the effectiveness of the letter of application, the teacher will need some information about the company to which the student is applying. Again, the teacher may decide to evaluate the background information that the student supplies as part of the unit. For the actual preparation of the letter of application, the teacher may choose to evaluate a rough draft or require that the students have more than one person read their letter and provide feedback before submitting the final copy to the teacher. To ensure an appropriate level of quality for the final product, the teacher may wish to specify certain criteria as nonnegotiable.

Internship: Letter of Application

Requirements:

1. The letter of application must include the following:

   __Formal letter format according to the target culture.

   __The letter must be typed.

   __The letter must be limited to one page.

   __The letter must include the following elements:
   - Qualifications for the internship
   - Special qualities that make you an exceptional candidate
   - Evidence that the candidate is familiar with the company

   __The letter must be accompanied by a one- to two-page description of the company to which the person is applying, providing pertinent background information that will help the teacher evaluate the quality of the letter of application.

   __The letter must be critiqued by two classmates before the final copy is submitted for grading. A comment sheet with feedback from each classmate must accompany the letter.

2. The letter of application will be judged according to the following criteria:

Exceeds expectations: The letter of application is carefully and thoughtfully written in both choice of language and structure of language. The candidate has provided succinct evidence that he or she is familiar with the company to which he or she is applying. There are compelling reasons why the candidate should receive serious consideration for the internship.

Meets expectations: The letter of application is carefully and thoughtfully written; there may be a few minor word choice or language structure errors. The candidate has provided evidence that he or she is familiar with the company to which he or she is applying. There are good reasons why the candidate should receive serious consideration for the internship.

Needs work: The letter of application is correctly written; there are errors of word choice or language structures. The candidate has provided some evidence that he or she is familiar with the company to which he or she is applying. The candidate has included reasons why he or she should receive consideration for the internship.

Sample Thematic Curriculum Units: Grouped by Level

These samples are arranged by language level, presenting several examples from different grades appropriate for each level. Beginning students might be in elementary school, middle school, or senior high. Their difference in age affects the context chosen and the assessment and activity ideas suggested. The units illustrate a variety of thematic content for each language level, emphasizing the need to include all skills and content areas at all levels. Culture, current events, and varieties of literature are woven throughout all language levels.

The following curriculum units are based on examples suggested by teachers from their own classroom experiences. Many are units that teachers have developed and piloted with their students. These samples are organized by language level:

Beginning: This level is more receptive in nature, with the student taking in sounds and patterns and then beginning to imitate language heard. The situation is controlled; the speaker is parroting. In other words, a beginner can successfully participate in memorized dialogues and can respond with memorized answers to memorized questions. Thus, accuracy is high.

Developing: This level is characterized by language behavior that moves from imitative to reflective (that is, a more thoughtful rather than automatic response to a situation or a question). Students now begin to move out of the controlled box, recombining memorized or learned pieces. They begin to respond in more complete and purposeful ways to meet their practical needs. As students begin to create with language, their accuracy decreases.

Transitioning: This level is characterized by movement from reflective to interactive language behavior. Students are struggling to act more independently in their language, successfully creating with language to express their own thoughts instead of recombining other people's words.

Refining: This level is characterized by language behavior moving from interactive to initiative, where the speaker takes on full responsibility for engaging, maintaining, and furthering the conversation. Students can successfully act independently in the new language, initiating with language to meet a wide variety of purposes.

TABLE 4.2 **Key Questions: Thematic Topics**

Beginning	**Developing**
Who am I?	What is my life like?
Who are you?	What is your life like?
Identify similarities and differences	*Investigate similarities and differences*

Self and Community

• Biographical facts	• Geography, climate, political divisions
• Interests/hobbies	• Urban, suburban, rural
• Family	• Community, housing
• School/studies	• Stores/shopping/restaurants
• Friends/peers	• Travel, transportation

Transitioning	**Refining**
How do I look at the world?	What do I think and feel?
How do you look at the world?	What do you think and feel?
Share and compare perspectives	*Discuss and defend opinions*

Personal, Local, and Global Issues

• Intellectual and aesthetic pursuits	• Politics
• Religion, philosophy	• History
• Cultural heritage, traditions, practices, celebrations	• Current events
	• Ecology, environment
	• Work/career

These key questions reflect the four levels of development described in the performance standards. The nature of the language level is captured in the kind of question and thematic topics students can explore within the limits of their language proficiency.

What might this look like in a classroom? Family as a thematic unit could provide rich content for the development of language skills throughout a program. What the student is able to do with the language is what changes over time, each level including elements of the previous level in increasingly strong and sustained ways. Each level is summarized by a key question that helps the curriculum writer target the expected performance to the proficiency goals.

Theme: Family

Level:	Key Question:	Students' Language:
Beginning	"Who am I? Who are you?"	"Do you have brothers (sisters)? How many?"
Developing	"What is my life like? What is your life like?"	"What activities does your family do together?"
Transitioning	"How do I look at the world? How do you look at the world?"	"What are the advantages of living at home versus living in a boarding school or dorm?"
Refining	"What do I think and feel? What do you think and feel?"	"What do you think are the benefits of nuclear versus extended families?"

Standards-Based Curriculum Units

These units force us as curriculum writers to bring students back again and again to issues of importance. The units deal with how the learner relates to others and the world.

These language levels are not linked to grade level or age. Beginners may be in any grade: kindergarten, seventh grade, ninth grade, or adults. Depending on the age, grade, and program model when students begin to learn a language, the speed, style, and way they learn will vary. Since proficiency is a function of time and experience, students will not reach the refining level without an early beginning (in elementary grades). High school beginners will barely enter the transitioning level.

The performance assessment tasks that are the core of each curriculum unit will be conducted entirely in the target language. Everything that students see, hear, and read and everything that they show, say, and write will be done in the target language. The performance assessment is not designed to find out what students know *about* the language, rather it is designed to find out what students can do *using* the language.

These sample curriculum units provide examples of how a variety of thematic content can be handled at different levels. Rather than focusing only on a limiting topic, such as food, a holiday, or family members, these curriculum units draw on richer content within which topics that were little more than vocabulary lists can be embedded. These units force us as curriculum writers to bring students back again and again to issues of importance. The units deal with how the learner relates to others and the world. In this way, information is recycled, topics return, and language structures are continuously practiced and refined. This spiraling of language and content allows for review and relearning, so students achieve a greater depth of knowledge and greater ease and comfort with the language.

This spiraling of language and content allows for review and relearning, so students achieve a greater depth of knowledge and greater ease and comfort with the language.

The following are sample curriculum units for each of the four levels of language development. The targeted point of progress along the proficiency continuum is shown by the graphic at the top of each curriculum unit. The descriptor that follows the graphic representation of the targeted language level describes the amount and type of prior instruction that would be necessary to lead students up to this point in their progress.

Beginning Level

This level is more receptive in nature, with the student taking in sounds and patterns and then beginning to imitate language heard. The situation is controlled; the speaker is parroting. In other words, a beginner can successfully participate in memorized dialogues and can respond with memorized answers to memorized questions. Thus, accuracy is high.

These six sample curriculum units are all within the beginning level, but targeted for students in elementary schools, middle schools, and high schools. While the overall expectation of language proficiency is similar, the cognitive and developmental characteristics of students in different grades must be taken into consideration. The first grade unit focused on colors would be taught with a different approach for beginning students in senior high. Likewise, the senior high unit focused on key features of countries through the context of being an exchange student would not be appropriate for primary grade students.

Beginning Level—Grade 1: Art Appreciation—Colors

Targeted very early in the development of language proficiency, students are starting to show achievement of these performance assessments based on the beginning level Standards and Performance Guidelines.

Beginning Level—Grade 3: Healthy Lifestyles—Food Pyramid

This unit is pegged at a moderate degree of achievement of the beginning level Standards and Performance Guidelines. Students would have begun their study of the language by first grade to be able to perform these assessment tasks.

Beginning Level—Grade 6: The City—Directions, Landmarks

This unit is designed for students beginning language study in sixth grade and having daily instruction throughout the year. They would not yet be secure in all the beginning level expectations and Performance Standards. They would be at a midpoint of development through the beginning level.

Beginning Level—Grade 8: Introducing Myself—Family, School, Home

These performance assessment tasks are targeted at students who have had the equivalence of one and a half years of daily instruction. They are able to show language skill solidly at the beginning level, exhibiting all the characteristics described as the beginning level Performance Guidelines.

Beginning Level—Grade 9: Daily Life—Free Time Activities

This unit is designed for students who did not have a substantial middle school language learning experience, the equivalence of less than a single year of instruction. These students would be starting to show the characteristics of beginning level Performance Guidelines.

Beginning Level—Grade 10: Geography—Key Features of Countries

These students enrolled in a second year high school language course would fully exhibit the characteristics of the beginning level Performance Guidelines. These performance assessment tasks clearly are targeted to the beginning level Performance Standards. Each assessment task has an open-ended component to allow students who are ready to begin to show language skills characteristic of the next level (developing).

Thematic Curriculum Unit—Performance Assessment and Planning Guide
Elementary School, Grade 1

Key Question: Who am I? Who are you? **Theme: Art appreciation** **Topic: Colors**

Beginning	Developing	Transitioning	Refining

Targeted very early in the development of language proficiency, students are starting to show achievement of these performance assessments based on the beginning level Standards and Performance Guidelines.

The intention is that all instruction and assessments are completed in the target language, with the exception of reading and listening comprehension assessments, which may require use of English to demonstrate understanding of the texts.

Communication Mode: *Performance Assessment*	Interpretive	Presentational	Interpersonal
	Listen to a song about colors and identify the colors as they are named in the song.	Recite a short poem or sing a short song about colors.	Look at art prints and tell each other what colors you see in each print. Say if you like the print or not.
Wisconsin Standards: Communication	**B2: Listening:** Students will comprehend simple daily conversations on familiar topics and selected, age-appropriate authentic recordings, broadcasts, videos.	**C1: Oral Presentations:** Students will dramatize student-created and/or authentic songs, short poems, skits, or dialogues.	**A3: Opinions:** Students will state personal preferences and feelings.
Target Performance (Key elements from the Performance Guidelines to consider in rubric development)	**Content:** *Complexity/sophistication:* Relies primarily on memorized phrases and short sentences on very familiar topics in both oral and written presentations. **Accuracy:** —	**Content:** *Situation:* Accomplishes a task directed by the teacher; can meet limited writing needs such as a short message or note. **Accuracy:** *Pronunciation:* Imitates sounds and intonation as part of a memorized process; understandable to someone accustomed to working with a language learner.	**Content:** *Vocabulary:* Uses a limited number of memorized words and phrases; relies on native language for unknown words and expressions; determines meaning by recognition of cognates, prefixes, and thematic vocabulary. **Accuracy:** *Ease:* Expresses memorized phrases with ease and with few errors; may show evidence of false starts and pauses as topics expand beyond memorized dialogues.

	Communication Strategies: *Comprehension:* Understands short, simple conversations and narration with highly predictable and familiar contexts; relies heavily on visuals, gestures, facial expressions in order to understand; generally needs repetition, restatement, and contextual clues in order to understand; relies heavily on background information. **Cross-Cultural Applications:** —	**Communication Strategies:** *Monitoring:* May self-correct on high-frequency items. **Cross-Cultural Applications:** *Awareness:* Understands a story line or event when it reflects a cultural background similar to own; begins to associate symbols, famous people, places, songs, etc. with a certain culture.	**Communication Strategies:** *Clarification:* Asks for repetition; may use gestures and facial expressions to show confusion. **Cross-Cultural Applications:** *Awareness:* Understands a story line or event when it reflects a cultural background similar to their own; begins to associate symbols, famous people, places, songs, etc. with a certain culture.
Links to **Culture** and the other Wisconsin Standards: ✓ *Connections* ✓ *Comparisons* ✓ *Communities* Evidence *(How these standards are incorporated in the instruction)*	**Culture: D2:** Cultural Activities Students will participate in and learn about age-appropriate cultural activities (such as games, songs, and holiday celebrations). (Memorize song, poem from the target culture.) **Connections: F1:** Speaking and Writing Students will use topics and skills from other school subjects to discuss and/or write in the language studied. (Look at and identify colors from art class.) **Comparisons: I1:** Cultural Variations Students will discuss the meaning of perspectives, products, and practices in different cultures. (Look at art prints from the target culture.) **Communities: K3:** Understanding Students will deepen their understanding of other cultures through various avenues such as cuisine, sports, theatre, dance, and art. (Look at art prints from the target culture.)		
Structures and Vocabulary: *What needs to be taught for students to be successful in the performance assessment*	**Structures:** ■ I see (color) ■ I like it/I don't like it		**Vocabulary:** ■ Colors ■ Pretty/ugly/strange

Standards-Based Curriculum Units

Thematic Curriculum Unit—Performance Assessment and Planning Guide
Elementary School, Grade 3

Key Question: Who Am I? Who are you? **Theme: Healthy lifestyles** **Topic: Food Pyramid**

This unit is pegged at a moderate degree of achievement of the beginning level Standards and Performance Guidelines. Students would have begun their study of the language by first grade to be able to perform these assessment tasks.

The intention is that all instruction and assessments are completed in the target language, with the exception of reading and listening comprehension assessments, which may require use of English to demonstrate understanding of the texts.

	Beginning	Developing	Transitioning	Refining
Communication Mode: *Performance Assessment*		**Interpretive**: When hearing the name of a food, take a picture of that food and correctly place it in its appropriate category on a food pyramid.	**Interpersonal**: Ask and answer questions with each other about foods you like/don't like to eat for breakfast, lunch, snacks, and dinner.	**Presentational**: Illustrate a healthy or unhealthy breakfast, lunch, snack, and dinner on four different paper plates. Present your illustrations to the class, naming the foods and saying why each meal is healthy or unhealthy.
Wisconsin Standards: Communication		**B1: Listening**: Students will understand spoken language on familiar topics that has strong visual support.	**A3: Opinions**: Students will state personal preferences and feelings.	**C2: Speeches**: Students will write and present a short narrative about themselves.
Target Performance *(Key elements from the Performance Guidelines to consider in rubric development)*		**Content:** *Situation*: Accomplishes a task directed by the teacher; can meet limited writing needs such as a short message or note. **Accuracy:** —	**Content:** *Complexity/sophistication*: Relies primarily on memorized phrases and short sentences on very familiar topics in both oral and written presentations. **Accuracy:** *Ease*: Expresses memorized phrases with ease and with few errors; may show evidence of false starts and pauses as topics expand beyond memorized dialogues.	**Content:** *Complexity/sophistication*: Relies primarily on memorized phrases and short sentences on very familiar topics in both oral and written presentations. **Accuracy:** *Pronunciation*: Imitates sounds and intonation as part of a memorized process; understandable to someone accustomed to working with a language learner.

Communication Strategies:

Comprehension: Understands short, simple conversations and narration within highly predictable and familiar contexts; relies heavily on visuals, gestures, facial expressions in order to understand; generally needs repetition, restatement, and contextual clues in order to understand; relies heavily on background information.

Cross-Cultural Applications:
—

Communication Strategies:

Clarification: Asks for repetition; may use gestures and facial expressions to show confusion.

Cross-Cultural Applications:

Verbal: Imitates appropriate linguistic patterns (register, formal vs. informal address, intonation) when modeled by the teacher.

Communication Strategies:

Impact: Focuses on successful task completion; uses gestures or visuals to maintain audience's attention and/or interest as appropriate to purpose.

Cross-Cultural Applications:

Verbal: Imitates appropriate linguistic patterns (register, formal vs. informal address, intonation) when modeled by the teacher.

Links to **Culture** and the other Wisconsin Standards: ✓ *Connections* ✓ *Comparisons* ✓ *Communities* *Evidence (How these standards are incorporated in the instruction)*	**Culture: E1:** Objects and Symbols Students will identify objects and symbols, such as flags or currency, that are used day-to-day and represent other cultures. (Place foods typical of the target culture on the food pyramid.) **Connections: F1:** Speaking and Writing Students will use topics and skills from other school subjects to discuss and/or write in the language studied. (Apply knowledge about healthy eating and the food pyramid from health class.) **Comparisons: I2:** Comparisons Students will compare the form, meaning, and importance of certain perspectives, products, and practices in different cultures. (Compare the food pyramid of the United States to the food pyramid of the target culture.) **Communities: K3:** Understanding Students will deepen their understanding of other cultures through various avenues such as cuisine, sports, theatre, dance, and art. (Prepare a healthy meal or snack from the target culture.)
Structures and Vocabulary: *What needs to be taught for students to be successful in the performance assessment*	**Structures:** ■ I like/I don't like ■ It is good/it is bad because …. ■ What do you like to eat? ■ I need **Vocabulary:** ■ Foods ■ Food categories of the food pyramid ■ Servings

Thematic Curriculum Unit—Performance Assessment and Planning Guide
Middle School, Grade 6

Key Question: Who am I? Who are you? **Theme: The city** **Topic: Directions, landmarks**

Beginning		Developing	Transitioning	Refining

This unit is designed for students beginning language study in sixth grade and having daily instruction throughout the year. They would not yet be secure in all the beginning level expectations and Performance Standards. They would be at a midpoint of development through the beginning level.

The intention is that all instruction and assessments are completed in the target language, with the exception of reading and listening comprehension assessments, which may require use of English to demonstrate understanding of the texts.

Communication Mode: *Performance Assessment*	Interpretive	Presentational	Interpersonal
	Read the written directions to a restaurant from the hotel where you are staying. Trace the route on your city map.	Explain to another person how to get from one place in the city where you are staying to a famous site within the city. Tell the person what can be seen at the famous site and why it is an interesting place to visit.	Using a city map, ask for directions from where you are to another place in the city. Trace the route on your map.
Wisconsin Standards: Communication	**B3: Reading:** Students will understand written materials on familiar topics that have strong visual support.	**C3: Directions:** Students will give simple commands and make requests of another person or group.	**A4: Problem-solving:** Students will express personal needs.
Target Performance (Key elements from the Performance Guidelines to consider in rubric development)	**Content:** *Situation:* Accomplishes a task directed by the teacher; can meet limited writing needs such as a short message or note. **Accuracy:** —	**Content:** *Vocabulary:* Uses a limited number of memorized words and phrases; relies on native language for unknown words and expressions; determines meaning by recognition of cognates, prefixes, and thematic vocabulary. **Accuracy:** *Pronunciation:* Imitates sounds and intonation as part of a memorized process; understandable to someone accustomed to working with a language learner.	**Content:** *Complexity/sophistication:* Relies primarily on memorized phrases and short sentences on very familiar topics in both oral and written presentations. **Accuracy:** *Ease:* Expresses memorized phrases with ease and with few errors; may show evidence of false starts and pauses as topics expand beyond memorized dialogues.

Communication Strategies:
Comprehension: Understands short, simple conversations and narration with highly predictable and familiar contexts; relies heavily on visuals, gestures, facial expressions in order to understand; generally needs repetition, restatement, and contextual clues in order to understand; relies heavily on background information.

Cross-Cultural Applications:
Awareness: Understands a story line or event when it reflects a cultural background similar to their own; begins to associate symbols, famous people, places, songs, etc. with a certain culture.

Communication Strategies:
Impact: Focuses on successful task completion; uses gestures or visuals to maintain audience's attention and/or interest as appropriate to purpose.

Cross-Cultural Applications:
Awareness: Understands a story line or event when it reflects a cultural background similar to their own; begins to associate symbols, famous people, places, songs, etc. with a certain culture.

Communication Strategies:
Clarification: Asks for repetition; may use gestures and facial expressions to show confusion.

Cross-Cultural Applications:
Verbal: Imitates appropriate linguistic patterns (i.e., register, formal vs. informal address, intonation) when modeled by the teacher.

Links to **Culture** and the other Wisconsin Standards: ✓ **Connections** ✓ **Comparisons** ✓ **Communities** Evidence (*How these standards are incorporated in the instruction*)	**Culture: E1:** Objects and Symbols Students will identify objects and symbols such as flags or currency that are used day-to-day and represent other cultures. (Places in a city in the target culture, street signs, landmarks within a city.) **Connections: F1:** Speaking and Writing Students will use topics and skills from other school subjects to discuss and/or write in the language studied. (Map-reading skills from geography class.) **Comparisons: H1:** Structures Students will identify cognates (words similar to English), word roots, prefixes, suffixes, and sentence structure to derive meaning. (Identify cognates in place names within the city.) **Communities: K1:** Media Students will use various media in the language studied for study, work, or pleasure. (Using Internet sites to learn about cities in the countries studied.)
Structures and Vocabulary: *What needs to be taught for students to be successful in the performance assessment*	**Structures:** ■ Directions ■ Prepositions of placement ■ Polite commands and requests **Vocabulary:** ■ Places in the city ■ Streets, avenues, corner, intersection

Standards-Based Curriculum Units

Thematic Curriculum Unit—Performance Assessment and Planning Guide
Middle School, Grade 8

Key Question: Who am I? Who are you? **Theme:** Introducing myself **Topic:** Family, school, home

Beginning	Developing	Transitioning	Refining

These performance assessment tasks are targeted at students who have had the equivalent of one and a half years of daily instruction. They are able to show language skill solidly at the beginning level, exhibiting all the characteristics described as the beginning level Performance Guidelines.

The intention is that all instruction and assessments are completed in the target language, with the exception of reading and listening comprehension assessments, which may require use of English to demonstrate understanding of the texts.

Communication Mode: *Performance Assessment*	**Interpretive** Watch a video of three students introducing themselves (videotaped when exchange students visited the school). Then, on a grid of topics that would logically be part of such an introduction, identify the topics actually mentioned and list any details understood on each topic.	**Presentational** Write a description of yourself accompanied by photos. The description will serve as a letter of introduction to a host family where you will be staying on a school trip abroad.	**Interpersonal** To prepare for the first night at a host family's home, pair up and practice what you might say and what you might be asked by the host family; introduce yourself by sharing the letter and photos prepared as the *presentational* assessment; ask questions about each other's likes and dislikes.
Wisconsin Standards: Communication	**B2: Listening:** Students will comprehend simple daily conversations on familiar topics and selected, age-appropriate authentic recordings, broadcasts, videos.	**C5: Forms of Writing:** Students will write personal journals and/or brief messages to friends (postcard, letter, E-mail).	**A3: Opinions:** Students will state personal preferences and feelings.
Target Performance (Key elements from the Performance Guidelines to consider in rubric development)	**Content:** *Vocabulary:* Uses a limited number of memorized words and phrases; relies on native language for unknown words and expressions; determines meaning by recognition of cognates, prefixes, and thematic vocabulary. **Accuracy:** —	**Content:** *Complexity/sophistication:* Relies primarily on memorized phrases and short sentences on very familiar topics in both oral and written presentations. **Accuracy:** *Spelling/orthography:* Can copy with accuracy memorized language; will not notice errors.	**Content:** *Spontaneity:* Responds automatically to high-frequency cues (i.e., hello, how are you, what's your name); can ask memorized questions (i.e., what's your name, how are you). *Vocabulary:* Uses a limited number of memorized words and phrases; relies on native language for unknown words and expressions; determines meaning by recognition of cognates, prefixes, and thematic vocabulary. **Accuracy:** *Ease:* Expresses memorized phrases with ease and with few errors; may show evidence of false starts and pauses as topics expand beyond memorized dialogues.

		Communication Strategies: *Comprehension:* Understands short, simple conversations and narration with highly predictable and familiar contexts; relies heavily on visuals, gestures, facial expressions in order to understand; generally needs repetition, restatement, and contextual clues in order to understand; relies heavily on background information. **Cross-Cultural Applications:** —	**Communication Strategies:** *Impact:* Focuses on successful task completion; uses gestures or visuals to maintain audience's attention and/or interest as appropriate to purpose. *Monitoring:* May self-correct on high-frequency items. **Cross-Cultural Applications:** *Verbal:* Imitates appropriate linguistic patterns (i.e., register, formal vs. informal address, intonation) when modeled by the teacher.	**Communication Strategies:** *Clarification:* Asks for repetition; may use gestures and facial expressions to show confusion. **Cross-Cultural Applications:** *Non-verbal:* Imitates non-verbal patterns of behavior appropriate to the target culture (i.e., gestures, proximity, eye contact) when they are modeled by the teacher.

Links to **Culture** and the other Wisconsin Standards: ✓ **Connections** ✓ *Comparisons* ✓ *Communities* Evidence *(How these standards are incorporated in the instruction)*	**Culture: D1:** Patterns of Interaction Students will observe and imitate appropriate patterns of behavior (such as greetings or gestures) used with friends and family in the cultures studied. (Watching videos of students their same age in countries where the language is spoken introducing themselves; students note how they greet each other, how close they stand, use of their hands and other gestures. Students practice using these same patterns of interaction when they ask and answer questions in pair activities.) **Culture: E2:** Contributions Students will identify major contributions and historical figures from the cultures studied in the target cultures. (For practice identifying biographical information, use CD-ROM encyclopedia descriptions of famous people from countries where the language is spoken. Besides the basic personal facts, learn categories of fame, e.g., science, the arts, entertainment, literature, inventors, etc.) **Connections: G1:** Popular Media Students will read, view, listen to, and talk about subjects contained in popular media from other countries in order to gain a perspective on other cultures. (Have students look for biographical summaries of contemporary famous people from target countries and compare the kind of information shared compared to what is found in U.S. popular magazines.) **Communities: J3:** Communication Students will exchange information with people locally and around the world through avenues such as pen pals, E-mail, video, speeches, and publications. (Students exchange their biographical information with pen pals or via E-mail, with a sister school if available.)

Structures and Vocabulary: *What needs to be taught for students to be successful in the performance assessment*	**Structures:** ■ Question words/question formation ■ To be ■ Expressing likes and dislikes ■ Using descriptive adjectives	**Vocabulary:** ■ Family members and descriptive adjectives ■ Biographical information ■ School and home facts

Standards-Based Curriculum Units

Thematic Curriculum Unit—Performance Assessment and Planning Guide
High School, Grade 9

Key Question: Who am I? Who are you?   **Theme:** Daily life   **Topic:** Free time activities

Beginning	Developing	Transitioning	Refining

This unit is designed for students who did not have a substantial middle school language learning experience, the equivalent of less than a single year of instruction. These students would be starting to show the characteristics of beginning level Performance Guidelines.

The intention is that all instruction and assessments are completed in the target language, with the exception of reading and listening comprehension assessments, which may require use of English to demonstrate understanding of the texts.

	Interpretive	Interpersonal	Presentational
Communication Mode: *Performance Assessment*	Watch a video of students from a target country describing what they do in their spare time. Check off on an answer sheet all of the activities that the students do in their spare time.	Complete a survey indicating which activities you like/don't like to do. Now predict which activities your partner likes/doesn't like. Ask your partner questions to see how accurate your predictions were.	Send a letter to another student (preferably one living in a country where the target language is spoken) telling what you like to do in your spare time. Ask what he/she likes to do.
Wisconsin Standards: *Communication*	**B2: Listening:** Students will comprehend simple daily conversations on familiar topics and selected, age-appropriate authentic recordings, broadcasts, videos.	**A1: Conversations:** Students will carry on a short conversation about personal interests, including what they have done, are doing, and are planning to do.	**C5: Forms of Writing:** Students will write personal journals and/or brief messages to friends (postcard, letter, E-mail).
Target Performance (Key elements from the Performance Guidelines to consider in rubric development)	**Content:** *Complexity/sophistication:* Relies primarily on memorized phrases and short sentences on very familiar topics in both oral and written presentations. **Accuracy:** —	**Content:** *Vocabulary:* Uses a limited number of memorized words and phrases; relies on native language for unknown words and expressions; determines meaning by recognition of cognates, prefixes, and thematic vocabulary. **Accuracy:** *Ease:* Expresses memorized phrases with ease and with few errors; may show evidence of false starts and pauses as topics expand beyond memorized dialogues.	**Content:** *Situation:* Accomplishes a task directed by the teacher; can meet limited writing needs such as a short message or note. **Accuracy:** *Spelling/orthography:* Can copy with accuracy memorized language; will not notice errors.

	Communication Strategies: *Comprehension*: Understands short, simple conversations and narration with highly predictable and familiar contexts; relies heavily on visuals, gestures, facial expressions in order to understand; generally needs repetition, restatement, and contextual clues in order to understand; relies heavily on background information. **Cross-Cultural Applications:** *Awareness*: Understands a story line or event when it reflects a cultural background similar to own; begins to associate symbols, famous people, places, songs, etc. with a certain culture.	**Communication Strategies:** *Clarification*: Asks for repetition; may use gestures and facial expressions to show confusion. **Cross-Cultural Applications:** *Verbal*: Imitates appropriate linguistic patterns (i.e., register, formal vs. informal address, intonation) when modeled by the teacher.	**Communication Strategies:** *Monitoring*: May self-correct on high-frequency items. **Cross-Cultural Applications:** *Verbal*: Imitates appropriate linguistic patterns (i.e., register, formal vs. informal address, intonation) when modeled by the teacher.
Links to **Culture** and the other Wisconsin Standards: ✓ *Connections* ✓ *Comparisons* ✓ *Communities* Evidence (*How these standards are incorporated in the instruction*)	**Culture: D2:** Cultural Activities Students will participate in and learn about age-appropriate cultural activities (such as games, songs, and holiday celebrations). (Discuss leisure activities of peers from the target culture.) **Connections: G1:** Popular Media Students will read, view, listen to, and talk about subjects contained in popular media from other countries in order to gain a perspective on other cultures. (Look at teen magazines that showcase leisure activities.) **Comparisons: I2:** Comparisons Students will compare the form, meaning, and importance of certain perspectives, products, and practices in different cultures. (Compare leisure activities through letter exchange.) **Communities: J3:** Communication Students will exchange information with people locally and around the world through avenues such as pen pals, E-mail, video, speeches, and publications. (Letter exchange.)			
Structures and Vocabulary: *What needs to be taught for students to be successful in the performance assessment*	**Structures:** ■ Verbs: to like, to prefer—affirmative and negative ■ Idioms with playing sports, musical instruments ■ Asking yes/no questions	**Vocabulary:** ■ Spare time activities	

Thematic Curriculum Unit—Performance Assessment and Planning Guide
High School, Grade 10

Key Question: Who am I? Who are you? **Theme: Geography** **Topic: Key features of countries**

Beginning	Developing	Transitioning	Refining
	▓▓▓		

These students enrolled in a second year high school language course would fully exhibit the characteristics of the beginning level Performance Guidelines. These performance assessment tasks clearly are targeted to the beginning level Performance Standards. Each assessment task has an open-ended component for students who are ready to begin to show language skills characteristic of the next level (developing).

The intention is that all instruction and assessments are completed in the target language, with the exception of reading and listening comprehension assessments, which may require use of English to demonstrate understanding of the texts.

	Interpretive	**Interpersonal**	**Presentational**
Communication Mode: *Performance Assessment*	In preparation to be an exchange student, watch a video giving an overview of countries where the target language is spoken. From a list of choices, circle the topics presented for each country presented in the video and add in any specific details they understood.	Investigate via the Internet the main features, weather, and activities in various countries where the target language is spoken. In small groups find out all you can about weather and activities you can do in the countries where the target language is spoken, in order to choose the country where you'd like to be an exchange student.	Make a poster illustrating the key features that made you choose one particular country where you want to spend your year as an exchange student. Present your choice to the class, highlighting why you chose the country.
Wisconsin Standards: Communication	**B2: Listening:** Students will comprehend simple daily conversations on familiar topics and selected, age-appropriate authentic recordings, broadcasts, videos.	**A2: Questions:** Students will ask and answer questions, including biographical information.	**C2: Speeches:** Students will write and present a short narrative about themselves.
Target Performance (Key elements from the Performance Guidelines to consider in rubric development)	**Content:** *Situation:* Accomplishes a task directed by the teacher; can meet limited writing needs such as a short message or note. **Accuracy:** —	**Content:** *Complexity/sophistication:* Relies primarily on memorized phrases and short sentences on very familiar topics in both oral and written presentations. **Accuracy:** *Ease:* Expresses memorized phrases with ease and with few errors; may show evidence of false starts and pauses as topics expand beyond memorized dialogues.	**Content:** *Complexity/sophistication:* Relies primarily on memorized phrases and short sentences on very familiar topics in both oral and written presentations. **Accuracy:** *Pronunciation:* Imitates sounds and intonation as part of a memorized process; understandable to someone accustomed to working with a language learner.

Communication Strategies:

Comprehension: Understands short, simple conversations and narration with highly predictable and familiar contexts; relies heavily on visuals, gestures, facial expressions in order to understand; generally needs repetition, restatement, and contextual clues in order to understand; relies heavily on background information.

Cross-Cultural Applications:

Awareness: Understands a story line or event when it reflects a cultural background similar to their own; begins to associate symbols, famous people, places, songs, etc. with a certain culture.

Communication Strategies:

Clarification: Asks for repetition; may use gestures and facial expressions to show confusion.

Cross-Cultural Applications:

Awareness: Understands a story line or event when it reflects a cultural background similar to their own; begins to associate symbols, famous people, places, songs, etc. with a certain culture.

Communication Strategies:

Impact: Focuses on successful task completion; uses gestures or visuals to maintain audience's attention and/or interest as appropriate to purpose.

Cross-Cultural Applications:

Awareness: Understands a story line or event when it reflects a cultural background similar to their own; begins to associate symbols, famous people, places, songs, etc. with a certain culture.

Links to **Culture** and the other Wisconsin Standards:	**Culture: E4:** Geography Students will identify countries, regions, and geographic features where the target language is spoken. (Unit theme addresses this standard.)
✓ **Connections** ✓ **Comparisons** ✓ **Communities** *Evidence (How these standards are incorporated in the instruction)*	**Connections: F2:** Reading and Listening Students will read material, listen to and/or watch programs in the language studied on topics from other classes. (Students read about and discuss key features of countries where the target language is spoken, in geography class.) **Comparisons: H1:** Structures Students will identify cognate (words similar to English), word roots, prefixes, suffixes, and sentence structure to derive meaning. (Students will compare geographic terms to identify cognates.) **Communities: K5:** Intercultural Experiences Students will travel to communities where the language studied is spoken and/or host someone from a country where the language studied is spoken. (Students investigate the possibilities or potential for being an exchange student.)
Structures and Vocabulary: *What needs to be taught for students to be successful in the performance assessment*	**Structures:** ■ Expressions of quantity ■ Prepositions with names of cities, countries ■ Idioms related with weather ■ Likes and dislikes ■ Comparisons (more/less) **Vocabulary:** ■ Geographical features ■ Weather expressions ■ Tourist activities

Standards-Based Curriculum Units

Developing Level

This level is characterized by language behavior that moves from imitative to reflective (that is, a more thoughtful rather than automatic response to a situation or a question). Students now begin to move out of the controlled box, recombining memorized or learned pieces. They begin to respond in more complete and purposeful ways to meet their practical needs. As students begin to create with language, their accuracy decreases.

These four sample curriculum units are all within the developing level, but targeted for students in elementary schools, middle schools, and high schools. While the overall expectation of language proficiency is similar, the cognitive and developmental characteristics of students in different grades must be taken into consideration. The art appreciation and artists unit is targeted for fifth grade; however, it could be used with middle school and senior high students with different practice activities, different art prints, and building on different prior knowledge and sophistication. Likewise, the senior high music unit could be used with elementary school and middle school students, changing the nature of the discussion activities while matching the music selections to what appeals to the students.

Developing Level—Grade 5: Art Appreciation—Artists

Fifth grade students who have studied the target language continuously since kindergarten would be secure at performing at the beginning level and would now begin to work on the developing level Standards and Performance Guidelines.

Developing Level—Grade 8: Cultural Celebrations—Seasonal Markets

By eighth grade, students who had instruction in the target language in Grades 4 through 7 would be showing a fair degree of achievement of the language performance described for the developing level. Some areas of language usage would be stronger than others, but most students would be solidly performing at the developing level.

Developing Level—Grade 10: Teenage Life—Family, School, Pastimes

Students who began study of the target language in sixth or seventh grade and entered a second year class as ninth graders would be showing moderate achievement of the developing level characteristics in tenth grade, beginning to use what they learned as memorized language in recombined and more creative ways.

Developing Level—Grade 12: Music—Contemporary Songs

This unit is designed for students who began their study of the target language as ninth graders. By Grade 12, these students will be secure in achieving the Performance Guidelines of the developing level.

Thematic Curriculum Unit—Performance Assessment and Planning Guide
Elementary School, Grade 5

Key Question: What is my life like? What is your life like? **Theme:** Art appreciation **Topic:** Artists

Beginning	Developing	Transitioning	Refining

Fifth grade students who have studied the target language continuously since kindergarten would be secure at performing at the beginning level and would now begin to work on the developing level Standards and Performance Guidelines.

The intention is that all instruction and assessments are completed in the target language, with the exception of reading and listening comprehension assessments, which may require use of English to demonstrate understanding of the texts.

Communication Mode: *Performance Assessment*

Interpretive
Read short biographies of artists from the target culture and make a timeline of the most important events in the artist's life.

Interpersonal
In small groups, compare art prints created by the artists studied. Describe the art prints, comparing colors, styles, subjects. Rate the art prints in order of personal preferences.

Presentational
Create original artwork that illustrates the color, style, and subject of the artist studied. Present your original art to the class, explaining how it reflects the artist studied and how it differs from the artist's style. A written description of the artwork along with an original title must accompany the project.

Wisconsin Standards: Communication

B4: Reading: Students will comprehend the main idea and some supporting ideas of selected authentic written materials.

A3: Opinions: Students will state personal preferences and feelings with some explanation.

C2: Speeches: Students will write and deliver a short presentation about their school or community.

Target Performance (Key elements from the Performance Guidelines to consider in rubric development)

Content:
Complexity/sophistication: Begins combining and recombining phrases into short strings of sentences on familiar topics in both oral and written presentations.

Content:
Vocabulary: Depends on vocabulary presented in class; may begin to use a dictionary to look up unknown words but will have difficulty selecting the correct translation; begins to use some common idiomatic expressions; may resort to native language to communicate unknown words and expressions.

Content:
Complexity/sophistication: Begins combining and recombining phrases into short strings of sentences on familiar topics in both oral and written presentations.

Accuracy:
Time/tense: Begins to distinguish present, past, and simple future tenses with cues and modeling; can express own ideas in the present tense with some errors.

Communication Strategies:
Comprehension: Understands general concepts and some supporting ideas of short conversations and narration on familiar topics; relies on visuals, gestures, facial expressions; may need repetition, restatement, and contextual clues in order to understand; uses background experience to help anticipate meaning.

Cross-Cultural Applications:
Awareness: Begins to use knowledge of own culture and the target culture(s) to help interpret oral and written texts.

Accuracy:
Ease: Restates and recombines memorized language with frequent pauses, hesitations, and false starts; many errors may occur as creativity increases.

Communication Strategies:
Comprehensibility: Understood by a sympathetic native speaker, though this may require special efforts by the native speaker at times.

Cross-Cultural Applications:
Verbal: Begins to recognize and produce linguistic patterns (i.e., placement of adjectives and adverbs, negation) appropriate to the target language.

Accuracy:
Pronunciation: May mispronounce words in new context or words being read for the first time; understandable to a sympathetic native speaker, though this may require special efforts by the native speaker at times.

Communication Strategies:
Impact: Asks follow-up questions; provides continuity to a presentation; begins to make choices of a phrase, image, or content to maintain the attention of the audience.

Cross-Cultural Applications:
Verbal: Begins to recognize and produce linguistic patterns (i.e., placement of adjectives and adverbs, negation) appropriate to the target language.

Links to **Culture** and the other Wisconsin Standards: ✓ *Connections* ✓ *Comparisons* ✓ *Communities* **Evidence** (How these standards are incorporated in the instruction)	**Culture: E2:** Contributions Students will identify major contributions and historical figures from the cultures studied that are significant in the target cultures. (Identify artists and their artwork from the target culture.) **Connections: F3:** Accessing Resources Students will access information in the language studied in order to gain greater insight about other cultures and/or their own. (Read short biographies of artists from the target cultures and talk about their styles of painting, in art class.) **Comparisons: I1:** Cultural Variations Students will discuss the meaning of perspectives, products, and practices in different cultures. (Discuss the importance of the artists and their works in the target culture.) **Communities: K3:** Understanding Students will deepen their understanding of other cultures through various avenues such as cuisine, sports, theatre, dance, and art. (Access museums on the Internet that have paintings by the artists studied.)
Structures and Vocabulary: *What needs to be taught for students to be successful in the performance assessment*	**Structures:** ■ Past tense ■ Adjective placement and agreement **Vocabulary:** ■ Painting, painter, to paint, brushstrokes, style ■ Colors with descriptors (dark blue, light green, etc.)

Standards-Based Curriculum Units

Thematic Curriculum Unit—Performance Assessment and Planning Guide
Middle School, Grade 8

Key Question: What is my life like? What is your life like? **Theme: Cultural celebrations** **Topic: Seasonal markets**

Beginning	Developing	Transitioning	Refining

By eighth grade, students who had instruction in the target language in Grades 4 through 7 would be showing a fair degree of achievement of the language performance described for the developing level. Some areas of language usage would be stronger than others, but most students would be solidly performing at the developing level.

The intention is that all instruction and assessments are completed in the target language, with the exception of reading and listening comprehension assessments, which may require use of English to demonstrate understanding of the texts.

Communication Mode: *Performance Assessment*	Interpretive	Presentational	Interpersonal
	Read information from a Web site about a specific cultural event in the target country (for example, Christmas Market in Nürnberg, Germany). To gauge comprehension, describe details understood under the categories given by the teacher (example: When does the event take place? Where? What activities take place?).	Prepare an entry to put in the Web site "guest book" including brief biographical data and a reaction to the Web site, making a comparison to similar cultural events in your own country.	Share the information learned about the cultural event and your own insights about what is similar and different compared to your own family experiences (example: Where they go to buy presents for birthdays, holidays, etc., and for whom.).
Wisconsin Standards: Communication	**B4: Reading:** Students will comprehend the main idea and some supporting ideas of selected authentic written materials.	**C5: Forms of Writing:** Students will write short compositions and letters.	**A1: Conversations:** Students will sustain a conversation including descriptions on selected topics about themselves and their state or country.
Target Performance (Key elements from the Performance Guidelines to consider in rubric development)	**Content:** —	**Content:** *Situation:* Meets basic communication needs in a controlled setting; can meet practical writing needs such as short letters and notes.	**Content:** *Spontaneity:* Responds with short answers to questions that have been rehearsed; asks simple yes/no questions, informational questions (i.e., who, when, where, what); begins to express reactions to responses (i.e., really, that's great, that's too bad).
	Accuracy: —	**Accuracy:** *Spelling/orthography:* Will begin to notice errors in well-learned items and can correct high-frequency items.	**Accuracy:** *Ease:* Restates and recombines memorized language with frequent pauses, hesitations, and false starts; many errors may occur as creativity increases.

	Communication Strategies: *Comprehension*: Understands general concepts and some supporting ideas of short conversations and narration on familiar topics; relies on visuals, gestures, facial expressions; may need repetition, restatement, and contextual clues in order to understand; uses background experience to help anticipate meaning.	**Communication Strategies:** *Monitoring*: Self-corrects on well-learned items.	**Communication Strategies:** *Clarification*: Asks for rewording, slowing of speech.
	Cross-Cultural Applications: *Awareness*: Begins to use knowledge of own culture and the target culture(s) to help interpret oral and written texts.	**Cross-Cultural Applications:** *Verbal*: Begins to recognize and produce linguistic patterns (i.e., placement of adjectives and adverbs, negation) appropriate to the target language.	**Cross-Cultural Applications:** *Awareness*: Begins to use knowledge of their own culture and the target culture(s) to help interpret oral and written texts.

Links to **Culture** and the other Wisconsin Standards:

Culture: D2: Cultural Activities
Students will experience cultural and social activities common to a student of similar age in the target cultures (such as holiday celebrations, school life, and pastimes). (Unit theme emphasizes celebrations.)

✓ **Connections**
✓ **Comparisons**
✓ **Communities**

Connections: G2: Accessing Resources
Students will access information in the language studied in order to gain greater insight about other cultures and/or their own. (Students use Internet to access information on cultural celebrations.)

Comparisons: I2: Comparisons
Students will compare the form, meaning, and importance of certain perspectives, products, and practices in different cultures. (Students compare shopping for celebrations in target cultures to those in the United States, such as birthdays, holidays.)

Evidence (*How these standards are incorporated in the instruction*)

Communities: J3: Communication
Students will exchange information with people locally and around the world through avenues such as pen pals, E-mail, video, speeches, and publications. (Students enter their response to the Internet site into a Web site guest book.)

Structures and Vocabulary:
What needs to be taught for students to be successful in the performance assessment

Structures:
- Comparisons
- Question formation
- Adjective agreement

Vocabulary:
- Celebrations
- Descriptive adjectives

Standards-Based Curriculum Units

Thematic Curriculum Unit—Performance Assessment and Planning Guide
High School, Grade 10

Key Question: What is my life like? What is your life like? **Theme:** Teenage life **Topic:** Family, school, pastimes

Beginning	Developing	Transitioning	Refining

Students who began study of the target language in sixth or seventh grade and entered a second year class as ninth graders would be showing moderate achievement of the developing level characteristics in tenth grade, beginning to use what they learned as memorized language in recombined and more creative ways.

The intention is that all instruction and assessments are completed in the target language, with the exception of reading and listening comprehension assessments, which may require use of English to demonstrate understanding of the texts.

Communication Mode:	Presentational	Interpersonal	Interpretive
Performance Assessment	Create a scrapbook sharing images (photos, magazine pictures, or drawings) of your parents' life as a teenager, including captions of what life was like.	Sharing your scrapbooks, in pairs discuss what your life is like today as a teenager, sharing similarities and differences with your parents' experiences.	Read an author's comments on his/her life growing up (from an autobiographical short story; from an interview; from excerpts given in a biography) and summarize what is the same or different compared to your parents and compared to your life.
Wisconsin Standards: Communication	**C4: Recounting Events:** Students will tell a story incorporating some description and detail.	**A1: Conversations:** Students will sustain a conversation including descriptions on selected topics about themselves and their state or country. **A3: Opinions:** Students will state personal preferences and feelings with some explanation.	**B4: Reading:** Students will comprehend the main idea and some supporting ideas of selected authentic written materials. **B5: Strategies:** In addition, students will begin to derive meaning through use of prediction, prefixes, suffixes, root words, words similar to English, contextual clues, and word order.
Target Performance (Key elements from the Performance Guidelines to consider in rubric development)	**Content:** *Vocabulary:* Depends on vocabulary presented in class; may begin to use a dictionary to look up unknown words but will have difficulty selecting the correct translation; begins to use some common idiomatic expressions; may resort to native language to communicate unknown words and expressions. *Situation:* Meets basic communication needs in a controlled setting; can meet practical writing needs such as short letters and notes.	**Content:** *Complexity/sophistication:* Begins combining and recombining phrases into short strings of sentences on familiar topics in both oral and written presentations. *Situation:* Meets basic communication needs in a controlled setting; can meet practical writing needs such as short letters and notes.	**Content:** *Vocabulary:* Depends on vocabulary presented in class; may begin to use a dictionary to look up unknown words but will have difficulty selecting the correct translation; begins to use some common idiomatic expressions; may resort to native language to communicate unknown words and expressions.

Accuracy:
Time/tense: Begins to distinguish present, past, and simple future tenses with cues and modeling; can express own ideas in the present tense with some errors.

Communication Strategies:
Comprehensibility: Understood by a sympathetic native speaker, though this may require special efforts by the native speaker at times.

Cross-Cultural Applications:
Verbal: Begins to recognize and produce linguistic patterns (i.e., placement of adjectives and adverbs, negation) appropriate to the target language.

Accuracy:
Time/tense: Begins to distinguish present, past, and simple future tenses with cues and modeling; can express own ideas in the present tense with some errors.

Communication Strategies:
Comprehension: Understands general concepts and some supporting ideas of short conversations and narration on familiar topics; relies on visuals, gestures, facial expressions; may need repetition, restatement, and contextual clues in order to understand; uses background experience to help anticipate meaning.
Clarification: Asks for rewording, slowing of speech.

Cross-Cultural Applications:
—

Accuracy:
Time/tense: Begins to distinguish present, past, and simple future tenses with cues and modeling; can express own ideas in the present tense with some errors.

Communication Strategies:
Comprehension: Understands general concepts and some supporting ideas of short conversations and narration on familiar topics; relies on visuals, gestures, facial expressions; may need repetition, restatement, and contextual clues in order to understand; uses background experience to help anticipate meaning.

Cross-Cultural Applications:
Awareness: Begins to use knowledge of own culture and the target culture(s) to help interpret oral and written texts.

Links to Culture and the other Wisconsin Standards:

✓ **Connections**
✓ **Comparisons**
✓ **Communities**

Evidence (*How these standards are incorporated in the instruction*)

Culture: D2: Cultural Activities
Students will experience cultural and social activities common to a student of similar age in the target cultures (such as holiday celebrations, school life, and pastimes). (Research the teenage lives of famous people through written interviews, autobiographies, or biographies, and describe any cultural or social activities that are different from the students' lives.)

Culture: D3: Beliefs and Attitudes
Students will identify some common beliefs and attitudes within the cultures studied and compare them to their own beliefs and attitudes.

Connections: G2: Accessing Resources
Students will access information in the language studied in order to gain greater insight about other cultures and/or their own.

Comparisons: I1: Cultural Variations
Students will discuss the meaning of perspectives, products, and practices in different cultures. (Discuss in class what attitudes students have in common toward their school work, working during the school year, driving, and other rites of passage. Then have groups of students select one attitude or belief and make it their unique focus for researching the teenage lives of famous people. Compare their attitudes with those of teenagers in another country.)

Structures and Vocabulary:
What needs to be taught for students to be successful in the performance assessment

Structures:
- Comparisons
- Expressing past time/tense

Vocabulary:
- Reentry of topics from beginning level (family, home, school, friends, pastimes)

Standards-Based Curriculum Units

Thematic Curriculum Unit—Performance Assessment and Planning Guide
High School, Grade 12

Key Question: What is my life like? What is your life like? **Theme: Music** **Topic: Contemporary songs**

Beginning	Developing	Transitioning	Refining
	▓▓▓▓▓		

This unit is designed for students who began their study of the target language as ninth graders. By Grade 12, these students will be secure in achieving the Performance Guidelines of the developing level.

The intention is that all instruction and assessments are completed in the target language, with the exception of reading and listening comprehension assessments, which may require use of English to demonstrate understanding of the texts.

Communication Mode: *Performance Assessment*	**Interpretive** Listen to a song (with lyrics as well as orchestration) from a country where the target language is spoken. Summarize in English what the song is about: What story does it tell? What issue does it explore? What mood does it create? Describe the target language key words, phrases, and ideas you understood that support your summary.	**Interpersonal** Discuss with another student what kinds of music you like. Be sure to ask specific questions of your partner and try to share as much information as you can. Talk about why you like or dislike certain types of music, what you listen for, and what you notice about songs when you listen. Ask about and refer to the songs you heard in class.	**Presentational** Given the song and summary (as prepared by another student in the interpretive task), write your review of that song: How popular would it be in your culture? Does the orchestration and style support the message of the lyrics? Describe whether the lyrics and the music work together to get across the same idea.
Wisconsin Standards: Communication	**B2: Listening:** Students will comprehend the main idea and some supporting ideas of selected authentic materials including recordings, broadcasts, videos.	**A3: Opinions:** Students will state personal preferences and feelings with some explanation.	**C5: Forms of Writing:** Students will write short compositions and letters.
Target Performance (Key elements from the Performance Guidelines to consider in rubric development)	**Content:** *Vocabulary:* Depends on vocabulary presented in class; may begin to use a dictionary to look up unknown words but will have difficulty selecting the correct translation; begins to use some common idiomatic expressions; may resort to native language to communicate unknown words and expressions.	**Content:** *Complexity/sophistication:* Begins combining and recombining phrases into short strings of sentences on familiar topics in both oral and written presentations. *Spontaneity:* Responds with short answers to questions that have been rehearsed; asks simple yes/no questions, informational questions (i.e., who, when, where, what); begins to express reactions to responses (i.e., really, that's great, that's too bad).	**Content:** *Vocabulary:* Depends on vocabulary presented in class; may begin to use a dictionary to look up unknown words but will have difficulty selecting the correct translation; begins to use some common idiomatic expressions; may resort to native language to communicate unknown words and expressions. *Situation:* Meets basic communication needs in a controlled setting; can meet practical writing needs such as short letters and notes.

Accuracy:	**Accuracy:**		**Accuracy:**
—	*Ease:* Restates and recombines memorized language with frequent pauses, hesitations, and false starts; many errors may occur as creativity increases.		*Time/tense:* Begins to distinguish present, past, and simple future tenses with cues and modeling; can express own ideas in the present tense with some errors.
	Time/tense: Begins to distinguish present, past, and simple future tenses with cues and modeling; can express own ideas in the present tense with some errors.		
Communication Strategies:	**Communication Strategies:**		**Communication Strategies:**
Comprehension: Understands general concepts and some supporting ideas of short conversations and narration on familiar topics; relies on visuals, gestures, facial expressions; may need repetition, restatement, and contextual clues in order to understand; uses background experience to help anticipate meaning.	*Impact:* Asks follow-up questions; provides continuity to a presentation; begins to make choices of a phrase, image, or content to maintain the attention of the audience. *Clarification:* Asks for rewording, slowing of speech.		*Monitoring:* Self-corrects on well-learned items.
Cross-Cultural Applications:	**Cross-Cultural Applications:**		**Cross-Cultural Applications:**
Awareness: Begins to use knowledge of own culture and the target culture(s) to help interpret oral and written texts. *Verbal:* Begins to recognize and produce linguistic patterns (i.e., placement of adjectives and adverbs, negation) appropriate to the target language.	*Verbal:* Begins to recognize and produce linguistic patterns (i.e., placement of adjectives and adverbs, negation) appropriate to the target language.		*Verbal:* Begins to recognize and produce linguistic patterns (i.e., placement of adjectives and adverbs, negation) appropriate to the target language. *Awareness:* Begins to use knowledge of own culture and the target culture(s) to help interpret oral and written texts.

Links to **Culture** and the other Wisconsin Standards: ✓ *Connections* ✓ *Comparisons* ✓ *Communities*	**Culture: E1:** Objects and Symbols Students will compare objects and symbols, such as flags or currency, from other cultures to those found in their own culture. (Compare forms of music and their popularity in different cultures, at least exploring the variety within U.S. culture, plus comparisons with target countries.) **Connections: G2:** Accessing Resources Students will access information in the language studied in order to gain greater insight about other cultures and/or their own. **Communities: K3:** Understanding Students will deepen their understanding of other cultures through various avenues such as cuisine, sports, theatre, dance, and art. (Check on the Internet for songs currently popular in different countries, draw conclusions about similarities and differences across cultures.) **Connections: F1:** Speaking and Writing Students will use topics and skills from other school subjects to discuss and/or write in the language studied. (After listening to a popular song in the target culture, write another stanza in the target language.)
Evidence (How these standards are incorporated in the instruction)	

Structures and Vocabulary: *What needs to be taught for students to be successful in the performance assessment*	**Structures:** ■ Comparisons ■ Likes/dislikes **Vocabulary:** ■ Musical terms ■ Emotions

Standards-Based Curriculum Units

Transitioning Level

This level is characterized by movement from reflective to interactive language behavior. Students are struggling to act more independently in their language, successfully creating with language to express their own thoughts instead of recombining other people's words.

These three sample units are provided to show what students who begin their language study before entering senior high school can achieve. The eighth grade unit on travel itineraries assumes strong language instruction that began by first grade. The senior high examples show what is possible for students to achieve when the middle school program is more than exploratory. The two senior high units assume a middle school program of year-long instruction in Grades 6 through 8. Middle school programs often provide an exploration of more than one language in sixth grade (or earlier) so that students can then begin the language of their choice by seventh grade. This model allows students to enter a traditional second year course as ninth graders. Such a program design makes it possible for students to be solidly in the transitioning level by Grade 12.

Transitioning Level—Grade 8: Geography—Travel Itinerary

For middle school students to reach the transitioning level, they had to begin their language instruction by first grade. These students will confidently use language at the developing level and thus will start to focus on the traits that will move their language skills into the transitioning level.

Transitioning Level—Grade 10: Cultural Heritage—Legends/Folktales

This unit is designed for students who began their language instruction by fourth grade. As tenth grade students, they will be able to handle all the language standards of the developing level and will be well on their way to accomplishing the characteristics of the transitioning level.

Transitioning Level—Grade 12: Famous People—Fame

Students who began study of the target language in sixth or seventh grade and entered a second year class as ninth graders would be secure in demonstrating the transitioning level characteristics in twelfth grade, beginning to successfully create with language, expressing thoughts in language that is closer to what they use in their native language.

Thematic Curriculum Unit—Performance Assessment and Planning Guide
Middle School, Grade 8

Key Question: How do I look at the world? How do you look at the world? **Theme:** Geography **Topic:** Travel itinerary

Beginning	Developing	Transitioning	Refining

For middle school students to reach the transitioning level, they had to begin their language instruction by first grade. These students will confidently use language at the developing level and thus will start to focus on the traits that will move their language skills into the transitioning level.

The intention is that all instruction and assessments are completed in the target language, with the exception of reading and listening comprehension assessments, which may require use of English to demonstrate understanding of the texts.

Communication Mode: *Performance Assessment*

Interpretive

Locate Internet sites for a region or country where the target language is spoken. Complete a fact sheet about the country. After completing the fact sheet, give your personal opinion about the ease of traveling/living in the region or country, justifying your opinion.

Interpersonal

In groups, locate the places that were researched on a map. Discuss the pluses and minuses of visiting each place in terms of location, climate, political situation, cultural and historic interest, etc. Share the information among groups.

Presentational

Prepare a plan to visit three of the places presented during the interpersonal phase of the unit. Indicate why you chose the three places, what you will do and see in each place, what to be aware of as a traveler in each place. Estimate the amount of time you will spend and the amount of money you will spend.

Wisconsin Standards: Communication

B3: Reading: Students will understand more complex written materials on a variety of topics and formats.

A1: Conversations: Students will discuss and defend an opinion on selected topics from the local to the international level.

C5: Writing: Students will write formal compositions and letters for a variety of purposes.

Target Performance (Key elements from the Performance Guidelines to consider in rubric development)

Content:
Vocabulary: Uses vocabulary from a variety of topics; if precise vocabulary is lacking, can often find another way to express an idea/term; uses a dictionary as needed and selects correct translation most of the time; shows some understanding and use of idiomatic expressions; may invent a word or phrase in order to stay in the target language.

Accuracy:
—

Content:
Spontaneity: Responds to unrehearsed comments, questions on familiar topics; asks a variety of questions and uses some expressive reactions and questions to elicit more information.

Accuracy:
Ease: Creates with both familiar and new language; presents thoughts and ideas with some pauses and hesitations; errors may occur but do not interfere with communication.

Content:
Situation: Meets communication needs on familiar topics in a variety of settings; can meet writing needs including letters, articles, short essays.

Accuracy:
Time/tense: Expresses own thoughts in present time with accuracy; with preparation can use present, past, and simple future times—some errors may be present.

Communication Strategies: *Comprehension*: Understands the main idea and some supporting ideas of conversations, lectures, and narration on familiar and some unfamiliar topics; uses contextual clues, inferences, key words and ideas and text types to aid understanding; uses background knowledge to help understand the discourse.	**Communication Strategies:** *Clarification*: May use paraphrasing, question asking, circumlocution.	**Communication Strategies:** *Comprehensibility*: Understood by a sympathetic native speaker, though this may require special efforts by the native speaker at times.
Cross-Cultural Applications: *Awareness*: Recognizes differences and similarities in the perspectives of the target culture(s) and their own as they are expressed in oral and written texts.	**Cross-Cultural Applications:** *Verbal*: Recognizes and produces linguistic patterns appropriate to the target language.	**Cross-Cultural Applications:** *Awareness*: Recognizes differences and similarities in the perspectives of the target culture(s) and their own as they are expressed in oral and written texts.

Links to **Culture** and the other Wisconsin Standards:	**Culture: E4:** Geography Students will explain the impact of the target country's geography on the people's beliefs, perspectives, and attitudes. (Discuss location and its implications.)
✓ *Connections* ✓ *Comparisons* ✓ *Communities*	**Connections: G2:** Accessing Resources Students will access information in the language studied in order to gain greater insight about other cultures and/or their own. (Use Internet sources for research purposes.)
Evidence (*How these standards are incorporated in the instruction*)	**Comparisons: I3:** Characteristics of Culture Students will understand the concept of culture as they compare other cultures to their own. (Compare countries to visit and pluses/minuses for these visits.) **Communities: K1:** Media Students will use various media in the language studied for study, work, or pleasure. (Use Internet resources.)
Structures and Vocabulary: *What needs to be taught for students to be successful in the performance assessment*	**Structures:** ■ Comparisons, superlatives ■ Prepositions of location ■ Articles/prepositions used with cities, countries **Vocabulary:** ■ Landforms ■ Climate

Standards-Based Curriculum Units

Thematic Curriculum Unit—Performance Assessment and Planning Guide
High School, Grade 10

Key Question: How do I look at the world? How do you look at the world?   **Theme:** Cultural heritage   **Topic:** Legends/folktales

Beginning	Developing	Transitioning	Refining

This unit is designed for students who began their language instruction by fourth grade. As tenth grade students, they will be able to handle all the language standards of the developing level and will be well on their way to accomplishing the characteristics of the transitioning level.

The intention is that all instruction and assessments are completed in the target language, with the exception of reading and listening comprehension assessments, which may require use of English to demonstrate understanding of the texts.

Communication Mode: *Performance Assessment*	**Interpretive** Read legends or folktales from the target culture. Draw a series of pictures to illustrate the sequence of events in the story. List characteristics of the legend or folktale that identify it with the target culture.	**Interpersonal** In groups, share the sequence of pictures that represents the legend or folktale that was read. Through discussion and question/answer, share the story lines of the legends.	**Presentational** Write an original legend or folktale that incorporates characteristics that are typical of the target culture's legends or folktales.
Wisconsin Standards: Communication	**B4: Reading:** Students will comprehend the main idea and key supporting ideas and begin to make inferences in selected authentic written materials.	**A2: Questions:** Students will ask and answer a variety of questions that require follow-up questions and responses for more information.	**C4: Recounting Events:** Students will recount a story with substantive description and detail.
Target Performance (Key elements from the Performance Guidelines to consider in rubric development)	**Content:** — **Accuracy:** —	**Content:** *Spontaneity:* Responds to unrehearsed comments, questions on familiar topics; asks a variety of questions and uses some expressive reactions and questions to elicit more information. **Accuracy:** *Ease:* Creates with both familiar and new language; presents thoughts and ideas with some pauses and hesitations; errors may occur but do not interfere with communication.	**Content:** *Vocabulary:* Uses vocabulary from a variety of topics; if precise vocabulary is lacking, can often find another way to express an idea/term; uses a dictionary as needed and selects correct translation most of the time; shows some understanding and use of idiomatic expressions; may invent a word or phrase in order to stay in the target language. **Accuracy:** *Spelling/orthography:* Pays more attention to correct orthography.

	Communication Strategies: *Comprehension:* Understands the main idea and some supporting ideas of conversations, lectures, and narration on familiar and some unfamiliar topics; uses contextual clues, inferences, key words and ideas, and text types to aid understanding; uses background knowledge to help understand the discourse. **Cross-Cultural Applications:** *Awareness:* Recognizes differences and similarities in the perspectives of the target culture(s) and their own as they are expressed in oral and written texts.	**Communication Strategies:** *Impact:* Personalizes to maintain or reengage audience; able to provide comparisons and/or contrasts to reinforce message. **Cross-Cultural Applications:** *Verbal:* Recognizes and produces linguistic patterns appropriate to the target language.	**Communication Strategies:** *Monitoring:* Begins to notice incorrect language structure and/or need for idioms but may not know how to correct the structure. **Cross-Cultural Applications:** *Verbal:* Recognizes and produces linguistic patterns appropriate to the target language.
Links to **Culture** and the other Wisconsin Standards: ✓ *Connections* ✓ *Comparisons* ✓ *Communities* Evidence (*How these standards are incorporated in the instruction*)	**Culture: D3:** Beliefs and Attitudes Students will discuss and compare beliefs and attitudes within the cultures studied and their own in relation to home, school, community, and nation. (Discuss characteristics of legends and folktales that are distinctive to the target culture.) **Connections: F1:** Speaking and Writing Students will use topics and skills from other school subjects to discuss and/or write in the language studied. (Discuss characteristics of legends and folktales from communication arts.) **Comparisons: H4:** Cultural Characteristics Students will identify cultural characteristics of language such as formalities, levels of politeness, informal and formal language. (Write a legend paying attention to formal/informal language among characters.) **Communities: K1:** Media Students will use various media in the language studied for study, work, or pleasure. (Folktales, legends.)		
Structures and Vocabulary: *What needs to be taught for students to be successful in the performance assessment*	**Structures:** ■ Past/imperfect tenses		**Vocabulary:** ■ Sequencing words

Standards-Based Curriculum Units

Thematic Curriculum Unit—Performance Assessment and Planning Guide
High School, Grade 12

Key Question: How do I look at the world? How do you look at the world? **Theme:** Famous people **Topic:** Fame

Beginning	Developing	Transitioning	Refining

Students who began study of the target language in sixth or seventh grade and entered a second year class as ninth graders would be secure in demonstrating the transitioning level characteristics in twelfth grade, beginning to successfully create with language, expressing thoughts in language that is closer to what they use in their native language.

The intention is that all instruction and assessments are completed in the target language, with the exception of reading and listening comprehension assessments, which may require use of English to demonstrate understanding of the texts.

Communication Mode: Performance Assessment	**Interpretive** Read magazine articles about well-known persons from the target culture; write a summary of the article highlighting the most important information about the person. State why the person is significant in the target culture and/or world.	**Interpersonal** In small groups, discuss what makes a person famous. References need to be made to the class presentations on well-known people from the target cultures. Further discussion must include the advantages and disadvantages of being famous. Include a personal opinion about the desirability of being famous some day.	**Presentational** Write a five-paragraph essay about fame. Give examples of people from the target culture who are famous and why they are famous. Note the difference between being famous within a country and being famous on an international level. Discuss the positive and negative aspects of fame.
Wisconsin Standards: **Communication**	**B4: Reading:** Students will comprehend the main idea and key supporting ideas and begin to make inferences in selected authentic written materials.	**A1: Conversations:** Students will discuss and defend an opinion on selected topics from the local to the international level.	**C5: Forms of Writing:** Students will write formal compositions and letters for a variety of purposes.
Target Performance (Key elements from the Performance Guidelines to consider in rubric development)	**Content:** —	**Content:** *Vocabulary:* Uses vocabulary from a variety of topics; if precise vocabulary is lacking, can often find another way to express an idea/term; uses a dictionary as needed and selects correct translation most of the time; shows some understanding and use of idiomatic expressions; may invent a word or phrase in order to stay in the target language.	**Content:** *Complexity/sophistication:* Expresses own thoughts to describe and narrate using sentences and strings of sentences on familiar and some unfamiliar topics in both oral and written presentations.

Chapter 4

Accuracy:
—

Communication Strategies:
Comprehension: Understands the main idea and some supporting ideas of conversations, lectures, and narration on familiar and some unfamiliar topics; uses contextual clues, inferences, key words and ideas, and text types to aid understanding; uses background knowledge to help understand the discourse.

Cross-Cultural Applications:
Awareness: Recognizes differences and similarities in the perspectives of the target culture(s) and their own as they are expressed in oral and written texts.

Accuracy:
Ease: Creates with both familiar and new language; presents their thoughts and ideas with some pauses and hesitations; errors may occur but do not interfere with communication.

Communication Strategies:
Clarification: May use paraphrasing, question asking, circumlocution.

Cross-Cultural Applications:
Verbal: Recognizes and produces linguistic patterns appropriate to the target language.

Accuracy:
Time/tense: Expresses own thoughts in present time with accuracy; with preparation can use present, past, and simple future times—some errors may be present.

Communication Strategies:
Impact: Personalizes to maintain or reengage audience; able to provide comparisons and/or contrasts to reinforce message.

Cross-Cultural Applications:
Verbal: Recognizes and produces linguistic patterns appropriate to the target language.

Links to Culture and the other Wisconsin Standards: ✓ *Connections* ✓ *Comparisons* ✓ *Communities* Evidence (How these standards are incorporated in the instruction)	**Culture: E2:** Contributions Students will examine the role and significance of the contributions of other cultures in today's world. (Discuss people from the target culture in terms of their local, national, and/or international fame.) **Connections: G1:** Popular Media Students will read, view, listen to, and talk about subjects contained in popular media from other countries in order to gain a perspective on other cultures. (Discuss people in the news from the target cultures.) **Comparisons: I2:** Comparisons Students will compare the form, meaning, and importance of certain perspectives, products, and practices in different cultures. (Discuss who is famous in other cultures and why they are famous.) **Communities: K1:** Media Students will use various media in the language studied for study, work, or pleasure. (Access articles about people from the target culture in the news.)
Structures and Vocabulary: What needs to be taught for students to be successful in the performance assessment	**Structures:** ■ Subjunctive: It is important that, I believe that, it is too bad that, etc. ■ Adverbs: completely, relatively, mostly, etc. **Vocabulary:** ■ Professions

Standards-Based Curriculum Units

Refining Level

This level is characterized by language behavior moving from interactive to initiative, where the speaker takes on full responsibility for engaging, maintaining, and furthering the conversation. Students can successfully act independently in the new language, initiating with language to meet a wide variety of purposes.

The three examples of the refining level would only be within reach of students who began their language study prior to middle school. Time is the single greatest factor impacting language proficiency. To feel secure at the refining level, students must begin their second language instruction by first grade and have continuous, frequent instruction aimed at developing language proficiency. These three sample units show the variety of content that should be included at the highest levels of an instructional sequence: a culture-focused unit, a current events emphasis, and an exploration of language and culture through literature.

Time is the single greatest factor impacting language proficiency.

Refining Level—Grade 12: Immigration—Border Issues

This unit is designed for students who began their language instruction by third grade. As twelfth grade students, they will be able to handle all the language standards of the transitioning level and will be starting to develop the characteristics of the refining level, focusing on these more challenging Performance Standards.

Refining Level—Grade 11: Cultural Perspectives—Cultural Celebration

For senior high school students to reach the refining level, they had to begin their language instruction in elementary grades. Students who began in first grade could be entering the refining level by Grade 11. These students will confidently use language at the transitioning level and thus will start to focus on the traits that will move their language skills into the refining level.

Refining Level—Grade 12: Prejudice—Short Story or Novel

Students who began their study of a second language in kindergarten or first grade will be able to successfully perform at the refining level by twelfth grade. These students are able to integrate their knowledge and understanding of the target culture as they use the target language in sophisticated and complex ways.

Thematic Curriculum Unit—Performance Assessment and Planning Guide
High School, Grade 12

Key Question: What do I think and feel? What do you think and feel? **Theme:** Immigration **Topic:** Border issues

	Beginning	Developing	Transitioning	Refining

This unit is designed for students who began their language instruction by third grade. As twelfth grade students, they will be able to handle all the language standards of the transitioning level and will be starting to develop the characteristics of the refining level, focusing on these more challenging Performance Standards.

The intention is that all instruction and assessments are completed in the target language, with the exception of reading and listening comprehension assessments, which may require use of English to demonstrate understanding of the texts.

Communication Mode: *Performance Assessment*	**Interpersonal** Have a conversation with two classmates about why citizens of other countries may be interested in coming to the United States. Share any stories known of family, friends, community members dealing with their immigration to the United States.		**Interpretive** Read two newspaper, magazine, or Web site editorials on immigration related issues (from two different countries). Describe the authors' opinions and supporting arguments. Compare their conclusions, expressing the argument made from the other country's perspective (not a U.S. perspective).	**Presentational** Prepare for an in-class debate on the topic of immigration by summarizing on note cards your key points and supporting data found through research. Be ready to state and defend your opinion pro or con on the debate question, such as the United States should allow immigration only for political or humanitarian reasons. In groups of two pro and two con, conduct the debate within a set time limit.
Wisconsin Standards: **Communication**		**A1: Conversations:** Students will discuss or debate a wide variety of topics from the local to the international level, hypothesizing, convincing, persuading, and negotiating to reach a conclusion. **A2: Questions:** Students will ask and answer a variety of questions that require elaboration and substantiation of opinions.	**B4: Reading:** Students will comprehend the main idea and supporting ideas and make inferences in a wide variety of authentic written materials. **B5: Strategies:** In addition, students will analyze the author's use of language to understand a written text.	**C2: Speeches:** Students will write and present a speech on a topic that has been researched.
Target Performance (Key elements from the Performance Guidelines to consider in rubric development)		**Content:** *Complexity/sophistication:* Reports, narrates, and describes using connected sentences with transitions to create paragraph-length discourse on a variety of topics in both oral and written presentations. *Spontaneity:* Initiates and maintains conversations using a variety of questions and rejoinders.	**Content:** *Vocabulary:* Demonstrates control of an extensive vocabulary, including a number of idiomatic and culturally authentic expressions from a variety of topics; can successfully explain/describe a term or idea when the precise words are not known; supplements vocabulary by using dictionaries and reference books; will not fall back into native language to express self.	**Content:** *Vocabulary:* Demonstrates control of an extensive vocabulary, including a number of idiomatic and culturally authentic expressions from a variety of topics; can successfully explain/describe a term or idea when the precise words are not known; supplements vocabulary by using dictionaries and reference books; will not fall back into native language to express self.

Accuracy:
Time/tense: Comfortable expressing own thoughts in the present and simple future times; may exhibit some inaccuracies when using past tenses; begins using memorized patterns for hypothesizing, wishing, stating options.

Communication Strategies:
Clarification: Uses a variety of strategies to maintain communication.

Cross-Cultural Applications:
—

Accuracy:
—

Communication Strategies:
Comprehension: Understands the main idea and most supporting ideas of conversations, lectures, and narration on a wide variety of topics; uses organizing principles, inferences, contexts, background knowledge to aid understanding.

Cross-Cultural Applications:
Awareness: Applies understanding of the target culture(s) and its unique perspectives to enhance comprehension of oral and written texts.

Accuracy:
Time/tense: Comfortable expressing own thoughts in the present and simple future times; may exhibit some inaccuracies when using past tenses; begins using memorized patterns for hypothesizing, wishing, stating options.
Ease: Expresses a wide variety of topics with few pauses and hesitations; errors may occur but do not interfere with communication.

Communication Strategies:
Impact: Provides multiple examples to present a more convincing argument; varies delivery style in order to maintain attention of the audience.

Cross-Cultural Applications:
Verbal: Recognizes and produces linguistic patterns appropriate to the target language; begins to show an awareness of the underlying meaning and importance of these patterns.

Links to Culture and the other Wisconsin Standards:

✓ **Connections**
✓ **Comparisons**
✓ **Communities**

Evidence (*How these standards are incorporated in the instruction*)

Culture: D3: Beliefs and Attitudes
Students will explain how beliefs, perspectives, and attitudes affect the target countries' position on global issues.

Connections: G1: Popular Media
Students will read, view, listen to, and talk about subjects contained in popular media from other countries in order to gain a perspective on other cultures. (Skim Web sites from outside the United States for immigration-related editorials and news stories; keep notes of how the issue is viewed in different countries, especially what is similar and different about the context of the discussion.)

Communities: J3: Communication
Students will exchange information with people locally and around the world through avenues such as pen pals, E-mail, video, speeches, and publications. (Interview community members who have recently immigrated to the United States and/or community members who are able to tell the story of their family's immigration.)

Culture: E4: Geography
Students will evaluate the target country's geography with respect to the impact on politics, economics, and history. (Read firsthand accounts written in the target language of immigrants' experiences, not only about coming to the United States. Focus on reasons behind immigration.)

Connections: G2: Accessing Resources
Students will access information in the language studied in order to gain greater insight about other cultures and/or their own. (Research and compare the immigration processes and requirements of different countries.)

Structures and Vocabulary:
What needs to be taught for students to be successful in the performance assessment

Structures:
■ Hypothesizing
■ Expressing opinions (in favor, against)
■ Compound sentence structures (conjunctions)
■ Making suggestions

Vocabulary:
■ Immigration causes
■ Data and charts (specialized vocabulary)

Standards-Based Curriculum Units

Thematic Curriculum Unit—Performance Assessment and Planning Guide
High School, Grade 11

Key Question: What do I think and feel? What do you think and feel? **Theme:** Cultural perspectives **Topic:** Cultural celebration

Beginning	Developing	Transitioning	Refining

For senior high school students to reach the refining level, they had to begin their language instruction in elementary grades. Students who began in first grade could be entering the refining level by Grade 11. These students will confidently use language at the transitioning level and thus will start to focus on the traits that will move their language skills into the refining level.

The intention is that all instruction and assessments are completed in the target language, with the exception of reading and listening comprehension assessments, which may require use of English to demonstrate understanding of the texts.

Communication Mode: *Performance Assessment*	**Presentational**	**Interpretive**	**Interpersonal**
	Prepare a five-minute speech on a topic that is deeply embedded in the target culture (psychologically, and in observable practices, such as *Día de los muertos*), contrasting and comparing the cultural practices and attitudes between a similar demographic group in the United States and in the target culture (e.g., teenagers, parents, socioeconomic groups).	Listen to three classmates' presentations. Summarize the key points made in their presentations. Contrast the perspective of each speaker with your personal perspective gained in your preparation for the presentational component.	Try to picture yourself in the target country during this cultural celebration. Share what you think your personal reaction would be and explain why. Clarify how your perspective is the same or different compared to that commonly held in the target culture and also compared to that of your conversation partner.
Wisconsin Standards: Communication	**C2: Speeches:** Students will write and present a speech on a topic that has been researched.	**B1: Listening:** Students will understand spoken language on a wide variety of topics. **B2: Listening:** Students will comprehend the main idea and supporting ideas of oral presentations and authentic spoken materials.	**A2: Questions:** Students will ask and answer a variety of questions that require elaboration and substantiation of opinions. **A5: Comprehension:** Students will ask for clarification and be able to paraphrase to ensure understanding.
Target Performance (Key elements from the Performance Guidelines to consider in rubric development)	**Content:** *Complexity/sophistication:* Reports, narrates, and describes using connected sentences with transitions to create paragraph-length discourse on a variety of topics in both oral and written presentations. **Accuracy:** *Pronunciation:* Converses with an accent and intonation that is understandable to a native speaker, though this may require special efforts by the native speaker at times.	**Content:** *Situation:* Meets communication needs in a variety of settings; can meet a variety of writing needs including compositions, reports. **Accuracy:** —	**Content:** *Spontaneity:* Initiates and maintains conversations using a variety of questions and rejoinders. **Accuracy:** *Time/tense:* Comfortable expressing own thoughts in the present and simple future times; may exhibit some inaccuracies when using past tenses; begins using memorized patterns for hypothesizing, wishing, stating options.

Communication Strategies:

Impact: Provides multiple examples to present a more convincing argument; varies delivery style in order to maintain attention of the audience.

Cross-Cultural Applications:

Awareness: Applies understanding of the target culture(s) and its unique perspectives to enhance comprehension of oral and written texts.

Verbal: Recognizes and produces linguistic patterns appropriate to the target language; begins to show an awareness of the underlying meaning and importance of these patterns.

Communication Strategies:

Comprehension: Understood by a native speaker, though this may require special efforts by the native speaker at times.

Cross-Cultural Applications:

Awareness: Applies understanding of the target culture(s) and its unique perspectives to enhance comprehension of oral and written texts.

Communication Strategies:

Clarification: Uses a variety of strategies to maintain communication.

Comprehensibility: Understood by a native speaker, though this may require special efforts by the native speaker at times.

Cross-Cultural Applications:

Awareness: Applies understanding of the target culture(s) and its unique perspectives to enhance comprehension of oral and written texts.

Links to Culture and the other Wisconsin Standards: ✓ *Connections* ✓ *Comparisons* ✓ *Communities* *Evidence (How these standards are incorporated in the instruction)*	**Culture: D2:** Cultural Activities Students will examine the role and importance of various social activities within the cultures studied (such as religious celebrations, historical events, rites of passage). (Find and summarize writings from within the target culture about the cultural celebration being studied; focus on the perspectives held by the culture that influence the celebration.) **Culture: D4:** Historical Influences Students will discuss historical and philosophical backgrounds that have influenced a culture's patterns of interaction. (Research historical and cultural roots of the cultural celebration being studied.) **Culture: E1:** Objects and Symbols Students will connect objects and symbols of other cultures to the underlying beliefs and perspectives. (Examine the objects associated with the cultural celebration being studied. Identify how available they are, and who buys [or makes] them for whom. Discuss the significance of the objects within the target culture.) **Comparisons: I1:** Cultural Variations Students will discuss the meaning of perspectives, products, and practices in different cultures. **Comparisons I2:** Comparisons Students will compare the form, meaning, and importance of certain perspectives, products, and practices in different cultures. (Examine how the cultural celebration is manifested in different cultures, including their own.)
Structures and Vocabulary: *What needs to be taught for students to be successful in the performance assessment*	**Structures:** ■ Expressing opinions ■ Hypothesizing ■ I would _____ if _____ ■ Expressing agreement/disagreement **Vocabulary:** ■ Topical vocabulary of cultural celebration ■ Terms to describe cultural phenomenon

Standards-Based Curriculum Units

Thematic Curriculum Unit—Performance Assessment and Planning Guide
High School, Grade 12

Key Question: What do I think and feel? What do you think and feel?   **Theme:** Prejudice   **Topic:** Short story or novel

Beginning	Developing	Transitioning	Refining

Students who began their study of a second language in kindergarten or first grade will be able to successfully perform at the refining level by twelfth grade. These students are able to integrate their knowledge and understanding of the target culture as they use the target language in sophisticated and complex ways.

The intention is that all instruction and assessments are completed in the target language, with the exception of reading and listening comprehension assessments, which may require use of English to demonstrate understanding of the texts.

	Interpersonal	Interpretive	Presentational
Communication Mode: *Performance Assessment*	In small groups, give examples of prejudice in today's society. Discuss reasons for the prejudice and possible ways to combat prejudice. Also note if the prejudice has historic roots or not.	Read a short story or novel from the target culture that deals with the theme of prejudice. Outline how the author depicts prejudice through the story line and through the individual characters. Indicate the resolution presented by the author.	In an essay, state how the people and the values of the target culture are presented in the short story or novel. Discuss if the theme of the story can be applied to all people or only to the target culture.
Wisconsin Standards: Communication	**A1: Conversations:** Students will discuss or debate a wide variety of topics from the local to the international level, hypothesizing, convincing, persuading, and negotiating to reach a conclusion.	**B4: Reading:** Students will comprehend the main idea and supporting ideas and make inferences in a wide variety of authentic written materials.	**C5: Forms of Writing:** Students will write formal compositions, research papers, and letters for a variety of purposes.
Target Performance (Key elements from the Performance Guidelines to consider in rubric development)	**Content:** *Spontaneity:* Initiates and maintains conversations using a variety of questions and rejoinders. **Accuracy:** *Ease:* Expresses a wide variety of topics with few pauses and hesitations; errors may occur but do not interfere with communication.	**Content:** *Vocabulary:* Demonstrates control of an extensive vocabulary, including a number of idiomatic and culturally authentic expressions from a variety of topics; can successfully explain/describe a term or idea when the precise words are not known; supplements vocabulary by using dictionaries and reference books; will not fall back into native language to express self. **Accuracy:** —	**Content:** *Complexity/sophistication:* Reports, narrates, and describes using connected sentences with transitions to create paragraph-length discourse on a variety of topics in both oral and written presentations. **Accuracy:** *Spelling/orthography:* Can proofread to write the target language with few errors.

		Communication Strategies:	**Communication Strategies:**
		Impact: Provides multiple examples to present a more convincing argument; varies delivery style in order to maintain attention of the audience.	*Impact*: Provides multiple examples to present a more convincing argument; varies delivery style in order to maintain attention of the audience.
		Comprehension: Understands the main idea and most supporting ideas of conversations, lectures, and narration on a wide variety of topics; uses organizing principles, inferences, contexts, background knowledge to aid understanding.	
		Cross-Cultural Applications:	**Cross-Cultural Applications:**
		Non-verbal: Acts in a culturally correct manner in a variety of contexts with sensitivity and understanding of the implied meanings.	*Awareness*: Applies understanding of the target culture(s) and its unique perspectives to enhance comprehension of oral and written texts.
		Awareness: Applies understanding of the target culture(s) and its unique perspectives to enhance comprehension of oral and written texts.	
Links to **Culture** and the other Wisconsin Standards:	**Culture: D3:** Beliefs and Attitudes Students will explain how beliefs, perspectives, and attitudes affect the target countries' position on global issues. (Discussion of prejudice.)		
✓ **Connections** ✓ **Comparisons** ✓ **Communities**	**Connections: F2:** Reading and Listening Students will read material, listen to and/or watch programs in the language studied on topics from other classes. (Read short story or novel; discuss prejudice.)		
	Comparisons: I3: Characteristics of Culture Students will understand the concept of culture as they compare other cultures to their own. (Discuss prejudice as it appears in the target culture.)		
Evidence (How these standards are incorporated in the instruction)	**Communities: K3:** Understanding Students will deepen their understanding of other cultures through various avenues such as cuisine, sports, theatre, dance, and art. (Study the literature of the target culture.)		
Structures and Vocabulary: *What needs to be taught for students to be successful in the performance assessment*	**Structures:** ■ Subjunctive ■ If . . . then statements ■ Literary past tense	**Vocabulary:** ■ As needed for discussion	

Standards-Based Curriculum Units 137

Part II
Issues Impacting Instruction

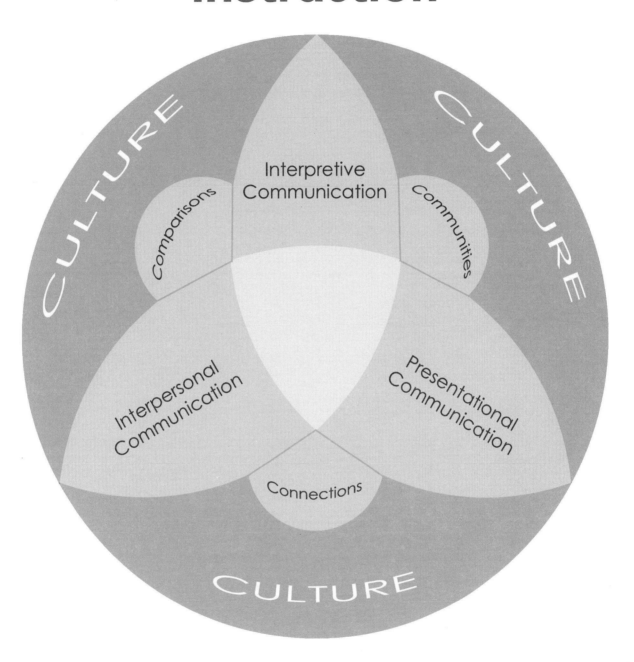

The Role of the Student in a Standards-Based Curriculum

5

Instruction Flowing from a Curriculum of Standards-Based Assessment
Brain-Compatible Learning
Welcoming Brain-Friendly Learning
Tuning Teaching to Learning, Memory, Attention, and Motivation
The Impact of Threat on Inhibiting Language Acquisition
The Role of Enrichment in Enhancing Language Acquisition
Working with the Brain for World Language Acquisition and Learning
Lesson Planning for Brain-Compatible World Language Acquisition
References and Resources

Instruction Flowing from a Curriculum of Standards-Based Assessment

"Okay. I understand the goals of the standards for student performance; I can even recite all five C's. I have a curriculum that captures those standards in the form of clear assessments for each unit I'm going to teach. Now I have to plan my daily lessons. I'd just like to have some ideas to get me started. I have some great activity ideas and I think I have a pretty good idea now of how to match those activities to the particular unit I'm teaching. I also have a better idea of how to be selective in using the textbook and other materials that I have at my disposal. I'd just really like a repertoire from which to design each day's lesson plan. I don't want someone to just hand me his or her lesson plans; I know I have to fit my plans to my students and to the unit I'm teaching. I know I have to decide how to teach based on where my students are, like what they already know, and where I want to get them, that is, what they will have to do at the end of this unit. Got any ideas?"

Clearly this teacher has placed her instructional dilemma in the context of a curriculum of standards-based assessment. Two important influences to help a teacher make those instructional decisions are recent research-based discoveries of how students learn and the corresponding evolution in language teaching methods. With a curriculum centered on standards-based assessment in place, a teacher's next step is to design lessons from a mind-set of compatible methodology. Although the standards themselves do not prescribe any particular methodology, there are clear implications that affect a teacher's instructional choices.

The standards represent a next step in our developing professional consensus, based on experience and research, around how students learn languages. Because the standards focus so much on the three modes of communication, a methodology that focuses on learning the language mainly by talking about it is not going to produce such goals. Students need to be involved in using the new language in order to really learn it. This chapter and the next one discuss two key elements to influence a teacher's instructional decisions:

- The implications for second language acquisition from research on how the human brain learns (Chapter 5)
- The evolution in teaching methods for the language learning classroom (Chapter 6)

Brain-Compatible Learning

By understanding how the brain learns naturally, language teachers may be better able to enhance their effectiveness in the classroom.

Genesee 2000, 1

Education is discovering the brain.... Anyone who does not have a thorough, holistic grasp of the brain's architecture, purposes and main ways of operating is as far behind the times as an automobile designer without a full understanding of engines.

—Leslie Hart

The purpose of this section is to identify brain-based processes of learning and language acquisition that foster second language acquisition. If we are knowledgeable of how the brain learns and acquires language, we are more likely to select learner-friendly teaching strategies for more effective second language acquisition by *all* students. Compatible with *Wisconsin's Model Academic Standards for foreign Languages*, the suggested strategies can be adapted to accommodate any language program, age, ability, and grade level.

Welcoming Brain-Friendly Learning

The latest neuroscientific research strongly supports a learning model that is harmonious with natural brain function, known as *brain-compatible* or *brain-based* learning. Thanks to discoveries in neuroscience and medical technology since 1980, scientists can observe and measure brain activity and function more precisely than ever before. A more comprehensive understanding of how the brain works has influenced the development of a brain-friendly paradigm for learning and second language acquisition. It recognizes biological factors that can affect learning. This paradigm offers alternatives to many methods based on the behavioral science beliefs of the 1950s, 1960s, and 1970s that might now be incompatible with how the brain works best.

What Are the Implications for Second Language Teachers?

Our flexibility to vary, modify, or even change our teaching styles and strategies in sync with current learning and second language acquisition research, methodologies, materials, and technology can help all of our students to reach their second language potential.

Tuning Teaching to Learning, Memory, Attention, and Motivation

Have you ever wondered why some students can easily attain their target language potential and others never do, or why some enjoy lifelong language retention and others have difficulty retaining the language beyond their classroom experience? We might ask ourselves:

- Are our teaching strategies focused on real-life, integrated, challenging activities, or are they merely grammar drills?
- Are we attentive to the way the brain (or a particular student) learns and recalls best?
- Do we seriously consider individual learning styles, challenges, and needs?
- Do we teach what is really relevant?
- Do we acknowledge emotions and encourage them to be expressed?
- Are we aware of important learning variables that can help us meet the needs of our students and reach the goals of proficiency in a second language?

How Do We Learn?

Learning, in general, is a means to gather new information with which to increase our knowledge, stimulate our actions, or affect our behavior. Current literature in brain-compatible learning suggests that learning involves an electrochemical process. Very simply, a stimulus, such as having a brainstorm, solving a puzzle, or decoding a message, produces electrical energy that in turn stimulates the release of chemicals. These chemicals help to stimulate brain cell growth. The neuron (brain cell) is signaled to activate either short- or long-term memory in the physical process that recalls learning. As we activate, repeat, and reinforce learning experiences, we stimulate dendrite growth—the connections or branching of brain cells—creating pathways that facilitate and increase our ability to perform a given task. The key to getting smarter is in growing more connections between brain cells and not losing ex-

Today's teachers ought to be a catalyst for learning or a choreographer of curriculum, not a talking textbook. The best learning happens in the midst of immense stimulation, variety of experience, rich multi-sensory real-life stimulation, music, role-play, art and movement.

—Freeman Dhority 1998

Language learning engages the whole brain in an integrated system.

isting connections, according to author, presenter, and trainer on brain-compatible learning Eric Jensen (1998, 15). The more we learn, the more connections we make. The more language connections we make, the greater the potential there will be for successful second language acquisition.

Language learning engages the whole brain in an integrated system. Research indicates that most brain functions once attributed solely to either the left or the right hemisphere actually overlap. Also, learning is not limited to the brain. The whole body works with the brain in the learning and language acquisition process. Integrated into the body, learning and language tend to be better integrated into life, easier to retrieve, and longer lasting.

How Do We Remember What We Have Learned?

Memory and recall, the proof of successful learning and language acquisition, are not simply the result of studying and memorizing. They occur as a result of a physiological retrieval process. An awareness of this process can remind us to align our teaching style more closely with the way our students learn and recall best.

The brain does not store memories but recreates them from learning that is coherent, relevant, and meaningful to the learner. Each type of learning requires its own electrochemical triggering for retrieval from its particular memory pathway. Some pathways, however, are more easily retrieved than others. Some students may be better at accessing one pathway over another, according to their individual learning and processing styles.

How Do We Access Memory Needed for Language Comprehension and Output?

Some memory pathways have a more natural retrieval system for recall than others. They are best accessed through contextual, event-oriented situations and performance-task activities that do not require complex processing. Memory is strengthened by learning activities that

- Are novel, interesting, and relevant to students
- Engage imagination, emotions, and senses
- Are accompanied by music, rhythm, or movement
- Include changing physical positions: standing, sitting on the floor or in another seat
- Include a variety of settings, such as changing the lighting, wearing costumes, going outside or on a field trip, and bringing in guest speakers
- Are hands-on (incorporating visual arts, projects, experiments, etc.)
- Involve manipulatives
- Include stretch breaks
- Use drama, theater, and role play
- Involve the body (i.e., total physical response [TPR], which develops comprehension through body movements in response to commands (Asher 1988)

Our semantic memory, in contrast, is accessed through pathways that retrieve more structured learning of vocabulary and grammar. Used for textbook, rote, and traditional grammar/translation-based learning, it has the weakest of the retrieval systems. It involves complex processing, requires more processing time, is short term and limited, often lasting only 5–20 seconds, and better accessed in the morning (Jensen 1998, 104). Relying only on recall from texts and rote memorization of vocabulary, grammar, translation, and other information can be frustrating, discouraging, and difficult or impossible for many students.

Some semantic learning is inevitable and might even be useful for

- Serial vocabulary—such as numbers
- Some categories of vocabulary—calendar, family, clothes, colors
- Grammatical language structures—verb forms, word order, gender and number agreement
- Reading for information

Studies suggest that we limit activities that require only semantic learning and teach our students specifically how to process it for quick recall. Semantic memory is strengthened by

- Using acronyms, key words, word associations, cognates, "language ladders"
- Providing meaningful, real-life contexts
- Mapping, journaling, or having discussion to process reading as it is read
- Categorizing, grouping, or illustrating words, ideas, or concepts

Textbooks may or may not present language in a meaningful, real-life, or task-oriented context. Textbooks are useful for reference, like an encyclopedia, dictionary, or instruction and practice manual, rather than as the sole source or guide for instruction.

How Can We Help Make Memory Pathways More Accessible?

Pathways are more accessible if the amount of material to be learned and the amount of time to learn it are reasonable. Plan lessons and units with fewer topics or tasks and less new language to be presented at one time but more depth in the coverage of what is presented. Allow time to

- Engage student thinking before instruction
- Incorporate varied teaching and learning strategies
- Integrate new learning
- Foster student proficiency and confidence by focusing on simpler language before adding more complex structures
- Share feedback

How Do We Affect Our Students' Ability to Pay Attention?

Classrooms should be busy, interactive environments where learners are teaching and teachers are learning. By using a multisensory approach consistently, teachers keep students actively engaged in their learning.

Sousa 1998

Paying attention and sustaining it are more complicated than the outwardly visible actions of cooperative, self-disciplined, well-focused students. Whether students are attentive or inattentive, focused or distracted, interested or bored, their physiological makeup dictates that the brain is always paying attention to something. Human survival depends on it. We, however, may influence our students' attentiveness and attention span in the second language classroom. If we present information and provide learning and language activities in ways that students perceive as relevant and engaging, they will then be more likely to focus on these stimuli over other competing stimuli and give us the attention we desire.

We are more likely to focus student attention through our role as a learning guide or facilitator of a variety of visual, auditory, and kinesthetic student-centered activities. These approaches help to create and sustain students' attention:

- Incorporate past learning to help students attend to new learning and make it relevant.
- Encourage positive feelings to maximize attention devoted to new learning.
- Play language games.
- Play appropriate background music.
- Include movement such as stretching, team activities, charades, role play, and mime.
- Use new or familiar aromas to trigger attention. (Smells have unfiltered access to the brain.)
- Intersperse novel and routine activities.
- Do cooperative learning activities in pairs or small groups to increase language production.
- "Dress" the classroom with target language-rich posters, signs, visual exhibits, and decorations to promote brain interest and support subconscious peripheral learning and incidental language acquisition. Periodically change them for novelty.

What Are the Brain's Natural Limits for Prolonged Attention?

The brain is not designed to sustain continuous, high-level, focused external attention. Approximately 10 minutes or less is the limit. It would, therefore, be unreasonable to expect students to pay attention to direct instruction by a teacher giving information or lecturing too often. Much of direct instruction is geared toward auditory learning (and semantic memory)—a strength for only 18 to 22 percent of classroom populations, according to California speech pathologist and educator Shirley Handy (1999).

Direct instruction is also one of the least effective methods for encouraging students to speak the target language. Excessively used, it may intimidate or bore students. It also reduces precious opportunities for them to speak, allowing as little as only two minutes per student per class period.

The guideline for direct instruction without a break or change in activity is:

    Kindergarten to Grade 2:   5–7 minutes
               Grades 3 to 7:   8–12 minutes
              Grades 8 to 12:   12–15 minutes

(Jensen 1998, 49)

How Does Individual Attentiveness Vary During the Day?

Our ability to pay attention varies during the day with repetitive cycles of varying degrees of highs and lows, lasting for about 90 to 110 minutes. We are much more attentive at the top of each cycle than at the bottom when energy, attention, and learning drop. Students at the end of a cycle may become less alert or drowsy. It would be unreasonable to expect high student attentiveness or output during that time. (Jensen 1998, 44–45)

How can we accommodate attentional cycles?

- Include movements such as standing and stretching (TPR activities) or "mental breaks" that can help focus attention.
- Allow students to get drinks of water or to bring and use a water bottle during class. Our brains are 80 percent water.
- Periodically, allow students a few minutes for personal processing of new information and target language.

Why Is Personal Processing Time So Important in a Second Language Class?

We cannot pay attention to external input and internalize new information for meaning at the same time. Bombarding students with more language or grammar rules than they can process would be overwhelming and counterproductive, compromising their potential for long-term retention and recall. Much of what we learn cannot be processed consciously. We need time to create meaning by subconsciously internalizing new learning and language patterns. That is why some of our best ideas or recall often occur spontaneously, long after the initial learning experience and in a completely different setting—seemingly "out of the blue." Our brain is constantly processing information, even as we sleep (Jensen 1998, 46).

How might we provide personal processing time in the target language?

- Ask questions or conduct class discussion in the target language to help process language.
- Provide extensive communicative, task-oriented practice of simpler language before introducing new or more complex structures.

- Promote language retention with a rest time for the brain. This should be an opportunity for each student to choose a target-language activity that requires only previously acquired language or rest time with no or noncompeting stimuli. If work is assigned or new language is required, it is not rest or "down time" for the brain. Possibilities might include
    - Reading
    - Personal reflection
    - Writing
    - Watching a video
    - Drawing
    - Listening to music
    - Physical activity
    - Language games
    - Conversation corners for small-group interpersonal discussion

How Do Emotions Affect Language Acquisition?

Expressing emotions, such as joy, pleasure, fear, surprise, disgust, anger, and sadness, can trigger chemical changes that alter our moods and behaviors. "Emotions drive attention, create meaning, and have their own memory pathways" (Jensen 1998, 72). Positively expressed, they get us passionate enough to carry out our goals with "the flow of the vital feel-good unifying chemicals that run both our biology and behavior" (Jensen 1998, 79). Repressed or denied they can cause adverse chemical changes, impair learning, and inhibit language.

How can we encourage positive expression of emotions in target-language activities?

- Frequently express our own love of learning and enthusiasm for teaching.
- Set up "controlled" controversy such as debate, dialogue, or argument.
- Encourage introspection through journal writing, discussion, and sharing.
- Read, tell, and discuss stories.

What Motivates Students to Achieve Success in the Target Language?

Intrinsic motivation and natural rewards are most likely to motivate complex, higher-order thinking, learning, and language.

Intrinsic motivation and natural rewards are most likely to motivate complex, higher-order thinking, learning, and language. Positive thinking, for example, can trigger the release of pleasurable chemicals (dopamine) and natural opiates (endorphins) that regulate pain and stress. Students who succeed usually feel good and experience "natural highs." That "feeling" serves as self-reward and motivation (Jensen 1998, 64).

Although effective for conditioning simple physical actions, external rewards for academic achievement can impair learning by motivating students to work more for the reward than the academic success. The perceived value and expectations of external rewards also limit their effectiveness.

How can we reinforce intrinsic motivation for second language acquisition?

- Eliminate threat and high stress.
- Encourage students' positive beliefs about themselves, the learning, the target language, and target-language cultures.
- Manage emotions with the use of routine activities, drama, and movement.
- Instill a love of learning with "celebrations." Celebrate learning after it has taken place with a surprise activity or treat. Celebrations promised in advance as an incentive become external rewards and lose their effectiveness. Such "post-learning" celebrations might include songs and music, cheers, language games, student-designed celebrations, or outings.

Students who have had a history of violence, threat, or stress, however, are not usually rewarded internally. They have more receptors for noradrenaline, which can cause behaviors such as overarousal, aggressiveness, and strong attention to body language. However, they tend to show more positive behaviors when put in cooperative or team roles when they can be both a leader and follower on the same day.

The Impact of Threat on Inhibiting Language Acquisition

High stress and threat have the greatest negative impact on learning and language. Though a little stress that produces a moderate rush of adrenaline is good for learning, high stress and threat can

- Change the body's chemistry so that the brain shuts down.
- Kill brain cells and reduce neural connections.
- Alter, impair or inhibit attention, learning, memory, and behavior.
- Raise anxiety and lower self-image, morale, and motivation. It raises the "affective filter" (Krashen 1983) whereby target language experiences are "filtered" through the body's responses to threat. A high affective filter reduces openness to language input, especially after age 10, raising language anxiety, lowering self-confidence and motivation, and limiting second language acquisition potential.

Students sensing threat will find it nearly impossible to stay focused on academic learning because the brain's priority becomes self-preservation from the immediate threat or stressor. "When a human being feels threatened, that human being's brain will shift out of rational processing into instinctive mode. The actions, then, that the human being performs will be the result of instinct, irrational-but-practiced behavior, or impulse." (Josten 2001, p. 209). The automatic physiological response triggered by the brain can be the same whether the perceived "danger" is bodily harm or any of the following:

Threat throws the brain into survival mode at the expense of developing higher-order thinking skills.

—Eric Jensen

- Punishment
- Embarrassment or humiliation (especially before peers)
- Finger-pointing
- Sarcasm
- Unrealistic deadlines
- Inappropriate learning styles
- Detention or loss of privileges
- Lowered grades
- Fear of failure
- Test anxiety
- Negative interaction (with a parent, teacher, or classmate)

For some students, the target language itself may be a threat! Threats can occur anywhere—in class, outside the classroom, at home—and no matter what the source and when or where they occur, the physiological and behavioral effects may carry over into our classes. How we as teachers deal with threat may influence each student's academic progress and ultimate success or failure in the target language.

What Can We Do in Our Language Classes to Eliminate Threat?

- *Reduce our own threats* by setting reasonable rules and expectations and enforcing them with an immediate, reasonable response or consequence—not the threat of one. We can extend deadlines and help students set specific, reasonable, and measurable goals. We can give "test tips" and reminders of what students should be doing to optimize their success such as good test-taking practice or words of encouragement. We can ask students, in English, what is interfering with their learning and then modify our teaching strategies for those who experience target-language anxiety or difficulties. We can also speak privately to individual students about learning or behavior problems, help them to see the connection between their actions and outcomes, and offer them choices for alternative possibilities.
- *Minimize the effects of outside threats and reduce stress* with a short target-language transition time at the beginning of class to help elevate mood: small or large group discussion, games, music, dance, journal or creative writing, stretching or physical exercise (i.e., TPR activities). Provide experiences and tasks that are "fun." Having fun decreases stress and improves immune system functioning for three days after the fun (Jensen 1998, 87).
- *Reduce the possibility of threats from other students* by setting clear behavioral expectations: rules, appropriate language (whether target language or English), conflict resolution strategies, and zero-tolerance for threatening or hurting one another. Use and vary partners. Groups and teams are good not only for minimizing the threat potential but also for cooperative learning, an effective second language acquisition strategy.
- *Recognize our limitations as teachers.* If repeated attempts to reduce threat or stress fail with certain students, their situations may be be-

yond our expertise. They might require a referral to an appropriate health care professional for evaluation and medical treatment, therapy, or a classroom behavior management program.

In the Classroom:
How Can We Create a Low-Anxiety Environment to Help Lower the Affective Filter for Language Acquisition?

Use the target language consistently and appropriately.
- Post a sign that the target language is being spoken to serve as a conscious reminder of the language in use.
- Provide target-language input that is interesting "in meaningful, communicative contexts that carry significance for the student" (Curtain and Pesola 1994, xiii).
- Use abundant visuals, props, realia, and hands-on activities to assist students' comprehension.
- Allow language output to begin with a combination of nonverbal responses, gestures, and target-language words or phrases.
- Provide daily expressions using the "password" technique: Students say a given expression before leaving the room. The daily expressions are posted in a designated area of the room and numbered. From then on, students must say that expression in the target language. If students say an item in English, the teacher can easily cue them by calling out the appropriate number.
- Provide students with classroom "survival expressions":
   - Giving greetings and leave-takings
   - Asking permission (i.e., "May I go to the bathroom? Sharpen my pencil?")
   - Reacting to classroom events by expressing enthusiasm/dissatisfaction
   - Expressing confusion and asking for clarification (i.e., "I don't understand, more slowly, please, How do you say____? What does this mean? Can you explain?")
   - Interacting with the teacher and other students (i.e., please, thank you, excuse me)

Place greater emphasis on comprehension and communication than on grammatical accuracy or form when focusing on interpersonal communication.
- Subtly and selectively correct speech errors that do not interfere with communication. Overcorrection can inhibit language production. Subtly restate the phrases correctly by verifying the information or requesting clarification without focusing attention on the error. More overt error correction may be appropriate if it does not interfere with the overall message or if it is important for interpretive or presentational tasks.
- Discuss and practice alternatives for other errors that require more attention for correction *after* completing the interpersonal conversation activity.

Place greater emphasis on comprehension and communication than on grammatical accuracy or form when focusing on interpersonal communication.

Allow students to progress at their own pace.

Use English cautiously and sparingly only if needed
- To do a comprehension check (interpretive standard) on students who are not yet able to speak in the target language.
- To help reassure insecure students who are afraid to speak in the target language.
- To allow occasional clarification time for students who have difficulty processing learning or understanding directions in the target language.
- To refocus students in the target language if they are using too much English.

This should be a brief period of time, strategically chosen by the teacher to redirect students in using the target language or to facilitate an activity for maximum target-language use (i.e., taking 2 minutes to discuss a problem or explain an activity in English so that students have 10 minutes on task in the target language verses 10 minutes for a target-language explanation by the teacher and only 2 minutes on task for students). Too much time in English reduces time in the target language and may ultimately limit proficiency.

Posting a sign that says "English is in use" is one technique that can help teachers make a conscious choice to allow and limit the use of English.

The Role of Enrichment in Enhancing Language Acquisition

How Can We Enrich Our Students' Second Language Experience While Making Learning and Teaching Meaningful, Relevant, and Fun?

We, as professional educators, have the means to enhance or limit the lifetime second language potential of our students.

Enrichment has the greatest positive impact on learning and language. Current brain research indicates that although heredity is responsible for 30 to 60 percent of our brain's wiring, 40 to 70 percent is influenced by environmental factors (Jensen 1998, 30). Studies suggest that the brain can grow new connections at any age with environmental stimulation. Given moderate challenge and high feedback, all students have the potential to grow an enriched brain. All students, including those with exceptional learning needs—that is, underachievement, attention deficit disorder, learning disabilities—can enjoy and successfully acquire a second language if teaching strategies are adequately attuned to their learning styles. Students seeking greater challenges might reach more advanced proficiency levels on the standards continuum as well as acquire additional languages.

Eliminating threat is a critical first condition for learning. Students will then benefit from "enrichments" of the learning environment. Providing a supportive environment for learning, supporting the learning process, varying the learning process, and providing feedback are the most important factors for such enrichment.

Provide a supportive environment for learning. Too much challenge can cause students to give up and too little can cause boredom, which reduces brain cell connections. To provide sufficient challenge but within a supportive environment, try the following suggestions:

- *Follow the "immersion model,"* conducting most, if not all, class time and activities in the target language. Use abundant visuals and realia.
- *Engage the senses* with a variety of visual, auditory, olfactory, gustatory, tactile, and kinesthetic experiences to create novelty and open additional memory pathways.
- *Do content-based, thematic activities and projects* in mathematics, science, social studies, literature (including stories, storytelling, comic books, "Big Books," poetry, and plays), physical education, and so on. They create a meaningful context for target language acquisition and a link to the Connections standard. They also provide simultaneous learning or reinforcement of other disciplines.
- *Use strategies that include the arts.* Music, visual arts, drama, dance, and theater promote a variety of learning styles and can have a powerful, positive impact on language acquisition. They can each serve as a medium for content-based learning and teaching to Wisconsin's world language standards while fostering the development of other valuable skills and attitudes.

Music: Research shows parallels between the structures of language and musical development: "an inseparably linked single system of processing sounds acquired from the earliest stages of infancy" (Garfias 1990). What turns sounds into language depends on what the brain does with them. Music is a carrier of language and culture and everything about it carries a message and provides a memory hook.

Music (through both singing and listening) has been shown to encourage physiological states that are learning receptive; it

- Increases or decreases chemicals that affect attention, mood, attitude, and emotions
- Enhances inflow of new information and language, reasoning, comprehension, prespeaking, speaking, reading, and long-term memory
- Alters brain waves that produce electrical energy to energize, focus attention, or stimulate creativity

Songs and rhymes link language and action in both planned and incidental learning. Information spoken in a rhythmic pattern can easily hold together as a unit (unlike isolated or unrelated words) and be recalled in a greater volume of material (Campbell 1997). Repetition in songs and rhythmic patterns helps embed language.

The melody of a song can serve as a vehicle for the words, ideas, concepts, or language patterns that are imparted through its lyrics. Songs provide a context for language and can also be a catalyst for interpersonal

All students, including those with exceptional learning needs, can enjoy and successfully acquire a second language if teaching strategies are adequately attuned to their learning styles.

Music is a carrier of language and culture and everything about it carries a message and provides a memory hook.

conversation and presentational reading and writing (communication standards) as well as other language content and multimodal activities.

Listening to songs can develop interpretive listening and reading skills. Songs help students improve auditory attention, sound discrimination, and even comprehension. Providing song lyrics can also foster reading comprehension.

Culturally authentic or "adopted" sing-along target-language songs and target-culture dance-along music create a sense of fun, build community, and connect language and culture. Teachers might use traditional folk songs, popular songs, and folk dances, linking the standards under Culture with language learning.

In the classroom
- Use sound stimuli in conjunction with other activities to promote brain interest
- Listen to soft classical or Baroque background music during discussion or as a transition activity to foster abstract thought and divergent thinking
- Use story, poetry or finger-play formats
- Encourage creative writing, composing original song lyrics, rhymes, poems, stories
- Teach vocabulary, grammar, phonics, and pronunciation in meaningful contexts
- Help memorize language patterns by the use of
  - Chaining songs, rounds, and countdown (or up) songs
  - Singing any language patterns to a familiar tune

Visual arts teach thinking and build emotive expressiveness and memory. "By learning and practicing art, the human brain actually rewires itself to make more and stronger connections" (Jensen 1998, 38). The visual arts also promote creativity and concentration.

In the classroom
- Coordinate target-language and art activities that foster the communication as well as culture standards and others that may apply

Visual arts can also be coordinated with target-language activities in the content areas and performing arts to integrate learning. Possibilities include
- "Art vocabulary" and observation activities focusing on subject, object, color, line, shape, size, texture, and so on, using art prints, slides, and three-dimensional objects
- Simple art projects or activities that imitate, recreate, or simulate a concept, style, or theme of an artist from the target culture
- Art history and artist biography activities
- Oral and written critiques of artwork
- Field trips to art or architecture exhibits with related pre- *and* posttrip activities

Dance, drama, and theater experiences provide opportunity for movement, producing chemical effects that reduce stress, stimulate the brain and learning, promote meaning, and open pathways for memory. Sensory-motor target-language experiences feed directly into the brain's pleasure centers, creating a sense of fun and providing emotional linkages. They also promote self-confidence, creativity, and coordination. The use of imagination can motivate communication in the target language. Including a focus on target-culture artists, playwrights, and their works enhances the cultural perspective and provides an opportunity to integrate other content.

In the classroom, examples of dance, drama, and theater activities for the world language classroom include

- Target-culture dances (folk and popular)
- TPR commands to the rhythm of instrumental music (see page 168, Chapter 6)
- Gouin Series (see page 169, Chapter 6)
- Creating movements to accompany vocal or instrumental music
- Pantomime
- Charades
- Role play
- Imaginary fantasy trip to or in a target culture
- Using puppets and props to stimulate conversation or accompany target-language activities
- Acting in a skit or play
- Storytelling
- Oral interpretation of poetry or prose
- Attending a live performance
- Watching a movie or videotaped performance

Support the learning process.
- Encourage use of problem solving, critical thinking, relevant projects, and complex activities when presenting new information or experiences.
- Do activities that require asking questions and searching for responses from trial and error rather than an immediate, correct answer. More neural connections are formed in the search for answers than from the actual right answers themselves.
- Include opportunities for multiple correct responses.
- Design performance tasks for practice and assessment so students can demonstrate what they can do with the target language:
    - Individual or group presentations
    - Peer teaching
    - Student-designed tests
    - Projects
    - Portfolios
    - Mindmaps
    - Videos/audios
    - Skits/role play
- Design tests that are consistent with the way in which information and language is presented and learned. For example, a vocabulary and grammar multiple choice test is probably not a good measure of language presented through a story format or practiced through role-play.

Vary the learning process.
- Provide activities that vary in time, materials, degree of difficulty, expectations, or teacher support.
- Change instructional strategies often for novelty: location, movement, pairings, groups, games, students teaching a lesson or leading an activity, journaling, multiage or multigrade level projects, field trips, guest speakers, even changing room décor.
- Balance activities: novel activities with those that are predictable, repetitive, routine, or ritual (class openings, closings, repetitious procedures, etc.).
- Provide choice in the learning process to recognize and accommodate students' multiple intelligences (Gardner 1999, 147). What is challenging for one student may not be for another. Include self-paced learning. Allow students to select the complexity or type of project and help in decisions regarding use of computers or videos, partners, seating, and criteria for the end product (Jensen 1998).
- Expose students to many different learning styles, regardless of what they choose on their own, for variety and novelty. Rotate individual and group work, drama, music, art, computers, presentations, guest speakers, and travel to new locations (even if it's just to the hallway or another classroom in the school).
- Set limits for "screen time" on computers and television. Although they can enhance some learning activities, overuse restricts eye movement, reduces opportunities for gross motor activities and face-to-face contact, and may compromise the development of neural connections helpful for other learning experiences.

Expose students to many different learning styles, regardless of what they choose on their own, for variety and novelty.

Provide feedback that is frequent, immediate, and interactive. The greatest intrinsic motivation, feedback reduces uncertainty and can produce positive chemical and behavioral responses, enhancing student second language potential. Feedback from outside the classroom links to the Communities standard. Feedback needs to focus on the quality of a student's performance, informing students specifically how their performance meets the expectation, does not meet it, or exceeds it. Feedback should help students identify what they can do to improve their performance.

Feedback might come from a variety of sources, including
- Second language teacher
- Partner(s)
- Jury of peers
- Other teachers
- Peer applause, affirmations, cheers
- Parents
- Community members

To vary the feedback process, incorporate feedback techniques such as
- Rubrics
- Peer review or critique
- Tutoring
- E-mail responses

- Surveys

Rather than only providing feedback on textbook activities or tests, consider a variety of projects that could provide opportunities to give feedback on students' language performance:
- Portfolios
- Discussion
- Cooperative learning
- Projects outside the classroom
- Public performance or display
- Community service
- Audio- and videotaping

Develop regular feedback rituals in the classroom with students using a series of verbal and nonverbal signals that provide positive and constructive commentary for use in self-assessment of performance. Thumbs up, handshakes, and editing comments can be helpful in acknowledging success, while another signal might indicate more work is needed to meet the objectives.

Working with the Brain for World Language Acquisition and Learning

What Is the Difference Between Learning and Acquisition?

Although the terminology "learning" and "acquisition" are often used interchangeably, recent pedagogical thought in brain-based learning and language acquisition frequently distinguishes more specifically between them.

Language learning is generally characterized by conscious, cognitive, explicit acts about language by instruction, study of rules, and form. Early foreign language methodology was predominately conscious, grammar-based learning. However, cognitive second language approaches such as audio-lingual or grammar-translation do not usually produce meaningful input for long-term language acquisition or interpersonal communication. They are effective primarily for learning about language and performance on grammar tests.

Language acquisition involves the implicit, often unconscious, natural physiological processes through which we internalize language, mostly through communication, experience, and interaction with others. The 1980s introduced acquisition through brain-based processes for more message-centered, communicative language. Brain-based second language acquisition strategies and methodologies include TPR, the natural approach, storytelling with TPR, Suggestopedia, Gouin Series, whole language, and cooperative learning.

Studies suggest that the potential for long-term retention of a second language with proficiency appears to require a much greater proportion of acquisition to learning. Most successful world language programs incorporate multiple acquisition and learning strategies and methodologies with a variety of teaching and learning styles for a more student-centered, eclectic, and communicative approach.

Most successful world language programs incorporate multiple acquisition and learning strategies and methodologies with a variety of teaching and learning styles for a more student-centered, eclectic, and communicative approach.

What Can We Infer from Our Native Language Acquisition Experiences?

Native language acquisition is a natural brain-based instinct. It happens relatively quickly and easily without a single grammar lesson or any formal instruction by specially trained language teachers. We learned to speak our native language mostly by just hearing it, trial and error responses, interaction, and feedback from others. Recent second language acquisition studies suggest that some of our attempts to acquire a second language might be more rapid, meaningful, and long lasting if we pattern the process to replicate many of our first language experiences.

> ### For Reflection
> - How do parents communicate with their infants and check comprehension of English?
> - Why can even many of the youngest infants understand messages they hear before they are able to speak?
> - What kinds of early language experiences do babies have before they make initial attempts at language production?
> - Is English translated into baby babble so that infants can verify their comprehension?
> - Do parents speak in baby babble to ensure their child's comprehension of English?
> - Do we expect babies to consult a cradle grammar textbook to improve their language proficiency?
> - Why does hearing more than one language in infancy facilitate second language acquisition later on?
> - Why is toddler talk usually spoken with relative ease and grammatical accuracy by two- and three-year-olds who have had no formal language instruction?
> - Why is the presentation of formal grammar delayed until 5 to 10 years after a child begins speaking?

At the same time, language teachers must consider the higher-level cognitive abilities and expanded life experiences of their second language learners in designing programs that are developmentally appropriate and challenging, matched to the age and grade level of the students.

What Is the Window of Opportunity for Optimal Second Language Acquisition?

The optimal time for beginning the second language acquisition process is between ages 5 and 10. By this age, the brain has already acquired the vocabulary, sounds, structure, and syntax of one language and still has new language architecture intact (Freeman Dhority 1998). Though a new language can be acquired at any age, it is usually more difficult to acquire a nativelike accent and to hardwire the patterns of another language with each passing year after

And schools might rethink the practice of waiting to teach foreign languages until kids are nearly grown and the window of native command of a second language is almost shut.

Brownlee 1998

puberty. By this time, the brain prunes or reallocates the neurons used for language acquisition.

Everything we learn well, we have learned over an extended period of time. Children learn language slowly, in stages, enabling them to surpass the proficiency of older learners over time. The earlier they begin a language, the more time on task students have for realizing higher levels of achievement and proficiency on the standards continuum. (Beginning in kindergarten and continuing through Grade 12, a student is more likely to reach the refining level, whereas a student beginning in Grades 7 or 9 may only reach as far as developing or transitioning.) When students begin to learn a second language in elementary grades, their ability to communicate is more likely to become consistent, sustained, and spontaneous with greater comfort and ease. Also, the younger the student, the less likely there will be significant interference of high anxiety and low self-confidence.

The incremental learning style of children helps them pick up new languages more easily than adults.
Azar 1996

What Are the Implications for Second Language Acquisition After Age 10?

The brain appears to be malleable and continues to rewire itself throughout our lives. It can grow new connections at any age, including those for language. Younger beginners might expect to reach higher levels of long-term second language proficiency and retention. Older beginners (high school and adult) are sometimes faster in attaining initial proficiency but are often later impeded by complex language processing interference. Motivation, life experience, and brain-compatible methodologies can provide them with a sufficient foundation for second language acquisition; however, their potential for proficiency and long-term retention is closely related to the amount of time immersed in the target language.

Does a Student's Age Affect the Second Language Acquisition Process?

Whether second language students begin at age 5, 10, 15, or beyond, studies indicate that the acquisition process is the same. Exposed to developmentally appropriate, brain-compatible strategies and an appropriate language acquisition environment, students are more likely to pick up additional languages, implicitly, by similar processes used for their native language. Like any other learning experience, however, the potential for proficiency and retention increases the earlier they begin and the longer they continue.

The standards-based language classroom described in this guide will easily match a variety of learning styles.

What Are the Implications for Second Language Acquisition by Students with Exceptional Needs?

Students with special needs can effectively acquire a second language despite their unique challenges or academic standing. The learning component may be difficult for underachievers and students with exceptional needs such as learning disabilities or attention deficit disorder. However, the acquisition process can provide the ease, flexibility, and motivation with which to realize their second language potential for greater overall academic achievement, foreign travel, recreational activities, career opportunities, and so on. The brain-compatible strategies discussed in this chapter provide multiple ways to learn in the language classroom. The standards-based language classroom described in this guide will easily match a variety of learning styles.

How Can We Simulate the Native Language Acquisition Process in the Classroom?

Allow students sufficient time to focus on receptive language readiness (interpretive communication standard) before speaking. During this time, teachers provide meaningful, comprehensible target language input (Krashen 1983) while students increase comprehension, build confidence, participate in listening and prespeaking activities, and accumulate patterns of syntax, grammar, and pronunciation that will eventually enable them to produce language. The amount of receptive readiness time needed can vary from a few hours to several months, depending on personality, age, and developmental stage.

During this receptive period

- Use the target language for communication and instruction.
- Do pre-speaking activities, such as TPR and listening activities that elicit nonverbal responses.
- Read and tell stories, sing songs, and play games.

Teachers can help make the input comprehensible and meaningful when they

- Provide listening and reading activities that are interesting and with visuals or graphic organizers to aid comprehension.
- Include activities at a level that is usually slightly beyond the students' competency level to foster increasing proficiency.
- Create real-life, interactive situations that motivate students to communicate.

Students may offer some target-language output during this time and should be encouraged to do so, because they want to use the new language to express themselves in ways that they can in their first language. However, the language they produce will be controlled, automatic, and memorized. The motivation comes from making it at the same time personal.

We can expect students' early speech efforts to emerge with simple words or phrases that are often flawed. Spoken and written language production will become increasingly more complex, grammatically accurate, spontaneous, and creative as students receive more and more language input. Students move beyond words and phrases as they build language confidence and as tasks require increasingly more demanding language.

What Is the Role of Formal Grammar Study with Language Learning?

A grammar focus is helpful for prepared speech or writing (the presentational standard) when there is enough time to apply conscious knowledge to improve language accuracy. Language learning via grammar and rules is appropriate as a "monitor" to edit language (Krashen 1983). The monitor provides a means to improve grammatical accuracy after language is acquired in two ways:

- to make alterations and corrections before a sentence is spoken or written (for prepared language).
- for self-correction and editing after a sentence is spoken or written.

What Are the Limitations of the Monitor?

While the monitor is important for increased language proficiency, it has a limited function in the interpersonal mode of communication. Three conditions must be met for the monitor to kick in:

- Students must have time to inspect language before it is spoken.
- Students must be consciously concerned about correctness.
- Students must know the rule.

These three conditions, however, are rarely met in natural conversation. The flow is too rapid, and speakers usually focus on what is said, not on how it is said. Being overly conscious or concerned about grammatical rules may disrupt communication and fluency, frustrating the speaker and raising the affective filter.

When and How Should Grammar Be Presented?

> If teachers of foreign languages have their way, never again will adults have reason to complain, "I took two years of French or German or Spanish, but I can't speak a word of it." That cliché will become obsolete, as the focus of foreign language instruction shifts from grammar and vocabulary to communication.
>
> *Willis 1998, 211*

The brain is good at learning grammar but poor at being taught it. The rules are too complex. The brain will naturally seek to find grammatical language patterns and meaning even without formal instruction. While students' knowledge of grammar rules is important for increasing their language proficiency and appropriate cultural or social usage, as well as carrying out communicative tasks and functions, we can encourage and facilitate a brain-friendly process for learning them with the following principles:

- Always model and present grammatically correct language.
- Design lessons to include real-life communicative tasks and functions that prompt the desired or necessary language patterns in a contextualized framework.
- Delay formal presentation of grammar and rules until a significant amount of comprehensible, meaningful, communicative, contextual language input has been acquired and practiced by students.
- Encourage students to notice language patterns, and create rules together. (Note that they recur cyclically and that they will be revisited and expanded periodically.)
- Encourage use of the monitor as an editor for prepared speech and writing.
- Consult the textbook for reference and clarification as needed.

What are the implications of these findings for teaching? First, effective teaching should include a focus on both parts and wholes.... Relating the mechanics of spelling to students' meaningful use of written language to express themselves during diary writing, for example, provides important motivational incentives for learning to read and write.... For example, teaching students simple emotional expressions (vocabulary and idioms) can take place in the context of talking about different emotions and what situations elicit different emotions. Students' vocabulary acquisition can be enhanced when it is embedded in real-world complex contexts that are familiar to them. Third, students need time and experience ("practice") to consolidate new skills and knowledge to become fluent and articulated.

Genesee 2000, 3

Instruction for beginning language learners, in particular, should take into account their need for context-rich, meaningful environments.

Genesee 2000, 4

Lesson Planning for Brain-Compatible World Language Acquisition

1. Prime students for learning and success. We are more likely to see something if we are prompted what to look for or where it's located and when we feel likely to succeed.
   - Preexpose students to new topics and language weeks and days in advance of the actual presentation.
   - Give students an introduction to the content, skills, and language that they will experience.
   - State your expectations and give examples. Share your own positive beliefs or relevant personal stories about what students will learn.
   - Prepare students for success (with phrases, in the target language, like: "It's not difficult," "You can do it," etc.).
2. Focus attention and attitude.
   - Post daily class topics and do goal setting (offering some student choice).
   - Suggest possible value and relevance of topics to students.
   - Engage students with a variety of multimodal, fun, challenging learning experiences (balance of novel and routine).
   - Lead "brain wake-ups," periodic short stretch or exercise and deep breathing between activities, and allow students to drink water as desired.
3. Process learning consciously.
   - Make thematic ties.
   - Create mindmaps.
   - Discuss previous activities.
   - Connect new learning and language to prior learning and language.
4. Incubate learning with time for personal processing: 2–5 minutes for every 10–15 minutes of heavy, new content.
5. Review for maximum recall potential. It is best to store learning in multiple pathways and review 10 minutes, 2 days, and 1 week later (Jensen 1998, 109).
6. Verify what students know through
   - performance tasks
   - assessments
   - feedback
   - self-evaluations
7. Celebrate after learning with a special activity or acknowledgement.

References

Asher, James. 1988. *Learning Another Language Through Actions*. Los Gatos, Calif.: Sky Oaks Productions, Inc.

Azar, Beth. 1996. "Sound Patterns: Learning Language Keys." *Monitor* (January).

Brownlee, Shannon. 1998. "Baby Talk." *U.S. News and World Report*. 15 June.

Campbell, Don. 1997. *The Mozart Effect*. New York: Avon Books.

Curtain, Helena, and Carol Ann Pesola. 1994. *Languages and Children: Making the Match*. White Plains, N.Y.: Longman.

Freeman Dhority, Lynn, and Eric Jensen. 1998. *Joyful Fluency*. San Diego, Calif.: The Brain Store, Inc.

Gardner, Howard. 1999. *Intelligence Reframed: Multiple Intelligences for the 21st Century*. New York: Basic Books.

Garfias, Robert. 1990. "An Ethnomusicologist's Thoughts on the Processes of Language and Music Acquisition." In *Music and Child Development: Proceedings of the 1987 Denver Conference*, edited by Frank R. Wilson and Franz L. Roehmann. St. Louis, Mo.: The Biology of Music Making, Inc.

Genesee, Fred. 2000. "Brain Research: Implications for Second Language Learning." *ERIC Digest*. Washington, D.C.: ERIC Clearinghouse on Languages and Linguistics.

Handy, Shirley. 1999. Presentation at The Singing-Reading Connection workshop, Milwaukee, Wis.

Jensen, Eric. 1998. *Teaching with the Brain in Mind*. Alexandria, Va.: Association for Supervision and Curriculum Development.

———. 1999. *Introduction to Brain-Compatible Learning*. San Diego, Calif.: The Brain Store, Inc.

Josten, Monica L. 2001. "Human Brains, Language, and Learning." In *Planning Curriculum in English Language Arts,* by Ellen Last. Madison: Wisconsin Department of Public Instruction.

Krashen, Stephen D., and Tracy Terrell. 1983. *The Natural Approach: Language Acquisition in the Classroom*. Hayward, Calif.: Alemany Press.

Sousa, David A. 1998. "Is the Fuss About Brain Research Justified?" *Education Week* 18(16). http://www.edweek.org/ew/vol-18/16sousa.h18, accessed April 2002.

Willis, Scott. 1998. "Learning to Communicate in the Real World." In *Revitalizing the Disciplines: The Best of ASCD's Curriculum Update,* edited by John O'Neil and Scott Willis. Alexandria, Va.: Association for Supervision and Curriculum Development.

Resources

Marzano, Robert J., Debra J. Pickering, and Jane E. Pollock. 2001. *Classroom Instruction That Works: Research Strategies for Increasing Student Achievement*. Alexandria, Va.: Association for Supervision and Curriculum Development.

Sousa, David A. 2001. *How the Brain Learns*. Thousand Oaks, Calif.: Corwin Press, Inc.

Tomlinson, Carol Ann. 1999. *The Differentiated Classroom*. Alexandria, Va.: Association for Supervision and Curriculum Development.

———. 2000. "Reconcilable Differences? Standards-based Teaching and Differentiation." *Educational Leadership* 58 (1): 6–11.

The Role of Methodology in a Standards-Based Curriculum

6

> Factors Shaping Language Teaching and Learning Today
>   Looking Back and Looking Ahead
>   Traditional Approaches to Teaching and Curriculum
>   Communicative Competence
>   Notional–Functional Approach
>   Second Language Acquisition: The Monitor Theory
>   Total Physical Response (TPR) and TPR-Storytelling
>   Content-Based Instruction
>   The Proficiency Movement
>   ACTFL Performance Guidelines for K–12 Learners
>   Research Outside the Discipline
> From Theory to Practice
> References

Factors Shaping Language Teaching and Learning Today

Looking Back and Looking Ahead

In order to understand language teaching and learning in the twenty-first century, it is important to consider where we have been, where we are and where we want to be as a profession. This chapter will provide an overview of major professional initiatives, research, and methods of the past 30 years. The discussion will show how the profession has progressed from traditional practices to our current focus on standards-based instruction and assessment. We will reflect upon these developments by addressing the lessons we have learned about effective language instruction.

Traditional Approaches to Teaching and Curriculum

World language methodology has changed significantly over the years. Classrooms were once characterized by the grammar-translation or audio-lingual approach to teaching. Teachers using the grammar-translation approach advocated learning languages through the memorization of grammar rules and vocabulary lists. This memorized material was then applied in translation exercises. Advocates of the audio-lingual approach considered habit formation to be essential to learning languages. Basic language patterns were taught through dialogue memorization, drills, and repetition. While the merits of these methods have not been forgotten, the world language classrooms of today are much more diverse, interactive, and creative.

Similarly, world language curricula and assessment reflect changes in the profession. While it was once common for a curriculum to be organized around the material to be taught, we now focus on the language learners and what they are able to do with the language. Assessment practices have evolved from discrete point grammar tests to authentic assessments involving both meaningful content and active language use. Given such changes, few educators now advocate a single method of instruction. Rather, we take an eclectic approach to teaching and learning that integrates a variety of influences and effective techniques.

Communicative Competence

In the 1970s, Sandra Savignon (1972) and other leaders in the profession began to emphasize the development of communicative competence in language learners. They defined such competence as the ability to interact appropriately, both linguistically and socially, in a spontaneous interchange involving the exchange of realistic information and ideas. They noted that in the grammar-translation and audio-lingual approaches, students may have developed linguistic competence—the ability to produce sounds, vocabulary, grammatical forms, even whole sentences—but not necessarily communicative competence. They stressed that students learn to communicate only if they engage in communicative and meaningful activities in which information is shared.

In her subsequent work Savignon (1983) further developed the notion of communicative competence by identifying four distinct components:

—*Grammatical competence* involves the recognition and production of grammatical features and language sounds. Rather than merely stating grammatical rules, students use them to form words and sentences.
—*Sociolinguistic competence* is an understanding of register levels (e.g., formal and informal language) and of the social rules and roles that govern interaction in a language.
—*Discourse competence* entails recognizing and using organizational patterns of linguistic interaction and the sequencing of these patterns.
—*Strategic competence* involves coping and survival techniques such as circumlocution, asking for repetition or clarification, paraphrasing, and acting out meaning.

> *Communicative competence shows us the importance of developing meaningful and realistic activities in which students exchange information.*

Lessons Learned

Communicative competence shows us the importance of developing meaningful and realistic activities in which students exchange information. Moreover, it illustrates that effective communication involves a variety of factors and not simply knowledge of grammatical structures and vocabulary.

Notional–Functional Approach

Some individuals in the profession have defined language use by communicative acts and exchanges. Developers of a notional–functional syllabus believe that language consists of the *functions* in which we engage and the *notions* we wish to convey. For example, we use language to greet and take leave, persuade, and inquire (typical functions), and we use language in given situations to express specific meanings. Therefore, users of a notional–functional syllabus select and organize learning materials according to common situations in the target culture, notions (topics for discourse and meanings to be conveyed), and functions (linguistic and social acts conducted through language).

Many instructional materials have been given a notional–functional dimension. In some cases grammar is presented in terms of purpose or effect. For example, direct commands are taught as a way of expressing orders while the future tense is taught with the function of expressing plans. Similarly, many exercises requiring a communicative exchange are framed in notional–functional terms, for example, "You have just met an exchange student from France in the school cafeteria. Ask five personalized questions to find out more about the student."

The notional-functional approach shifts course design from a focus on the teacher to a focus on the learner.

> ### Lessons Learned
>
> The notional–functional approach shifts course design from a focus on the teacher to a focus on the learner. We consider what students can *do* with the language and what information they convey in real-life situations involving specific purposes for using the language.

Second Language Acquisition: The Monitor Theory

Research in the field of second language acquisition has led to a greater understanding of how students develop language proficiency. Of the significant body of second language acquisition research developed in recent decades, the work of Steven Krashen has been especially influential and at times controversial. The connection of his monitor theory with brain-compatible learning was already discussed in Chapter 5. Krashen's monitor theory of language acquisition (1982) presents five key hypotheses:

— *The acquisition-learning distinction:* Language acquisition is a subconscious process in which one develops ability in a language by using it in natural, communicative situations. For example, children *acquire* their native language. In contrast, language learning is rule based and involves a conscious knowledge and application of grammar.
— *The natural order hypothesis:* A predictable order for acquiring grammatical structures exists when acquisition is natural (versus a contrived sequence that is established for formal learning).

[The natural approach] allows speech production to emerge in stages and encourages a focus on communicative competence rather than grammatical perfection.

—*The monitor hypothesis:* Language learning provides a monitor or editor for language output. The effectiveness of the monitor depends on knowledge of rules, a situation that focuses on form, and the necessary time to use the monitor. While the monitor is useful in certain instances, acquisition is what leads to more nativelike language utterances and fluency.

—*The input hypothesis:* Acquisition is facilitated by input at the level of $i + 1$. This formula refers to input a bit above the current level of the students, input that is made comprehensible through context cues and background knowledge. Through extensive input (by listening and reading), language production and accuracy will develop over time.

—*The affective filter hypothesis:* Comprehensible input and acquisition are possible only when there is an environment characterized by low anxiety, high motivation, and self-confidence.

Lessons Learned

The key points of the monitor theory have been applied to the classroom through the *natural approach* developed by Krashen and Tracy Terrell (1983). This method encourages extensive input at the $i + 1$ level in a supportive environment for language acquisition. It allows speech production to emerge in stages and encourages a focus on communicative competence rather than grammatical perfection.

Total Physical Response (TPR) and TPR-Storytelling

In relation to input in the language classroom, the work of James Asher (1986) also has been influential. Asher advocates an extended period of listening before students speak the target language. He proposes the use of *total physical response,* a technique in which students listen to commands and act out their corresponding actions. Asher maintains that such linking of language and physical movement facilitates comprehension and retention. In a typical TPR sequence students first listen to a series of commands and observe the related actions performed by the teacher. They next respond to the teacher's commands in large and small groups through physical action. As the students become familiar with the commands the teacher no longer has to model the actions and eventually the students will verbally produce the commands as well.

A recent variation of TPR involves storytelling. In this approach spoken language is linked to physical actions and visual images that tell a story. Over time, students go from input and comprehension to output (language production) as they create and tell stories. The focus is on linking meaning to a gesture that aids memorization, with an emphasis on creatively retelling the story as originally presented. After sufficient practice of the original story and accompanying gestures, students can creatively retell the story, recombining memorized elements to create new stories.

> ## Lessons Learned
>
> Combining language use with physical movement can be both enjoyable and beneficial for the memory. In addition to TPR, other activities to link language and gestures include singing songs with gestures and the Gouin Series in which a logical series of actions is dramatized as it is spoken. These techniques along with TPR and TPR-storytelling are useful methods for helping students absorb and use language, but they are not exclusive curricula.

Content-Based Instruction

The two *Connections* standards of the world language standards serve to highlight the natural ties that languages have to other academic disciplines. Given such connections, teachers at different levels of instruction have pursued the integration of world language and other academic subjects through *content-based* or *content-related* instruction. For example, FLES teachers can incorporate material from the science and art curriculum in their French lessons, thus providing meaningful material for using the language and reinforcing other academic content. In elementary grades, content-related connections with the general grade level curriculum create a valued place for world language instruction. Rather than competing for minutes in the school day with core subject areas, the world language teacher becomes an ally supporting the instruction of the elementary classroom teacher. The most complete form of content-based instruction is found in immersion schools, where the entire school curriculum is taught via the target language.

> ## Lessons Learned
>
> There are multiple opportunities to connect world language study to content from other disciplines. Such connections can provide interesting content, authentic materials, unique cultural perspectives, and the opportunity to apply language skills in meaningful tasks. By choosing topics from other disciplines, the language teacher has an endless list of themes to choose from to provide high-interest topics for student discussion and content for cognitively challenging lessons.

The Proficiency Movement

Since the 1980s there has been an ongoing dialogue in the profession about language proficiency. If communicative competence explored *what* it is to know and use a language, the proficiency movement added the issue of *how well*. At the heart of this discussion are the *ACTFL Proficiency Guidelines* that were published in a provisional form in 1982 and then in a completed form in 1986 by the American Council on the Teaching of Foreign Languages. While guidelines exist for the four skills of listening, speaking, reading, and writing, the *Oral Proficiency Guidelines* are by far the most widely utilized and as such were updated in 1999.

The *Oral Proficiency Guidelines* are divided into the four major levels of *novice, intermediate, advanced,* and *superior.* All levels with the exception of superior also have corresponding sublevels (for example, novice low-mid-high). The guidelines advocate no particular language-teaching method or approach. Rather, they describe the functional competence of language users at different levels of proficiency, regardless of where, when, or how the language was acquired. As detailed in Table 6.1, the guidelines consider language functions, context, content, accuracy, and text type in order to assign a level of oral proficiency. While these factors are present at all levels, they become increasingly developed as a speaker moves up to higher levels of proficiency.

In relation to the *Oral Proficiency Guidelines,* it is important to note the widespread use of the Oral Proficiency Interview (OPI). The OPI was first developed by the Foreign Service Institute and later adapted to academia and other fields in which the assessment of language proficiency is required. The interview takes the form of an interpersonal conversation in which interviewees are asked to perform increasingly complex functions. Their highest sustained performance is then rated according to the *Oral Proficiency Guidelines*. A variation of the OPI for testing at the novice and intermediate levels is the Modified Oral Proficiency Interview (MOPI).

TABLE 6.1 **Assessment Criteria: Speaking Proficiency**

Global Tasks/ Functions	Context	Content	Accuracy	Text Type
Superior: Can discuss extensively by supporting opinions, abstracting, and hypothesizing	Most formal and informal settings	Wide range of general interest topics and some special fields of interest and expertise; concrete, abstract and unfamiliar topics	Errors virtually never interfere with communication or disturb the native speaker	Extended discourse
Advanced: Can describe and narrate in major time/aspect frames	Most informal and some formal settings	Concrete and factual topics of personal and public interest	Can be understood without difficulty by speakers unaccustomed to nonnative speakers	Paragraph discourse
Intermediate: Can maintain simple face-to-face conversation by asking and responding to simple questions	Some informal settings and a limited number of transactional situations	Topics related primarily to self and immediate environment	Can be understood, with some repetition, by speakers accustomed to nonnative speakers	Discrete sentences and strings of sentences
Novice: Can produce only formulaic utterances, lists, and enumerations	Highly predictable common daily settings	Common discrete elements of daily life	May be difficult to understand, even for those accustomed to nonnative speakers	Discrete words and phrases

Source: American Council on the Teaching of Foreign Languages 1999b. Used with permission.

Lessons Learned

The *ACTFL Proficiency Guidelines* provide a rich profile of what it means to know and use a language by describing the functional competence of language users at different levels of proficiency. We learn, for example, that proficiency is tied to time and experience and involves a variety of factors. In terms of instruction, the proficiency-oriented classroom is characterized by meaningful communication *in* the language as opposed to talking *about* the language. We use, recycle, and expand materials and topics in order to develop increasingly sustained, spontaneous performance by our students.

ACTFL Performance Guidelines for K–12 Learners

Given that the *ACTFL Proficiency Guidelines* were designed to describe the language performance of adult language users, many educators sensed a need for guidelines appropriate to younger language learners. The *ACTFL Performance Guidelines for K–12 Learners* (1999) meet this need by describing the characteristics of younger language users at various stages of learning and development. While the guidelines are designed to reflect and advocate an uninterrupted sequence of language learning from kindergarten through grade 12, they also take into account the different entry points corresponding to the most common language sequences in U.S. schools.

Like the *Standards for Foreign Language Learning* (National Standards for Foreign Language Education Project 1996), the *Performance Guidelines* have the organizing principle of three modes of communication: Interpersonal, Interpretive, and Presentational. In turn, the corresponding guidelines outline each mode at three benchmarks (novice range, intermediate range, and preadvanced range) in relation to the following domains:

—*Comprehensibility* (How well is the student understood?)
—*Comprehension* (How well does the student understand?)
—*Language control* (How accurate is the student's language?)
—*Vocabulary* (How extensive and applicable is the student's vocabulary?)
—*Cultural awareness* (How is the student's cultural knowledge reflected in language use?)
—*Communication strategies* (How does the student maintain communication?)

Lessons Learned

The *ACTFL Performance Guidelines for K–12 Learners* provide guidelines appropriate for younger language learners that help teachers target an appropriate level of language usage in both designing classroom activities and assessments and in evaluating them. This document and the Wisconsin proficiency standards from the first edition of *Wisconsin's Model Academic Standards for Foreign Languages* were key resources used in the development of the Wisconsin Performance Guidelines found in this guide.

Research Outside the Discipline

A growing body of research outside of the immediate discipline of world languages also has impacted the profession in recent years. Two examples of such research include Howard Gardner's theory of multiple intelligences (1985) and Robert Marzano's dimensions of learning (1992).

Gardner's theory suggests that people have different abilities in different areas of thought and learning, and that these varying abilities impact people's interests and how quickly they assimilate information and develop skills. Gardner believes that we all have at least eight different intelligences that operate in varying degrees depending upon each individual profile. The intelligences include bodily kinesthetic, interpersonal, intrapersonal, linguistic, logical-mathematical, musical, naturalist, and spatial (visual) intelligence.

Marzano's work presents an instructional framework based on the premise that there are five types of thinking essential to successful learning. The five integrated dimensions include

—*Positive attitudes and perceptions about learning:* For example, a student must feel comfortable and have a positive attitude in order to learn effectively.
—*Acquiring and integrating knowledge:* For example, students need to connect new content to prior knowledge, organize new knowledge in meaningful ways, and make it a part of long-term memory.
—*Extending and refining knowledge:* Learners extend and refine their knowledge by making further connections through activities such as comparing, classifying, analyzing, and making inductions and deductions.
—*Using knowledge meaningfully:* The most effective learning occurs when students use knowledge in meaningful tasks. The types of tasks include decision making, investigation, experimental inquiry, problem solving, and invention.
—*Productive habits of mind:* Students must develop mental habits that will help them be critical, creative, and self-regulated thinkers. Examples of such productive habits include being clear, being open minded, restraining impulsivity, being aware of your own thinking, evaluating the effectiveness of your actions, and engaging intensely in tasks.

Lessons Learned

Multiple intelligences research allows for similarities and differences between students. It encourages inclusion and enrichment opportunities while emphasizing respect for individuals and their abilities. It also helps create a classroom environment that allows students to learn through their strengths and to share their talents. *Dimensions of Learning* helps teachers utilize knowledge of how students learn in order to more effectively plan curriculum and instruction. Most recently, Marzano has connected the five dimensions of learning to performance assessment by describing how a performance assessment system can support the *Dimensions of Learning* instructional framework.

From Theory to Practice

The lessons learned from research, theory, methods, and our classroom experience have led us to move from certain practices toward other practices (Table 6.2). It is not to place these as polar opposites, with one side labeled as bad and the other as good; rather it is to seek a balance in our instruction, with the goal of helping all students move toward greater proficiency in using their target language.

In this chapter we have seen that *communicative competence* stresses that students should engage in meaningful activities in which information is exchanged. The *notional–functional approach* tells us that language instruction should provide real-life situations in which students have specific purposes for using the language. The *monitor model* emphasizes the importance of extensive and interesting input along with a supportive environment for language acquisition. *Total physical response* illustrates the benefits of associating language use with physical movement, employing active responses to improve memory. *Content-based instruction* demonstrates the possibility of connecting foreign language study to other academic disciplines. The *ACTFL Proficiency Guidelines* and *Performance Guidelines* help us understand what it means to know and use a language by describing the functional competence of language users at different levels of proficiency. *Research* on multiple intelligences and how students learn tells us that our classrooms should have variety in order to accommodate students' different personalities, interests, and intelligences.

These diverse but interrelated factors have helped inform our instructional practices and they continue to have strong implications for effective teaching. Moreover, they have been instrumental components in the journey that led to the development of the world language standards and the standards-based classrooms of the twenty-first century. The lessons learned from such research and initiatives have transformed our classrooms into language learning environments characterized by performance assessments, creative approaches to instruction, real-life tasks, and meaningful communication.

The lessons learned from such research and initiatives have transformed our classrooms into language learning environments characterized by performance assessments, creative approaches to instruction, real-life tasks, and meaningful communication.

TABLE 6.2 **Changing Our Classroom Practices**

Moving from	**Moving toward**
■ text-bound (content-controlled)	■ standards-based (content-rich)
■ norm-referenced (bell curve)	■ criterion-referenced (expect achievement)
■ discrete point assessment	■ global assessment
■ achievement testing	■ proficiency assessment
■ focus on "learned"	■ focus on "acquired"
■ testing that sorts	■ assessment that guides

Source: Donna Clementi, Appleton West High School (2001).

References

American Council on the Teaching of Foreign Languages. 1982. *ACTFL Provisional Proficiency Guidelines*. Hastings-on-Hudson, N.Y.: American Council on the Teaching of Foreign Languages.

———. 1986. *ACTFL Proficiency Guidelines*. Hastings-on-Hudson, N.Y.: American Council on the Teaching of Foreign Languages.

———. 1999a. *ACTFL Performance Guidelines for K–12 Learners*. Yonkers, N.Y.: American Council on the Teaching of Foreign Languages.

———. 1999b. *ACTFL Proficiency Guidelines—Speaking*. Yonkers, N.Y.: American Council on the Teaching of Foreign Languages.

Asher, James. 1986. *Learning Another Language Through Actions: The Complete Teacher's Guidebook*. 3d ed. Los Gatos, Calif.: Sky Oaks Production.

Gardner, Howard. 1985. *Frames of Mind: The Theory of Multiple Intelligences*. New York: Basic Books.

Krashen, Stephen D. 1982. *Principles and Practice in Second Language Acquisition*. New York: Pergamon Press.

Krashen, Stephen D., and Tracy Terrell. 1983. *The Natural Approach: Language Acquisition in the Classroom*. Hayward, Calif.: Alemany Press.

Marzano, Robert. 1992. *A Different Kind of Classroom: Teaching with Dimensions of Learning*. Alexandria, Va.: The Association for Supervision and Curriculum Development.

National Standards in Foreign Language Education Project. 1996. *Standards for Foreign Language Learning: Preparing for the 21st Century*. Lawrence, Kans.: Allen Press.

Savignon, Sandra. 1972. *Communicative Competence: An Experiment in Foreign Language Teaching*. Philadelphia, Pa.: Center for Curriculum Development.

———. 1983. *Communicative Competence: Theory and Classroom Practice*. Reading, Mass.: Addison-Wesley.

Part III
Issues Impacting Language Programs

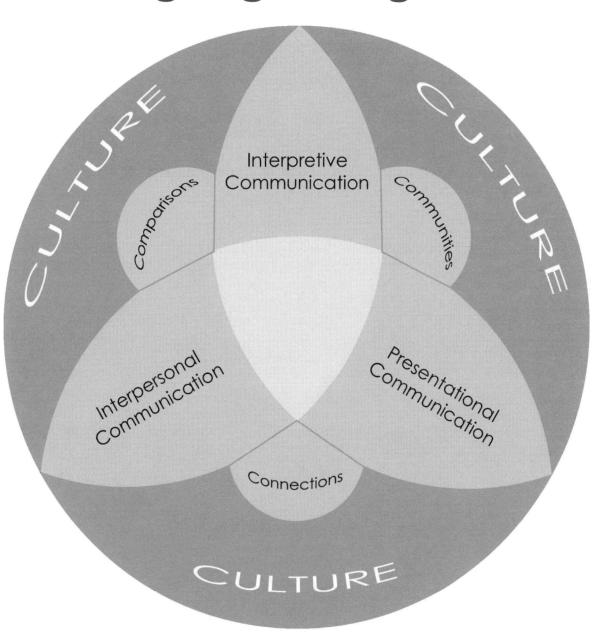

Considerations for Building Effective Programs

Components of High Quality World Language Programs
Practical Considerations
Characteristics of Effective Foreign Language Instruction
Program Enrichment Opportunities
Considerations for Designing Foreign Language in the Elementary School (FLES) Programs
References

Components of High Quality World Language Programs

These guidelines list elements that are critical to the success of world language programs in elementary schools, middle schools, and senior high schools. The guidelines may be used in the program planning phase or as the basis for the ongoing evaluation of an existing program. These are the essential elements that must be addressed in order for a program to be effective in building students' language proficiency. A district self-study should look at all of these components, which form the foundation for a quality world language program. The elements listed here represent the professional consensus in Wisconsin and nationally, based on research and position statements from national and state world language teaching organizations.

1. **Standards.** *Wisconsin's Model Academic Standards for Foreign Languages* provides the basis upon which quality programs are built. Using the philosophical framework of the national *Standards for Foreign Language Learning*, Wisconsin's standards describe content and performance standards to serve as guideposts in curriculum planning and development.
2. **Teachers.** The language teachers should be certified teachers who are fluent in the target language and understand effective teaching practices for the age group being taught. They should have spent an extended time living in a country where the target language is spoken, to gain firsthand knowledge of the target culture as well as the language skills to conduct a classroom in the target language. They should remain up to date in current trends and methodologies in the field through membership in professional organizations, attendance at workshops and conferences, and participation in professional development programs.

3. ***Methodology.*** The goal of instruction is for students to understand and communicate successfully in another language. Methodologies should reflect a student-centered classroom to maximize the opportunities for students to be actively engaged listening, speaking, reading, and writing in the target language, all within a meaningful context that strengthens students' understanding of the target culture.

4. ***Length of study.*** The goal of every world language program is to have a K–12 uninterrupted sequence in at least one language. A minimal expectation is a 7–12 uninterrupted sequence in at least one language. Long, uninterrupted sequences of high-quality instruction lead to higher degrees of proficiency in a language. Because students will more easily learn a third or fourth language after learning a second language, all languages offered by a district do not have to begin in kindergarten.

5. ***Number of languages offered.*** As we increase connections with the countries all over the world, it becomes more and more important for students to have the opportunity to learn more than one language. Districts must consider how many languages their student population can support effectively. Offering two years each of four different languages does not provide the opportunity to achieve the high levels of proficiency that will be most useful to students. Offering at least four years each of two different languages is both preferable and valuable.

6. ***Model of delivery.*** Daily instruction for a minimum of 20 minutes per day is recommended at the elementary level; any schedule of less than three times a week for 30 minutes per session will not efficiently develop students' language proficiency. At the middle school level, daily instruction for a minimum of 40 minutes per day is recommended. At the high school level, daily instruction for a minimum of 50 minutes per day is recommended.

7. ***Languages offered.*** The most important factor in determining which languages to include in a quality program is the availability of excellent teachers who are fluent in the target language and understand effective teaching practices for the age group being taught. The following criteria should also be considered:
    - Employment opportunities where the language is beneficial
    - Local demographics
    - Local business and community needs
    - Local ethnic interests
    - National needs
    - Possibility of supporting a bilingual program
    - Connection to a program for speakers of other languages (ESL)
    - Opportunity to support heritage speakers' language abilities

Less commonly taught languages such as Arabic, Chinese, Japanese, Korean, and Russian are viable options provided that excellent teachers are available. The district must have a strong commitment to maintain these programs over time.

Latin is also a viable language option. Latin is often viewed as a path to decoding other languages. It strengthens English vocabulary and provides a rich historic foundation to many aspects of Western civilization. It

> *As we increase connections with the countries all over the world, it becomes more and more important for students to have the opportunity to learn more than one language.*

also provides a unique learning experience because it places less emphasis on speaking and listening than other languages.

American Sign Language (ASL) may be offered in a Wisconsin school district for world language credit. ASL should be included on an equal basis with other languages in a district's language program.

8. ***Equal opportunity.*** All students should have the opportunity and should be encouraged to learn a second language. Language instruction can be modified to meet the needs of students with special needs. As our communities become increasingly diverse, all citizens will need to use the language skills and cultural understanding skills taught in a language classroom.
9. ***Technology.*** Language programs should have access to current technology to enhance instruction. A quality program will take advantage of the resources on the Internet to provide current, relevant information in the target language concerning the countries where the language is spoken. Multimedia language centers that include components of a language lab also help students work at their own pace to improve their speaking and listening skills and monitor their own progress.

Practical Considerations

These points, while also important to the success of a world language program, are the implementation issues that make a good program run more smoothly, reach more students, and improve the quality of the experience for students. These are issues that often arise in established programs. The outline given here provides districts with talking points to frame the local discussion of these issues. The overarching principle is to provide world language instruction that is available to and appropriate for *all* students.

1. ***Class size.*** While class size is not the single defining characteristic of a quality program, districts should work to stay as close to 15 students per section as possible to allow adequate opportunities for students to practice the target language and receive meaningful feedback on their performance.
2. ***Classrooms.*** Creating an atmosphere that reflects the countries where the target language is spoken is a critical component in quality language programs. In addition, teachers must have a myriad of props and visuals on hand to help students understand what is being said in the target language. Because of these two characteristics, it is extremely important that language teachers have their own classrooms that allow students to step into another culture when they enter the room.
3. ***Multilevel courses.*** Teaching more than one level of language within one class is not desirable. The students at each level are not receiving the teacher's full attention, nor can the curriculum for each level be delivered in its entirety. Planning for a multilevel course requires a great deal of extra time in order to consistently challenge the students at each level to make progress. If a multilevel course becomes a necessity, there must be time for the curricula of each level to be modified so that the students can work together as a single group for at least a portion of the class.

4. ***Multiple entry points.*** A strong world language program has more than one opportunity for students to begin language study and offers more than one language for students to learn. This accommodates students who move into the district after a sequence is begun. It also allows students to add another language to their program of studies.
5. ***Acceleration.*** Students who master the concepts of a language at the level in which they are enrolled should be allowed to move ahead to a more challenging course during the year. Proficiency rather than grammatical knowledge must be the basis for such placement decisions. While these students may not have the same learning experiences and vocabulary practice as other students, if they have command of the language functions at a given level, they should be advanced in order to learn more complex language functions. Vocabulary is important as it relates to the context for language use and not the level of instruction.
6. ***Remediation.*** Students who are struggling with the concepts of a language at their level of enrollment should be allowed to move to a level that is not beyond their ability. All students do not learn languages at the same rate. Taking time to become successful with the language at a given level may mean that all students do not automatically move to a higher level in September of each year.
7. ***Articulation.*** A strong program develops curriculum in a collaborative effort among department members within a school and among department members at all levels of instruction within a district. Goals for each level of instruction should be developed cooperatively by teachers representing all levels of instruction in the district. There should be a continuum of progress that guides the instructional practices of all teachers in the department.

Characteristics of Effective Foreign Language Instruction

The National Association of District Supervisors of Foreign Languages has identified the following characteristics of effective world language instruction. These guidelines provide a basis for common understanding and communication among evaluators, observers, and practitioners in classrooms where languages are taught. The characteristics focus on the students who are the recipients of effective world language instruction. The characteristics reflect the national *Standards for Foreign Language Learning* (1996) and focus on the five goal areas of Communication, Connections, Comparisons, Cultures, and Communities. The characteristics also reflect the importance of language learning strategies, diverse learning styles, the use of authentic cultural documents, and the use of technology as an instructional tool. The characteristics are a companion resource to the national *Standards for Foreign Language Learning,* state frameworks, and local curriculum guides. The *Characteristics of Effective Foreign Language Instruction* is based on an earlier document developed with the world language teachers of the Montgomery County, Maryland, Public Schools.

- The teacher sets high expectations for all students, designs assessment and instruction to engage and motivate all learners.
- The teacher and students communicate purposefully in the target language as listeners, speakers, readers, writers, and viewers.
- There is more student activity than teacher activity in most lessons. Student activity includes student-to-student interactions as well as teacher-to-student interactions. Students work independently, in pairs, and in groups. Students ask and answer questions and they create with language.
- Students take risks as language learners because the learning environment is positive and supportive.
- When error correction is appropriate, students are given opportunities, including wait time, to self-correct. Teacher correction of student errors is often done through follow-up review and reteaching strategies.
- Assessments are ongoing. Students are assessed formally and informally on how well they are able to meet the objectives of the lesson. Continuous self-assessments for students and teachers are encouraged.
- Students use language-specific learning strategies and are encouraged to assess their own progress.
- Culture is a natural component of language use in all activities.
- All students are guided to use all levels of thinking skills, for example, they repeat, recognize, and recall as well as apply, create, and predict.
- The diverse learning styles of all students are considered in the teacher's instructional planning.
- Students have positive attitudes toward cultural diversity, which are often demonstrated in the learning environment.
- The physical environment including displays of student work is instructional, motivational, and informative.
- Students and teachers are not text bound during instructional time. It is obvious that the text is a tool, not the curriculum.
- Students and teachers use a variety of print and nonprint materials including authentic target language sources.
- Technology, as appropriate and available, is used by students and teachers to facilitate learning and teaching.

Note: Listening, speaking, and authentic nonprint materials are emphasized, but to a lesser degree, in Latin and Classical Greek instruction.

[Reprinted with permission: National Association of District Supervisors of Foreign Languages. Revised 1999. http://ivc.uidaho.edu/nadsfl/characteristics.html]

> ## Using the Characteristics of Effective Foreign Language Instruction
>
> —Share with your principal when he or she comes to observe your classroom.
> —Ask for feedback on two or three characteristics during a classroom observation.
> —Discuss successful strategies that support one characteristic at a departmental meeting.
> —Plan an action research project to explore one characteristic.
> —Focus your professional development plan (for license renewal) on one characteristic or a cluster of related ones.

Program Enrichment Opportunities

Beyond the traditional sequential program, students benefit from a variety of enrichment opportunities. Some of these are extensions to the regularly scheduled sequence of classes, usually beyond the fourth year of study, including the Advanced Placement (AP) program, the International Baccalaureate (IB) Diploma Programme, and the Cooperative Academic Partnership Program (CAPP). Others are enhancements that bring a real-world motivation to the study of a language, including school partnerships, travel programs, field trips, and other cultural experiences. Both types of enrichment provide students with reasons to continue the study of a language until they reach a useful level of proficiency. In the United States, the myth persists that two years of a foreign language is required for high school graduation or college admission, neither of which is commonly true. Rather than being motivated by some external requirement, these program enrichment opportunities provide intrinsic motivation in which students realize that ongoing study of a language is necessary in order to reach the levels of proficiency that will make them independent and lifelong users of this new language skill.

1. ***Advanced Placement (AP) courses.*** AP courses offer challenging college-level curriculum to high school students. Currently AP courses are offered in French Language, French Literature, German Language, Latin Vergil, Latin Literature, Spanish Language, Spanish Literature. Quoting from the AP Guide: "The Advanced Placement Program is a cooperative educational endeavor between secondary schools and colleges and universities. Since its inception in 1955, the Program has provided motivated high school students with the opportunity to take college-level courses in a high school setting. Students who participate in the Program not only gain college-level skills, but in many cases they also earn college credit while they are still in high school.... Over 90 percent of the nation's colleges and universities have an AP policy granting incoming students credit, placement, or both, for qualifying AP Exam grades" (College Board 2002). Many colleges award sophomore standing to an incoming

first-year student who has successfully completed three or more AP courses.

2. ***International Baccalaureate (IB) Diploma Programme.*** Quoting from the IB Web site: "The International Baccalaureate Organization's Diploma Programme, created in 1968, is a demanding pre-university course of study that leads to examinations. It is designed for highly motivated secondary school students aged 16 to 19. The programme has earned a reputation for rigorous assessment, giving IB diploma holders access to the world's leading universities. The Diploma Programme's grading system is criterion-referenced: each student's performance is measured against well-defined levels of achievement consistent from one examination session to the next.... The programme is a comprehensive two-year international curriculum, available in English, French and Spanish, that generally allows students to fulfill the requirements of their national or state education systems" (International Baccalaureate Organization 2002). As of 2001, there are five IB high schools in Wisconsin: Case in Racine; Rufus King, Madison University, and John Marshall in Milwaukee; and Wausau East.

3. ***Cooperative Academic Partnership Program (CAPP) courses.*** College-level courses can be offered in high school as part of an agreement between the high school and a university. Currently, University of Wisconsin–Oshkosh offers this arrangement with over 30 high schools. These courses must be taught by someone authorized by the university to deliver its college-level curriculum in a high school setting.

4. ***School partnership programs.*** Schools may establish partnerships with their counterparts in countries where the target language is spoken. Pen pals, E-mail exchanges, and classroom hookups via television provide opportunities for students in Wisconsin to exchange ideas with students from around the world. Ultimately students from the sister schools may exchange visits to each other's city.

5. ***Travel programs.*** School partnerships may be established that bring students from other countries to schools in Wisconsin and allow Wisconsin students to travel to countries where the target language is spoken. Teachers may opt to take their students to countries where the target language is spoken on an organized travel and study program. These opportunities allow students to experience the culture of another country firsthand and use their language skills to communicate with native speakers.

6. ***Field trips.*** Students can learn more about the countries where the target language is spoken by visiting museums, restaurants, and regional attractions that reflect these cultures. The students will also learn more about the diversity and richness of their own state or region through these experiences.

7. ***Cultural experiences.*** Teachers can bring aspects of other cultures into the classroom through music, dance, artwork, games, videos, and food. Native speakers of the target language should be invited to class to share their backgrounds and experiences with the students. Cultural enrichment may also occur through oral pronounciation or poetry contests.

Considerations for Designing Foreign Language in the Elementary School (FLES) Programs

In large and small districts throughout Wisconsin, in rural, urban, and suburban settings, citizens are asking for world language instruction to begin in elementary grades. Research supports starting instruction in a second language prior to the age of 10, in order to take advantage of the brain's language forming function. Certainly, students who begin at this earlier age will have more nativelike pronunciation as well as more automatic responses and patterns as compared to the more analytic approach to learning a language that typifies high school and adult students.

The political climate in the late 1950s and early 1960s spurred a movement in the United States to implement widespread early world language programs across the country. Realizing that communicating in world languages was an asset if not a prerequisite for survival as a world power, it seemed to follow that requiring world language instruction for young children would help us to ensure our political status and even give us a competitive edge. The rationale was sound. Unfortunately, the planning was not. Many of those early world language programs succumbed to the pitfalls of poor planning.

Today's world acknowledges even greater justification for communicating in more than one language as well as the validation and necessity of early world language instruction. Growing numbers of thriving early world language programs nationwide serve as models of success. The following article provides important considerations for districts planning an early world language program, based on experiences and research in Wisconsin and beyond. The good news is that we've learned from our past mistakes and know just how to avoid them!

Today's world acknowledges even greater justification for communicating in more than one language as well as the validation and necessity of early world language instruction.

Planning for Success: Common Pitfalls in the Planning of Early Foreign Language Programs

Helena Curtain
  University of Wisconsin–Milwaukee

Carol Ann Pesola Dahlberg
  Concordia College, Moorhead, MN

There has been a significant increase in new foreign language programs at the elementary school level in recent years. Many of these programs, often referred to as foreign language in the elementary school or FLES programs, have been implemented to comply with state mandates, while others have been developed in response to parental pressure for early language learning opportunities for their children. The growing body of information about the cognitive and academic benefits of early bilingualism will no doubt fuel the continued development and expansion of these programs. Unfortunately, many will not succeed over an extended period of time because of planning decisions that were not carefully thought out or that were based on inaccurate assumptions about foreign language learning. The purpose of this digest is to identify some common pitfalls in program planning and to focus attention on issues that must be considered in the planning stages if early foreign language programs are to succeed.

Pitfall: Scheduling foreign language classes too infrequently or in sessions that are too short.

There is a widespread misperception that children learn foreign languages easily even with very limited exposure. As a result, some programs operate on the assumption that a little bit of language instruction is better than no language instruction at all. This perception contradicts the recommendations of foreign language professionals and the experience of successful programs (Gilzow and Branaman 2000). A sequence of instruction that includes sufficient instructional time is needed for students to achieve proficiency in another language. Met and Rhodes (1990) suggest that "foreign language instruction should be scheduled daily, and for no less than 30 minutes" (438). A national group of experts, convened by Goethe House New York, recommended a minimum of 75 minutes per week for any program designated as

FLES; they agreed that these classes should meet all year, during the school day, at least every other day (Rosenbusch 1992). More recently, the *ACTFL Performance Guidelines for K–12 Learners* (Swender and Duncan 1998) proposed a higher standard: elementary programs that meet from 3 to 5 days per week for no less than 30–40 minutes per class; middle school programs that meet daily for no less than 40–50 minutes; and high school programs that equal four units of credit.

Pitfall: Treating foreign languages differently from other academic subjects.

In most countries around the world, languages have the same status as other academic subjects and are a regular part of the curriculum of every school. Instruction usually starts no later than Grade 5, and often earlier. Given that most of these countries are much more successful than the United States at producing adults who can speak more than one language, we would do well to follow their example. Foreign languages should be recognized as valid academic subjects and be accorded the same status and priority for instructional time as other school subjects.

Pitfall: Offering only commonly taught languages, without considering other important world languages.

Spanish is by far the most commonly taught language in the United States, followed by French (Rhodes and Branaman 1999). While there is no denying the importance of these two languages both domestically and globally, there is a tremendous need for individuals who speak many other world languages. The United States interacts with virtually every nation in the world; the need for proficiency in the languages of these countries has never been higher (Brecht and Ingold 1999). It is impossible to know which language will be most useful to any given elementary school student or which will be most important for our country in the future. It is important, therefore, to offer a variety of languages in order to provide choices for individual students and to broaden the range of languages spoken by U.S. citizens.

Pitfall: Implementing a new program in all grades at the same time.

There are many stresses in launching a new foreign language program at the elementary school level. Unlike teachers in other curriculum areas, foreign language teachers cannot turn to existing textbook series and standardized materials as they plan a program. This is partly because elementary school programs differ markedly from one place to another. Locating and adapting appropriate materials is a formidable task even when the language is introduced in only one or two grades at a time. If a new program is introduced in all grades at once, the task is much greater. Although all students are beginners in the first year, even introductory lessons need to be adapted to the different developmental levels of students in different grades. In the second year of the program, curriculum for every grade level after the first one needs to be written. This process continues yearly until the entire program is in place. It is much more effective to implement a new program in only one or two grades during the first year, then add another grade each year until it is in place at all levels.

Pitfall: Ignoring the needs of students who enter the program in later grades.

Students who enter the program after the second year require significant support to catch up with classmates who have already had 2 or more years of foreign language instruction. This support may be provided in the form of supplementary materials and additional instructional time. Without such support, newcomers are likely to experience considerable frustration and may never reach the level of language proficiency of their peers. If the proportion of newcomers to a program becomes too great, especially at more advanced levels, the language experience for all students may be diluted in a misguided attempt to make it comprehensible for the new students. Specific plans must be in place to provide appropriate support for newcomers before the language program enters its second year of operation.

Pitfall: Failing to plan for appropriate articulation from elementary to secondary school programs.

Articulation issues, when postponed, can lead to the eventual disintegration of an early language program (Abbott 1998). No child who has already studied a language for several years should be treated as a beginner after moving on to middle school. Admittedly, bridging the middle school years is a difficult challenge. Because middle schools typically receive students from several elementary schools, they may have some incoming students with extensive language experience in elementary school and others who have had no prior language instruction. This presents a significant scheduling challenge. Courses for students with prior language learning experience must be designed to build on the learning that has taken place in elementary school. If elementary school program planners involve secondary school teachers and administrators in addressing these issues in the early planning stages of their program, the potential for long-term success is much greater.

Pitfall: Hiring teachers who do not have both language and teaching skills.

There are two misconceptions that sometimes influence the hiring of foreign language teachers: that a native speaker is always a better choice than a teacher who has learned the language as a second language, and that teachers at beginning levels of instruction do not need the same degree of language proficiency as those who teach at more advanced levels. In reality, teachers at all levels need to be fully proficient in the language they teach. But native or near-native language proficiency is not the only requirement. Language teachers also need to be knowledgeable about second language acquisition, especially in children, and about appropriate second language teaching strategies and practices.

Teachers who cannot comfortably use the target language for classroom purposes will not be able to surround learners with language, an essential component of an effective language learning environment. They will also find it difficult to develop and create curricula and activities in the target language. Even fluent speakers of the language may be ineffective in the classroom if they are not knowledgeable about second language acquisition, child development, and teaching strategies for American elementary school students.

Pitfall: Planning and scheduling the foreign language program in isolation from the general curriculum.

An isolated foreign language program can justifiably be perceived as an intrusion on precious time in the elementary school day. By contrast, a content-related program can reinforce the goals of the general curriculum, provide additional practice with significant concepts, and give learners a second chance at understanding material from other curricular areas. A common characteristic of seven model early foreign language programs examined in Gilzow and Branaman (2000) is a close connection with the general elementary school curriculum.

Effective language instruction is thematic and builds on topics and contexts that are relevant to the students. These topics or contexts can vary greatly, from activities based on the regular school curriculum, such as those found in content-based or content-related instruction, to other activities typically found in early language programs, such as drama, role-play, games, songs, children's literature, folk and fairy tales, storytelling, and puppetry. All of these activities contribute to the other content areas and to the basic mission of the school, because they all contribute to the child's learning.

Pitfall: Planning schedules and workloads that lead to teacher burnout.

There is currently a shortage of qualified teachers for early language programs. To rectify this situation, it is imperative to build programs that are good for children and also good for teachers. With this in mind, the Georgia

Department of Education stipulated that FLES teachers in state-supported model programs should teach no more than eight classes per day, leaving time for the many additional responsibilities of a FLES teacher: interacting with numerous classroom teachers, developing curriculum and materials, communicating with parents and community, and building public relations for the program.

If language teachers work under unfavorable conditions, they are likely to burn out and leave the profession or opt for regular classrooms. There are dangers in the proliferation of early language programs when attention is not given to the stress factors involved in typical teacher workloads. Elementary school language teachers may find themselves teaching as many as 14 classes in a single day, seeing as many as 600 students in a week. Their classes are often scheduled back to back, and they rarely have their own classrooms. They often lack professional support and opportunities for inservice training, and their schedules rarely allow them time to collaborate with other language teachers.

Conclusion

While it is not possible in this short space to address every issue involved in planning an early language program, this digest identifies a number of important considerations that program planners need to address. Many of the issues discussed here may sound familiar—they are similar to the obstacles that plagued the early language learning movement 40 years ago: a shortage of qualified teachers, a tendency to establish programs without sufficient planning or careful selection of teachers and materials, a lack of clarity about the connection between program goals and the amount of time allocated to the program, and a willingness to promise whatever the public wants to hear. In order to avoid the mistakes of the past, it is critical that program planners have a clear understanding of all of the components necessary to create a positive environment for early language teaching and learning.

References

Abbott, M.G. 1998. "Articulation: Challenges and Solutions." In *Critical Issues in Early Second Language Learning*, edited by M. Met. Glenview, Ill.: Scott Foresman Addison Wesley.

Brecht, Richard D., and C.W. Ingold. 1998. *Tapping a National Resource: Heritage Languages in the United States. ERIC Digest*. Washington, DC: ERIC Clearinghouse on Languages and Linguistics.

Gilzow, D.F., and L.E. Branaman. 2000. *Lessons Learned: Model Early Foreign Language Programs*. McHenry, Ill., and Washington, D.C.: Delta Systems and Center for Applied Linguistics.

Met, M., and N. Rhodes. 1990. "Priority: Instruction. Elementary School Foreign Language Instruction: Priorities for the 1990s." *Foreign Language Annals*. 25: 433–43.

Rhodes, N., and L. Branaman. 1999. *Foreign Language Instruction in the United States: A National Survey of Elementary and Secondary Schools*. McHenry, Ill., and Washington, D.C.: Delta Systems and Center for Applied Linguistics.

Rosenbusch, M., ed. 1992. *Colloquium on Foreign Languages in the Elementary School Curriculum—Proceedings.* Munich, Germany: Goethe Institut.
Standards for Foreign Language Learning in the 21st Century. 1999. Yonkers, N.Y.: National Standards in Foreign Language Education Project.
Swender, E., and G. Duncan. 1998. ACTFL Performance Guidelines for K–12 Learners. *Foreign Language Annals.* 31: 479–91.

This digest was prepared with funding from the U.S. Dept. of Education, Office of Educational Research and Improvement, National Library of Education, under contract no. ED-99-CO-0008. The opinions expressed do not necessarily reflect the positions or policies of ED, OERI, or NLE.

ERIC Clearinghouse on Languages and Linguistics, 4646 40th Street, NW, Washington, DC 20016-1859 (202)362-0700/(800)276-9834 *eric@cal.org*

(Reprinted with permission: *ERIC Digest,* December 2000, EDO-FL-00-11)

> There has never been greater potential for creating successful foreign language programs as there is today. An awareness of both pedagogy and possible pitfalls are essential for planning effective and enduring early world language programs. Scheduling, academic status, variety of language choices, gradual program implementation, accommodating new students, articulation with secondary school programs, well-prepared teachers, content-related instruction, and favorable teaching conditions are some of the more important issues to consider in planning a path for progress and success.

References

College Board. 2002. "AP Central. The AP Program." http://apcentral.collegeboard.com/program/0, 1289, 150-0-0-0,00.html.
Curtain, Helena, and Carol Ann Pesola Dahlberg. 2000. "Planning for Success: Common Pitfalls in the Planning of Early Foreign Language Programs." ERIC Digest, EDO-FL-00-11. Washington, D.C.: ERIC Clearinghouse on Languages and Linguistics.
International Baccalaureate Organization. 2002. "The Diploma Programme" http://www.ibo.org/ibo/index.cfm?ObjectID=C6463F11-140A-4418-84053E942FCACAE2&language=EN
National Standards in Foreign Language Education Project. 1996. *Standards for Foreign Language Learning: Preparing for the 21st Century.* Lawrence, Kans.: Allen Press.
Wisconsin Department of Public Instruction. 1997. *Wisconsin's Model Academic Standards for Foreign Languages.* Madison: Wisconsin Department of Public Instruction.

Related Issues

8

Why Language Learning Matters
Why Learn Another Language?
Considerations for Heritage Speakers
Use of Technology in World Language Instruction
NCSSFL Position Statement on Distance Learning in World Languages

Why Language Learning Matters

To thrive in a global economy and a multicultural society, U.S. students need fluency in at least one language other than English.

Myriam Met

Current U.S. education policy focuses on a singularly important goal: to leave no child behind as we raise the achievement bar for all students and close the persistent achievement gap among groups of students. That policy, however, will neither close the achievement gap nor offer students a world-class education because it ignores the importance of communication in languages other than English.

Even schools in third-world countries are more effective than U.S. schools at producing students who demonstrate foreign language proficiency. A world-class education includes foreign language learning—a subject that many U.S. schools neglect. Moreover, among schools in the United States, there are disparities of equity and access to language learning that produce a language-proficiency gap. Yet, competence in languages and cultures is conspicuously absent from the U.S. education agenda.

Beyond Proficiency in English

All U.S. students need to be proficient and literate in English. In addition, students will need competence in at least one additional language and skills in cross-cultural interaction. The need for such competence, both in our current economy and in the one in which today's students will live and work, has been well documented. Research shows that multilingual societies have a competitive advantage over monolingual societies in international trade (Halliwell 1999). Economic success and security in the United States depend on our ability to understand the information we gather about the current status of or coming changes in foreign economies, about research and development efforts elsewhere, or about threats to security—information that is unlikely to be in English. More than 70 agencies and offices of the U.S. government currently require language-proficient professionals, including the State Department, the Central Intelligence Agency, and the National Security Agency.

In an international service-sector economy, many Americans need to interact regularly with people who are unlikely to know English. Research shows that in the service industries, more than half of U.S. professionals working in a multicultural environment—whether in the U.S. or abroad—are linguistically unprepared to do so (Lena and Reason Moll 2000). Language competence is important because, contrary to popular myth, everyone in the world does not speak English. In fact, a recent survey found that only 41 percent of Europeans speak English in addition to their native language (International Research Associates and the European Union 2001). Despite the early dominance of English on the Internet, the majority of electronic communications, such as Web sites and E-mail, are now carried out in languages other than English. Within the United States, increasing linguistic diversity means that knowing languages other than English is helpful to service providers, marketers, and workers in diverse businesses.

Unlike in the United States, most education systems around the globe prepare their students to function in their national language and at least one additional language. A survey of 19 countries found that 16 provide widespread or compulsory foreign language instruction to students by the upper elementary grades (Pufahl, Rhodes, and Christian 2001). In many of these countries, students may elect or be required to take an additional foreign language during the elementary school years. Europeans are paying substantial attention to multilingualism and the schools' role in developing a populace capable of communicating across multiple linguistic borders. But although European students are expected to be skilled in several languages, U.S. schools are barely able to produce students who have enough fluency in a language other than English to be polite tourists.

A Widening Gap

Not only does the omission of language and cultural education leave U.S. students behind their peers in other countries, but also it exacerbates the achievement gap within the United States. Many students come to school well prepared for the challenges of a rigorous academic program. Other students who are less prepared enter school already behind their peers. Educators have found that the knowledge and performance gap in evidence upon school entry has been difficult to close. In fact, the gap frequently widens in reading and mathematics achievement.

The gap is also evident in language learning. Across the United States, only about one in three elementary schools offers its students the opportunity to gain some measure of skill in another language. More than two-thirds of elementary schools offer their students no language learning opportunities at all. Even more disturbing is the disparity among the schools that do teach languages; more than half of private elementary schools offer a foreign language, but only about one-fourth of public elementary schools do. The inequities of access are even more pronounced in urban schools. About 25 per-

Languages should be part of the core curriculum in elementary, middle, and high school.

cent of urban public elementary schools teach a foreign language compared with 65 percent of suburban private elementary schools. At the secondary level, the pattern is similar. Although 96 percent of suburban private secondary schools and 91 percent of urban private secondary schools teach foreign languages, only 81 percent of urban public secondary schools do. Within schools that teach languages, there are differences as well: 78 percent of private secondary schools report that half or more of their students are enrolled in foreign language courses, yet only 51 percent of public secondary schools report that at least half their students are taking a foreign language (Branaman and Rhodes 1999).

Clearly, money matters. Even when schools have equal financial resources, disparities exist. Schools that serve students from high-poverty backgrounds need to devote more of their resources to addressing basic academic needs. In contrast, schools in low-poverty areas can use their resources to expand and enrich their offerings. The digital divide that separates poor and affluent communities has been well documented. Although much less has been said about the linguistic divide, it exists—and for many of the same reasons. Because the U.S. education agenda fails to address access to opportunities to develop high-level skills in languages other than English, the linguistic divide in our schools will likely be maintained or will expand.

The U.S. education agenda also ignores the inequities of access to the language competencies that students need. It will leave children in urban public schools trailing their peers in the suburbs, private schools, or other havens for those with choices. Whereas some students will have access to quality opportunities to develop competence in languages other than English, many will not. At present, most native speakers of English do not have the option of enrolling in a foreign language course until they enter high school, and the current education agenda is unlikely to change that. Even those students who already know other languages will be left behind those in other countries. In the United States, native speakers of languages other than English are rarely encouraged to maintain and extend their proficiency. Instead, schools work toward substituting proficiency in English for proficiency in students' native languages. This unwritten policy in our schools fosters monolingualism in English, even when bilingualism could be easily and inexpensively attained.

Enhancing Academic Performance

No one would seriously argue with the goal that all students should be proficient at reading and successful at mathematics. Fortuitously, languages in the school curriculum can contribute to producing academically successful students. A significant body of research has documented the academic and cognitive benefits of knowing more than one language:

- Bilingual students with strong competence in both languages are more likely to be successful readers (Lindholm-Leary 2000);
- Bilingualism enhances cognitive functioning, such as metalinguistic skills and divergent thinking (Robinson 1998);

- Study of a foreign language in the elementary grades has been associated with higher scores on standardized measures of reading and mathematics, even for students from high-poverty backgrounds (Caldas and Bourdeaux 1999; Robinson 1998).

Rather than diverting energy and attention from high-priority academic goals, inclusion of languages in the school curriculum furthers the education agenda.

Expanding the Agenda

As the U.S. Department of Education formulates plans to implement the national education agenda, the federal government, the states, and our schools should consider the following actions:

- *Create a language education policy that addresses the serious needs of our schools.* We can trace the success of language education programs outside the United States directly to strong policies at the national or regional levels. These policies determine who studies foreign languages (frequently, everyone); when they begin (generally, at an early age); and for how long (usually, for a long sequence of study). In many countries, foreign languages are part of the core curriculum. Additionally, some countries or regions have policies that focus on the maintenance of native languages.

    Not only have education systems around the world been proactive in developing language education policy, but they also have actively promoted such policies. Major initiatives by the Council of Europe have made substantial improvements in the quality of language learning and the extent of multilingualism among member nations. The Australian National Policy on Languages has been responsible for initiating, expanding, and supporting significantly more and better language programs for more than a decade. In England, the government has announced a major initiative to address the inadequacy of its education system in preparing its students to live in the modern world. The United States should do the same.

    Only a small number of U.S. states mandate or provide financial incentives for early language learning. And of the states that do, only a handful actually require the development of some degree of proficiency. Some enlightened districts and schools involve all students in language learning. These are sound first steps on the long road to parity with schools abroad.

- *Build on the assets that language minority students bring to school.* The languages children learn at home are a valuable national resource. The federal government invests hundreds of millions of dollars annually to teach languages to adults who work in commerce, agriculture, public health, diplomacy, and national defense. At the same time, U.S. schools do little to capitalize on the skills that many of their students, already fluent speakers of other languages, have mastered by the early grades. Unfortunately, the education system has a questionable policy regarding the maintenance of heritage or indigenous languages for those who have developed their skills outside the school. By building on the heritage that speakers bring to school, however, we can help all students become highly proficient in both English and one additional language.

- *Respond to parent interest.* Public surveys indicate parent interest in language learning opportunities (Brecht, Robinson, Robinson, and Rivers, unpublished), as do enrollments in magnet programs that feature foreign languages and the significant number of parents who pay out-of-pocket for their children to participate in language learning programs outside the regular school day.

Public demand for language magnet schools usually exceeds the seats available. Media reports have documented the extremes to which parents will go to ensure a place for their child in many of these schools.

Much has been discussed about the rights of parents to choose the kind of education program most appropriate for their children. For some time, public schools of choice, such as public charter schools and magnet programs, have flourished when languages have been included in the curriculum. Excellent language magnet programs can be found in Cincinnati, Ohio; Montgomery County, Maryland; Portland, Oregon; Lexington, Kentucky; and San Diego, California. Among the nation's most successful programs to promote desegregation have been immersion programs in which students can attain very high levels of foreign language proficiency (Met 1992). Montgomery County's (MD) total immersion magnet programs began in the 1970s and are currently housed at Maryvale, Sligo Creek, and Rock Forest elementary schools. Students in the French immersion program at Sligo Creek, for example, receive their subject matter instruction in French. In grades K–3, French is the only language used in the classrooms. In 4th grade, students receive instruction in English twice a week for 45 minutes during the second half of the school year. In 5th grade, students are given instruction in English for approximately three and a half hours each week. Art, music, and physical education are conducted in English. A 1996 internal study found that the immersion students in the district performed academically (in English) as well as or better than comparison students. Immersion students also demonstrated high levels of proficiency in French or Spanish.

In addition to magnet programs, numerous public charter schools offer foreign languages in their curriculum. Private schools are far more likely than public schools to offer languages, presumably because such offerings appeal to those seeking a high-quality school. Private school management companies, such as Edison Schools, include foreign language instruction in their core curriculum. Given the public interest in language learning and the increasing appeal of school choice, the U.S. Department of Education should encourage and expand public schools of choice that include or focus on languages.

About 25 percent of urban public elementary schools teach foreign language compared with 65 percent of suburban private elementary schools.

- *Hold schools accountable for producing language-competent graduates.* In large part, dollars tend to accompany accountability initiatives. With few exceptions, schools are not accountable for producing graduates with foreign language competence. Because high-stakes accountability and the national and state assessments that go with them have focused on reading, mathematics, social studies, and science, other subjects that are not tested have received little attention and few resources. For example, dollar investments in teacher professional development have been far greater in reading, science, and mathematics than in languages. Our schools should not only produce language-competent graduates—they should receive support to do so and be held accountable for the outcomes of the resulting programs.
- *Acknowledge the vital role that languages play in an information-based economy.* No one doubts that students must attain the highest levels of competence in mathematics and the sciences to thrive in a global economy. Language competence is also vitally important in a globalized economy that depends on easy access to information, in whichever language it may be available. Languages should be part of the core curriculum in elementary, middle, and high school.

Preparing for the 21st Century

It is almost a cliché to point out that education must prepare our students to lead and work in tomorrow's world. The past decades have brought technological advances and changes in the political landscape, and we can only assume that the world our students will inhabit will be unimaginably different from what teachers and parents have known. We can predict with some certainty, however, that communication across current linguistic and national borders will continue to increase as a matter of political and economic necessity. Of course, we cannot predict with precision which languages our students will need to know. We can, however, be sure that unless U.S. students are prepared with an education comparable to the best that schools around the world offer—one that includes foreign language study—we will have failed to achieve our goal to leave no child behind.

References

Branaman, L., and N. C. Rhodes. 1999, *Foreign Language Instruction in the United States: A National Survey of Elementary and Secondary Schools.* Washington, D.C.: Center for Applied Linguistics.

Brecht, R., J. L. Robinson, J. P. Robinson, and W. Rivers. n.d. *American's Attitudes Towards Language and Language Policy.* Forthcoming.

Brecht, Richard D., and Catherine W. Ingold. 1998. "Tapping a National Resource: Heritage Languages in the United States." *ERIC/CLL Digest.* Washington, DC: ERIC Clearinghouse on Languages and Linguistics. http://www.cal.org/ericcll/digest/brecht01.html, accessed April 1, 2002.

Caldas, S.J., and N. Bordeaux. 1999. "Poverty, Race, and Foreign Language Immersion: Predictors of Math and English Language Arts Performance." *Learning Languages* 5 (1): 4–15.

Halliwell, J. 1999. "Language and Trade." In *Exploring the Economics of Language*, edited by A. Breton. Ottawa, Ontario: Department of Cultural Heritage.

International Research Associates and the European Union. 2001. *"Les Européens et les langues."* Eurobaromètre 54 Spécial. Brussels: International Research Associates and the European Union.

Lena, M., and J. Reason Moll. 2000. *The Globalization of the Professions in the United States and Canada: A Survey and Analysis.* Washington, D.C.: The Center for Quality Assurance in International Education.

Lewelling, Vickie W., and Joy Kreeft Peyton. 1999. "Spanish for Native Speakers: Developing Dual Language Proficiency." *ERIC/CLL Digest.* Washington, D.C.: ERIC Clearinghouse on Languages and Linguistics.http://www.cal.org/ericcll/digest/spanish_native2.html, accessed April 1, 2002.

Lindholm-Leary, K. 2000. *Biliteracy for a Global Society: An Ideal Book on Dual Language Education.* Washington, D.C.: National Clearinghouse for Bilingual Education.

Met, M. 1992. "Second Language Learning in Magnet School Settings." In *Annual Review of Applied Linguistics,* vol. 13, edited by W. Grabe. Cambridge, U.K.: Cambridge University Press.

Pufahl, I., N. Rhodes, and D. Christian. 2001. *Foreign Language Teaching: What the United States Can Learn from Other Countries.* Washington, D.C.: Center for Applied Linguistics.

Robinson, D. W. 1998. "The Cognitive, Academic, and Attitudinal Benefits of Early Language Learning." In *Critical Issues in Early Language Learning,* edited by M. Met. Glenview, Ill.: Scott Foresman Addison Wesley.

[Reprinted with permission, Association of Supervision and Curriculum Development, *Educational Leadership,* October 2001, 59(2): 36–40.]

Why Learn Another Language?

Learning a second language leads to understanding another culture.
Learning other languages increases the number of people with whom one can communicate effectively.
The five C's of the national standards provide the talking points to answer the question: why learn another language?

Broadened Perspective:
Communication
- Learn why one language cannot be translated into another without losing the values and attitudes inherent in certain words and phrases
- Learn why people respect and listen to you more when you speak their language

Culture
- Learn another way of life and another view of the world
- Look at your own culture from another perspective

Connections
- Learn new perspectives for looking at other course content (for example, environmental issues in science, or the concept and make-up of families in social studies)
- Access new information (available only in a language other than English)

Comparisons
- Learn another means of communication and look at your first language with heightened awareness
- Learn unique perspectives and concepts attached to the language that give you a new way of looking at your own culture

Communities
- Develop awareness of other languages and cultures in your own community

Cognitive Benefits:
Communication
- Speaking and understanding more than one language stimulates the brain

Culture
- Through language, one has a deeper understanding of other cultures and is better able to compare and analyze cultural differences and similarities

Connections
- ACT and SAT scores increase

Comparisons
- Knowledge of language structure (how language works) increases
- Vocabulary in all languages increases

Communities
- Language opens the door to greater and richer participation in our increasingly diverse communities

Broadened Opportunities—Benefits in Careers and Jobs:
Communication
- Proficiency in more than one language addresses a shortage of workers qualified to use languages to communicate successfully, a shortage identified in virtually all fields

Culture
- Language study includes culture study which helps workers be aware of and understand the unique characteristics of markets and employees around the world

> **Connections**
> - Studying any discipline from a non-U.S. perspective enhances understanding of other people
>
> **Comparisons**
> - Comparing languages and cultures leads to greater understanding of the values and perspectives of other people
>
> **Communities**
> - As the U.S. becomes increasingly global, our communities and markets reflect not only an American perspective and workforce, but international ones
>
> **Lifelong Opportunities:**
> - Students will experience multiple contacts with a second language or a second culture at home and abroad
> - Learning another language helps students meet university and technical college graduation requirements, and qualify for internship opportunities
> - Studying other languages provides access to arts around the world
> - Students with proficiency in other languages are ready to travel and host international visitors, comfortably interacting with other cultures.

Considerations for Heritage Speakers

Increasingly in our schools, speakers of other languages look to the world language teachers to fill a unique role: Helping them continue the study of their heritage language. While the most common heritage language in the United States is Spanish, different areas have different concentrations of heritage speakers. Most world language teachers do not have preparation in how to meet the needs of the heritage speakers in their schools. Rather than losing the valuable language resource within these students, language programs should plan for how to best serve heritage speakers.

Who Are Our Heritage Speakers?

Heritage language students are often referred to as language minority students. They "speak a language other than English as their first language, either because they were born in another country or because their families speak another language at home" (Lewelling and Peyton 1999, 1).

A wide range of skill in using a language other than English exists among heritage speakers. Students fit somewhere along a broad continuum, each having unique needs:

- Third- or fourth-generation students who are born in the United States enter school with a full command of English, understanding the spoken heritage language but with limited productive skills (speaking or writing). A large number of Hispanic students in U.S. schools may have strong listening skills in Spanish, limited Spanish-speaking skills, and almost no reading or writing skills in Spanish, as they never experienced formal literacy instruction in Spanish.

- First- or second-generation bilinguals possess different ranges of proficiency in English and their native language. While their speaking and listening skills will be strong, these students generally have received their education in English and have developed few, if any, literacy (reading and writing) skills in Spanish.
- Recent immigrants to the United States will obviously have strong listening and speaking skills in their native language; however, reading and writing skills will be entirely dependent on the amount of formal education that preceded their arrival in the United States.
- A unique group of heritage speakers in the world language classroom may on occasion be exchange students, who are attending the school for a limited period of time. These speakers also provide linguistic and cultural models and can be involved in the activities of the world language classroom.

In all of these groups, language proficiency may vary from individual to individual and from language to language. Many students are completely fluent in oral Spanish (both speaking and comprehending), others speak and understand Spanish fairly well, while others possess only basic skills in the language.

Lewelling and Peyton 1999, 2

Meeting the Needs of Heritage Speakers

In our schools, heritage speakers of languages other than English may choose to participate in world language courses of their heritage language for a number of reasons:

- To learn more about their language and cultural heritage
- To acquire literacy skills in their language
- To develop or augment academic language skills in their language
- To enhance career opportunities
- To fulfill a world language requirement

Schools need to assess both the language background of heritage speakers and their identified purposes for learning and using their heritage language. Assessing the proficiency level of each student is critical for both placement and measurement of progress. As is the case for native speakers of English, a grammatically based assessment will not reveal what the speaker can really do with the language, and may, in fact, create the impression that the person has very little ability in the language. Assessment must focus on the performance of the student, providing tasks to be performed that use the language. Instruction can be designed for heritage language students only when the instructor truly knows what each student can *do with* the language, rather than only discovering what the student can *say about* the language.

Even though heritage language speakers also frequently lack some of the language skills and knowledge required in a professional context (e.g., literacy or the ability to use more formal language registers), their head start is substantial, making the cost in instructional time and dollars required to bring them to professional levels of competence significantly less than the cost for individuals without home language experience.

Brecht and Ingold 1998, 2

To meet these needs, world language programs need to offer adaptations to their traditional curriculum and means of assessment. Programs should consider any of the following:

- The opportunity to study the language formally in an academic setting in the same way that native speakers of English study the English language, including a component of exploring the literary and cultural heritage of the cultures that speak the students' heritage language.
- A focus for heritage speakers within a language course on specific identified language goals, ranging from learning the grammar and spelling rules and developing an academic vocabulary to learning how to analyze a literary text or write poetry, or acquiring information through the heritage language for application in different academic content courses (Lewelling and Peyton 1999, p. 2). Heritage speakers' strong listening and speaking skills should be utilized and honored in the language classroom, to the benefit of their self-esteem and the nonheritage students' cultural perspectives and awareness. The main challenge in such situations is to adjust tasks and assignments in the course to fit the strengths and needs of the heritage language students.
- Special courses for heritage language speakers, in addition to the existing world language offerings. This option could be provided via distance learning in schools where sufficient numbers of speakers of the same heritage language are not present.

Although the exact goal of different Spanish for Native Speakers courses may vary, most aim at maintenance and retrieval of functional abilities and further development of existing competencies.

Lewelling and Peyton 1999, 2

Language teachers need to admit the limitations to their command of the student's heritage language. At the same time, teachers should be confident of the formal knowledge of the language they possess. Being conscious of these realities allows a teacher to tap the language resources represented by the heritage speakers while confidently offering the instruction they need. Again, considering the majority of heritage speakers of Spanish, the nonnative-speaking Spanish teacher can call on heritage speakers to provide listening practice, expansion of vocabulary, and conversation practice within the classroom, while offering them the spelling, grammatical, and writing practice that will allow the heritage speakers to prepare their language skill for productive application in their future world of work.

The overarching characteristic needed to serve heritage language speakers is an awareness of who the heritage speakers are and what they bring to and need in the world language classroom. The teacher and the nonheritage

Heritage speakers' strong listening and speaking skills should be utilized and honored in the language classroom, to the benefit of their self-esteem and the nonheritage students' cultural perspectives and awareness.

students need to demonstrate a respect for the language skills and cultural knowledge that heritage speakers bring to the classroom. Heritage speakers, in turn, need to demonstrate their respect for the language skills and cultural knowledge the teacher brings to the classroom. The result is an enriched experience for all.

References

Brecht, Richard D., and Catherine W. Ingold. 1998. "Tapping a National Resource: Heritage Languages in the United States." *ERIC/CLL Digest.* Washington, D.C.: ERIC Clearinghouse on Languages and Linguistics. http://www.cal.org/ericcll/digest/brecht01.html, accessed April 1, 2002.

Lewelling, Vickie W., and Joy Kreeft Peyton. 1999. "Spanish for Native Speakers: Developing Dual Language Proficiency." *ERIC/CLL Digest.* Washington, D.C.: ERIC Clearinghouse on Languages and Linguistics. http://www.cal.org/ericcll/digest/spanish_native2.html, accessed April 1, 2002.

Resources on Heritage Speakers

American Association of Teachers of Spanish and Portuguese. 2000. *Spanish for Native Speakers.* Vol. 1, *AATSP Professional Development Series Handbook for Teachers K–16.* Orlando, Fla.: Harcourt, Inc.

National Council of State Supervisors of Foreign Languages. 2002. *Position Paper on Heritage Language Learners.* http://www.ncssfl.org, accessed April 1, 2002.

Peyton, Joy Kreeft, Vickie W. Lewelling, and Paula Winke. 2001. Spanish for Spanish Speakers: Developing Dual Language Proficiency. *ERIC/CLL Digest.* Washington, D.C.: ERIC Clearinghouse on Languages and Linguistics. http://www.cal.org/ericcll/digest/spanish_native.html, accessed April 1, 2002.

Roca, Ana. 2000. "Heritage Learners of Spanish." In *Teaching Spanish with the Five C's: A Blueprint for Success* edited by Gail Guntermann. Vol, 2, *AATSP Professional Development Series Handbook for Teachers K–16.* Orlando, Fla.: Harcourt, Inc.

Use of Technology in World Language Instruction

Incorporating Technology into Lesson Planning and Instructional Delivery

The technological revolution of the last 20 years brings both opportunities and challenges for world language curriculum and instruction. Teachers and students can access authentic material and communicate with others in locations worldwide. Advances in technology can enhance and enrich instructional delivery, affecting the traditional roles of students and teachers in the classroom. Technology alone, however, cannot supply the motivation for learning, nor can the use of technology be the instructional goal in the world language classroom. Technology must be employed only as a means to achieve the language and culture goals of the standards-based curriculum. Viewing the role of technology through the five C's of the standards provides a useful focus for implementing technology in the world language classroom.

Incorporating the Web into teaching provides new authentic material and a different motivation for communicative activities;...It should be regarded as what it is: a technological tool that gives students and teachers the option to explore worlds of authentic information, to strengthen their language skills, to acquire more knowledge about the target culture, and to keep abreast of new developments there in order to teach in an interesting and effective way and, last but not least, to become Internet-literate, i.e., to be up-to-date in dealing with a contemporary and ubiquitous medium.

Kost 1999, 317

> ## Defining Technology
>
> The term *technology* in this guide refers to many forms of technology tools that can be employed in the classroom. At this point in our technological development, we tend to think of the use of computers, and especially of Internet access, as employing technology in schools. The range of technology tools is, of course, much broader, from tape recorders and overhead projectors, to word processors, networked computers, digital cameras, and two-way interactive videoconferencing. For the purposes of this guide, the discussion of the role of technology in world language teaching refers primarily to the multiple uses of computers.

Technology as Part of the "Curricular Weave"

In identifying the process through which students learn to communicate in a world language, the *Standards for Foreign Language Learning* identify the use of technology as one of the strands in the "curricular weave."

> Students should be given ample opportunities to explore, develop, and use communication strategies, learning strategies, critical thinking skills, and skills in technology, as well as the appropriate elements of the language system and culture...The Standards provide a background, a framework for the reflective teacher to use in weaving these rich curricular experiences into the fabric of language learning.
>
> *National Standards in Foreign Language Education Project 1996, 28*

The scope of the content of the language instruction is broadened and enriched by the use of technology. Through experiences provided by CD-ROM and Internet, the students can immerse themselves in an environment that is rich in information, enhanced by visual and audio components, and is current, up-to-date, and constantly changing.

In each of the 5 C's of the standards, the use of technology can allow the learner to practice skills, communicate with others, and gather and share information. The Internet provides a rich, up-to-date resource of culturally authentic material, written primarily by native speakers for natives of the target culture. Web sites from around the world provide information that would not be otherwise available and enhance the existing curriculum content. A textbook may contain illustrations of clothing, but a Web page from a boutique or

Good computer education is not drastically different from what we already know about quality teaching and learning. The challenge, as with any new instructional tool, is to integrate computers with established educational objectives and practices.

Lebow and Dugger 1999, 31

fashion magazine shows current trends. A student can view the plazas of Spain not only in the textbook or on posters in the classroom, but can take a virtual tour of those locations with sound and video on the computer. While reading selections from "culture corners" of textbooks can quickly become outdated, the Internet provides reading selections that are current and of high interest to students. Via technology, students can read the front page of the newspaper, music and movie top 10 lists, and interviews—all created in the target language for native speakers of the language.

Students have the opportunity to react and respond to the written, visual, or audio information from the computer. For example, they may interact with a CD-ROM program, or add their personal message to an Internet bulletin board, or write in the "guest book" of a Web site. Students can practice writing skills and learn firsthand about the culture by communicating with a key pal. In the classroom, the teacher can use a television or projector screen to display the computer images to the entire class, providing a visual display as part of the teaching unit.

Using a Single Computer Screen Display in a Classroom

- Enhance the cultural connection of a typical textbook unit that introduces places in a city by using a virtual tour of an actual city in the target culture to learn vocabulary and provide discussion topics.
- Take a virtual tour of an art museum. Beginning students could name colors and express likes and dislikes, or advanced students could discuss the art objects, expressing and justifying their opinions.
- Students could work individually or in pairs in the computer lab to become familiar with one part of a multifaceted Web site, (such as a city Web site, a school Web site from the target culture, a newspaper or magazine, or a site that describes a holiday celebration). Each "expert" then presents and explains the part of the Web site with which they have become familiar, while the Web site is displayed to the entire class.

The overwhelming amount of information available also requires the students to apply critical thinking skills to determine the reliability and value of the material. This need for evaluation is addressed in the *Wisconsin Model Academic Standards for Information and Technology Literacy*.

Technology Content Standard B. INFORMATION AND INQUIRY: Students in Wisconsin will access, evaluate, and apply information efficiently and effectively from a variety of sources in print, nonprint, and electronic formats to meet personal and academic needs.

Rationale: Today's students face a present and future in which they will encounter unprecedented access to ever increasing amounts of information. Students must be prepared to evaluate critically each item of information in order to select and use information effectively in learning and decision making for personal growth and empowerment. This critical evaluation requires that students have frequent opportunities to learn how knowledge is organized, how to find information, and how to use information in such a way that others can learn from them. Mastery of information and inquiry skills will prepare students to participate in a rapidly changing, information-based environment.

Wisconsin Department of Public Instruction 1998, 8

The evaluation of information from electronic sources takes on an added challenge when applied to world language materials. Students must not only be able to interpret the language but also must employ knowledge of the culture to critically evaluate the information they have obtained. For example, information received about a city from a government information site may differ from information about the same city received from a tourist promotional site. The students must be taught to recognize the information source and to read the information through a filter of the purpose and goals of that source.

Using Technology to Enhance Learning and Instruction through Each of the Five C's

As the teacher plans curriculum, designs thematic units, and prepares daily lesson plans, it is vital to first determine the goals of the instruction, and then to decide how the use of technology can help the students attain those goals. An inordinate amount of instructional time should not be spent on employing the technological tools at the expense of the world language learning goals (Gonglewski 1999, 348).

The access to technology is not equal among school districts, or even among buildings or departments within the same district. It is vital that teachers are aware of the possibilities offered through use of technological advancements, even if the technology itself is not yet available to the individual teacher. Awareness of the possibilities for curriculum enhancement offered through the use of technology enables teachers to become effective advocates for technology when district funding is discussed or voted upon.

The following suggestions for employing technology in a world language curriculum based on the five C's of the standards are offered as possibilities that can be adapted to the opportunities and limitations of individual programs. Margaret Gonglewski originally presented this concept of viewing the use of technology through the lens of the five C's in 1999 (Gonglewski 1999).

Communication

Interpersonal: Via technology, students have the opportunity to engage in interpersonal communication with native speakers through E-mail exchanges, real-time "chats," videoconferencing, or video exchanges. Classes of language learners within the same country could be connected by E-mail to exchange information about their schools and towns, using a comparable level of proficiency in the foreign language to fill an information gap. Using the computer to communicate can provide a means of written conversation, in which short E-mail messages are exchanged, rather than letters. A class may set up a Web site through which they can communicate with each other or their teacher in the target language. Messages or homework questions can be posted and answered. Although the information is read, and is therefore also interpretive communication, the nature of the discourse is conversational, with the emphasis more on the message being communicated and the negotiation of meaning.

> In the traditional classroom, students write, exchange, and respond to "Dear Abby" letters as part of the teen problems unit. To enhance the same unit through the use of the computer, students could post the letters in a class "chat room." They would then have the opportunity to read more than one letter, read the advice offered, and comment on the letters and advice, working on the standard of Interpersonal Communication.

Interpretive: The vast amount of written information on the World Wide Web provides a wealth of content for interpretive reading experiences. News, weather, ads, song lyrics, virtual tours of cities or museums, comics, fan letters, historical documents, classical and popular literature, and correspondence are examples that represent only a small portion of accessible text. The graphic organization and rich use of accompanying photos and illustrations make text on Web sites more comprehensible to language students at even the beginning level. The diverse nature of the written information provides the opportunity for students to employ varying reading skills, such as reading for general meaning, reading for detail, skimming, scanning, deriving meaning from context, and evaluating material for authenticity. Teachers have access to authentic material that was previously only attainable through travel or personal connections to the target country. The level of sophistication and type of written material can be adapted to the student's level of proficiency and to the instructional goal. For example, advanced students might read a movie review, while beginning students could read movie theater ads to find opening and closing times, viewer age restrictions, or titles of movies they recognize.

Presentational: Students can use technology tools to create or compose presentations to demonstrate their performance of the learning goals. Using word processing to write in the target language enables students to edit and rewrite easily, encouraging them to incorporate the corrections and revisions made through peer and teacher editing into a final manuscript, representative of their best efforts. Just as these writing tools are commonly used in one's first language, students should learn how to use these tools in their second and third languages. In presentational mode, accuracy takes on added importance, because meaning cannot be negotiated. Technology can help students polish their writing, appropriate in the presentational mode.

Students can demonstrate their skill in the presentational mode through video and audio productions, PowerPoint or hyperstudio presentations, production of Web pages, use of digital camera photographs or scanned images in presentation documents or displays, or through numerous other types of technology-enhanced performance tasks.

Culture

The standard of Culture is the background in which we must embed the Communication standards. Technology can certainly enhance the student's ability to "develop an awareness of another people's way of life" (Wisconsin Model Academic Standard D, Culture: Practices). Viewing video presentations that depict traditional ideas and attitudes and how they influence behavior provides communication models for students. They develop observational skills by watching native speakers interacting with each other. They can see links between communication and culture, like the use of gestures, personal space, and register that would be missed in written text or audiotapes. Videoconferencing, video streaming, and other audio and video technologies that link classrooms can provide face-to-face interaction. This connection will open the door to learning about the culture through direct interaction with native speakers. Images from a digital camera can be incorporated into text documents or PowerPoint presentations to bring authentic materials, objects, and scenes into presentational materials. These images can also be exchanged by E-mail with a partner classroom, providing the basis for presenting information, concepts, and ideas (Standard C).

The wealth of authentic information available from Internet sites provides current cultural information in a real context. Until recently, the incorporation of culture into the classroom was limited by available material, the teacher's experience in the target culture, or the access to native speakers or field trips. The variety and ever-changing nature of Internet resources provide a multifaceted picture of the target culture, thus avoiding narrow cultural definitions that often reinforce stereotypes. Internet resources "provide invaluable information in understanding the diversity of the target culture, an aspect often left untouched in the traditional classroom due to lack of time or the instructor's incomplete knowledge, training or experience" (Gonglewski 1999, 355).

Connections

Using the Internet for research for other classes opens the door to an entire world of information for students. Information found only in foreign journals or Web sites can now be accessed as easily as the local newspaper. Using the target language to access material otherwise available only to native speakers provides the connection to other subject areas and clearly demonstrates the value of knowing another language and culture.

> A student who is researching the nutritional food pyramid for health or science could access that same information from another country to determine similarities and differences. Knowledge of the language and culture provides keys to interpreting the pyramid and finding reasons for the differences.

Comparisons

Communicating with individuals in the target culture or reading information from authentic sites enables the students to compare both the language and the culture of other countries. In an E-mail exchange with key pals in the target culture, students naturally refer to aspects of their school and personal lives, such as *study hall, homecoming, pep rally, detention,* or *driver's ed.* A German partner may refer to *Leistungskurs, Abistreich,* or going to the *Disko,* which is much different than an American student's image of *Disco.* When an E-mail partner does not understand the culturally specific terms and needs clarification, students are called upon to reexamine cultural and linguistic phenomena through the perspective of another culture. This experience reflects both Content Standards H and I, as students demonstrate understanding of the nature of language and concept of culture through comparisons of the language and culture studied and their own.

Communities

Through E-mail partnerships, Internet connections, or other communication with the target culture, students are employing the standard of Communities, reaching out to "multilingual communities at home and abroad." As students work on the presentational aspect of the communication standard, the nature of the performance task often creates a product that is readily shared with others. Students' productions, newsletters, or exhibits can be shared with other classes, other schools, parents, community groups, or in interschool competitions, such as Spanish Forensics, German Day at UW-Madison, or pronunciation and speaking contests. Students may be able to research language resources in their communities or regions that they would not be able to find without employing technology. This Communities standard is achieved through the very use of technology as a tool for language learning and for connecting to speakers of other languages.

Employing Technology: Implications for Teachers

Teachers must decide how to best incorporate the use of technology to enhance instruction in the foreign language classroom. The traditional use of audiotape, video, or overhead projectors may still be the most appropriate means of presenting some instructional material. In other situations, teachers may have the opportunity or need to use multimedia language lab systems that incorporate audio, video, and digital resources to students at individual computer workstations. Language software for authoring programs, practice and remediation, or reference can be delivered to individual students at their networked computers. Computer output can be displayed to an entire class through "smart classroom" design or by portable LCD projectors that can be shared within a building. In any case, the teacher must make the decision to incorporate technology based on the most effective way of teaching the instructional goal. The crucial question is whether the goal justifies the class time spent in activities that do not address the primary goal of communication.

The crucial question is whether the goal justifies the class time spent in activities that do not address the primary goal of communication.

Professional Development

School districts, administrators, and teachers must recognize the need for teacher development and involvement as we incorporate the use of technology in our schools. Teachers must receive ongoing, in-depth professional development to learn how to use various technology tools and develop instructional strategies enhanced or supported by technology.

> The business world typically spends 30 percent of staff time and resources on research and training, but in public education funding for staff development evaporates across this country.... Teachers from various content areas need structured time to discuss their common concerns, to share effective strategies, and to develop new instructional approaches...to infuse technology into teaching as well as to integrate curriculum content.
>
> *Lebow and Dugger 1999, 34–35*

Teacher and Student Roles in the Classroom

Incorporating technology tools into instruction can dramatically change the traditional roles of the teacher and student in the classroom. Software programs can provide a means for individualized or remedial instruction, allowing students to progress at different rates, to pursue varied interests, and to gain practice in different areas of language learning. When the technology is being employed as a means to achieve a well-defined performance task, it is possible for students to pursue different paths to the learning goal. The teacher functions as a facilitator and guide, or as a partner in the pursuit of information or learning. When the student is able to share technological knowledge and skill from which the teacher learns, the teacher models the qualities of a lifelong learner.

Assessment

As the teacher develops the rubric for assessing the performance task that has been enhanced, developed, or delivered through technology, it is essential to focus on the original language goal and how the student has demonstrated increased knowledge or progress toward that goal. The assessment may include an evaluation of the application of technology if that was truly part of the learning goal, but the student and teacher should not be distracted from the language goal by a glossy application of technology.

The use of video or audio portfolios can make progress toward proficiency more visible to both the teacher and the student. Samples of progress over time should include more than paper and pencil assessments, highlighting interpersonal communication skills and oral proficiency.

> Using either audio- or videotape, record the students at regular intervals as they complete varied performance tasks. It is particularly valuable to maintain the portfolios for the entire time the students are enrolled in the language program, providing an overview of their growing proficiency in the language. Using rubrics that clearly describe varying levels of performance provides feedback to the students about the areas in which they may excel or could improve.

Appropriate Use of Internet and Web Sites

As students use the information network available to them through advanced technology, teachers must define guidelines for determining the validity of the information and sources. As part of writing across the curriculum, students must follow accepted guidelines for citing sources from which they have gathered information. Because this verification can be especially problematic for students in a world language site, students need to learn strategies to help them identify and evaluate their sources. Students must employ critical thinking skills as they accept or reject information, based on their assessment of the source. For example, students were given the assignment to find and summarize an article from a German newspaper or magazine about the anniversary celebration of the fall of the Berlin Wall. Several students brought encyclopedia articles about the history of the Berlin Wall that they found by typing "Berlin Wall" into a search engine, while others brought articles that were clearly propaganda from extremist groups. While the content of the article may have been difficult for the students to understand at a critical level, they can learn general guidelines about Web sources from the target culture that can serve as validation or cautionary red flags.

Use of Translation Programs

Translation programs are readily available through the Internet. Text can be scanned or copied and automatically translated on the screen. Presently the results are usually limited to word-for-word translations, which can be embarrassing, culturally inappropriate, or inaccurate. The programs, however, are improving rapidly and their easy availability can be problematic for teachers. Pointing out the limitations of the translation programs to students effectively demonstrates to them the need to understand the culture of the target country to be able to communicate effectively. The need for face-to-face communication, or verbal communication on the telephone, will only become greater as the globalization of the economy progresses. Translation programs cannot take into account the role of register in communication with native speakers. A person who does not speak the language or understand the culture will not be able to identify the errors in meaning or cultural taboos that may appear in the rough electronic translation.

Students may be tempted to use translation programs to prepare written assignments. Teachers should publish clear guidelines about the use of translation programs, stressing the purpose of writing assignments as instruments that develop and assess a student's proficiency in the language. The guidelines should outline consequences for submitting work that is ostensibly original, but has been obtained from other sources.

District Computer Use Policy

Teachers and students must be alert to the school district's protocol regarding computer and Internet use, Web site postings, and the use of students' names and photos. These protocols are constantly changing and being revised as new challenges arise. In planning instruction, teachers must be aware of the possibility that some students in the class may not have the permission required to access the Internet and therefore make necessary adaptations to the lesson.

Distance Learning and World Languages

There is no alternative that can match the presence of a qualified teacher in a classroom. Districts considering distance learning programs to teach world languages must weigh the cost versus the benefits, keeping in mind that the ultimate goal is to provide the best learning opportunities for students. If students do not have the opportunity to learn a world language because of the size or remote location of the district, distance learning may be the only option available to them. In every situation in which distance learning is being considered, administrators, teachers, students, and parents need to consider and address a wide range of guidelines to provide a quality program. The same guidelines that describe a quality world language program (chapter 7) must be addressed when districts consider providing world language instruction through distance learning.

> Without exception, effective distance education programs begin with careful planning and a focused understanding of course requirements and student needs. Appropriate technology can only be selected once these elements are understood in detail. There is no mystery to the way effective distance education programs develop. They don't happen spontaneously; they evolve through the hard work and dedicated efforts of many individuals and organizations. In fact, successful distance education programs rely on the consistent and integrated efforts of students, faculty, facilitators, support staff, and administrators.
>
> *Willis 2002*

NCSSFL Position Statement on Distance Learning in Foreign Languages

Foreign language educators recognize the rapid growth and contributions of foreign language distance learning programs. Their concerns are:

- *The need for distance learning*
- *Involvement of foreign language specialists in program design and implementation*
- *Qualifications of the distance learning teachers and on-site facilitators*
- *Appropriate use of technology*

In this position statement, distance learning refers to instruction that relies on the use of telecommunications, rather than an on-site teacher, as the major delivery system for foreign language instruction.

This statement briefly outlines guidelines from specialists in foreign language education who work for state education agencies in the United States. The accompanying document (*Characteristics of Effective Foreign Language*

Distance Learning Programs) may be useful to anyone responsible for selecting and implementing distance learning programs.

- *The Need for Distance Learning*
  Distance learning classes should be used only when qualified teachers who are proficient in the target language(s) are not available or when qualified teachers want to enrich their programs. For example, distance learning might be a way to offer foreign language instruction in areas of population sparsity or when there are small numbers of potential students.
- *Involvement of Foreign Language Specialists in Program Design and Implementation*
  The expertise of the specialist is needed when considering curriculum, methodology, policies, and mandates. For distance learning to be a viable alternative to conventional classroom instruction, it must be consistent with current research and practice which focuses on developing the learner's language proficiency. Proficiency, what the learner can do with the language rather than what he or she knows about it, is the major principle around which today's foreign language teaching and curricula are organized. Distance learning programs must, therefore, provide a mechanism for a major portion of class time to be devoted to meaningful language use and practice and to authentic communication.
- *Qualifications of the Distance Learning Teachers and On-Site Facilitators*
  The distance learning teacher should be an experienced master teacher with proven proficiency in the target language. The classroom facilitator should participate in appropriate in-service and should have a working knowledge of the target language or should be committed to learning the language.
- *Appropriate Use of Technology*
  It is essential that technology be at the service of communication (i.e., acquisition of skills) and not an end in itself. The electronic technology in foreign language distance learning programs should allow for interactive instructional activities (i.e., one-way video and two-way audio or two-way audio-video). Live interaction is essential to quality foreign language teaching and learning.

The National Council of State Supervisors of Foreign Languages (NCSSFL) recognizes the potential of distance learning to overcome obstacles of distance, time, and human and material resources that limit access to foreign language learning opportunities. However, if the purpose of a distance learning program is to teach foreign language, then the program must provide instruction that fosters creative interaction both among and between learners and with a native or near-native speaker of the language. This interaction should occur in a range of contexts likely to be encountered in the target culture. In summary, when school districts choose distance learning programs due to the limited resources as described above, NCSSFL encourages selection of materials and opportunities which are designed to meet the goals of quality foreign language education.

NCSSFL Characteristics of Effective Foreign Language Distance Learning Programs

1. Foreign language distance learning programs offer at least two levels of each foreign language.
2. Foreign language distance learning programs are interactive (two-way audio and video or two-way audio and fax or computer terminal for interactivity) in the foreign language.
3. Foreign language distance learning classes are limited to no more than 10–15 students or interaction with groups of students is with groups of 12 or fewer students.
4. The program offers a variety of instructional activities to include listening, speaking, reading, and writing skills, as well as social and cultural information.
5. The program provides frequent (daily, if possible, but at least 2–3 times each week) oral interactions between each student and an adult proficient in the target language (i.e., a certified foreign language teacher, a native speaker, or other individual with training in interactive teaching/learning techniques).
6. There is immediate feedback on student oral performance. Program source grades and returns student work (tests, assignments, projects, etc.) within 7–10 school days.
7. Program source is extremely well-organized so that classroom facilitators and students are informed of scheduled activities well in advance. A calendar of lesson objectives, test dates, activities, etc., is printed prior to each semester.
8. Text and printed materials correlated with the distance learning class are used for review, drill, practice, and homework to strengthen the concepts being taught.
9. In addition to all program printed materials, program source provides classroom facilitators recent research on foreign language learning and foreign language teaching methodology.
10. Program source directly involves all schools and students by providing a vehicle for networking with each other and with program source.
11. Each distance learning class is formally evaluated each year. Program source provides data on program effectiveness.
12. The distance learning teacher is an experienced master teacher with proven proficiency in the target language.
13. The program source provides in-service training in course organization, classroom management, and technical aspects of the program for classroom facilitators.
14. Each distance learning class has a classroom facilitator who is a certified teacher (preferably in another foreign language or a related field).
15. Classroom facilitators have a working knowledge of the foreign language or are committed to learning the language (with students and/or through college/university classes).
16. School schedule coincides with program schedule.
17. Local education agencies have the facility and permission to tape programs for repetition and reinforcement of instruction.

Reprinted with permission: National Council of State Supervisors of Foreign Languages, 1990. http://www.ncssfl.org

References on Use of Technology

Gonglewski, Margaret R. 1999. "Linking the Internet to the National Standards for Foreign Language Learning." *Foreign Language Annals* 32 (3): 348–62.

Kost, Claudia R. 1999. "Enhancing Communicative Language Skills through Effective Use of the World Wide Web in the Foreign Language Classroom." *Foreign Language Annals* 32 (3): 309–20.

Lebow, Tasha, and David Dugger. 1999. "Successfully Merging onto the Information Super-Highway." *Equity Coalition* V (Fall): 31–36.

National Standards in Foreign Language Education Project. 1996. *Standards for Foreign Language Learning: Preparing for the 21st Century*. Lawrence, Kans.: Allen Press.

National Council of State Supervisors of Foreign Languages. 1990. "Position Statement on Distance Learning in Foreign Languages." http://www.ncssfl.org.

Osuna, Maritza M., and Carla Meskill. 1998. "Using the World Wide Web to Integrate Spanish Language and Culture: A Pilot Study." *Language Learning & Technology* 1 (2): 71–92.

Willis, Barry. 2002. "Guide #1—Distance Education: An Overview." *Distance Education at a Glance*. Moscow, Ida.: Engineering Outreach, College of Engineering, University of Idaho. http://www.uidaho.edu/evo/dist1.html, accessed February 27, 2002.

Wisconsin Department of Public Instruction. 1998. *Wisconsin's Model Academic Standards for Information & Technology Literacy*. Madison: Wisconsin Department of Public Instruction.

Part IV
Resources

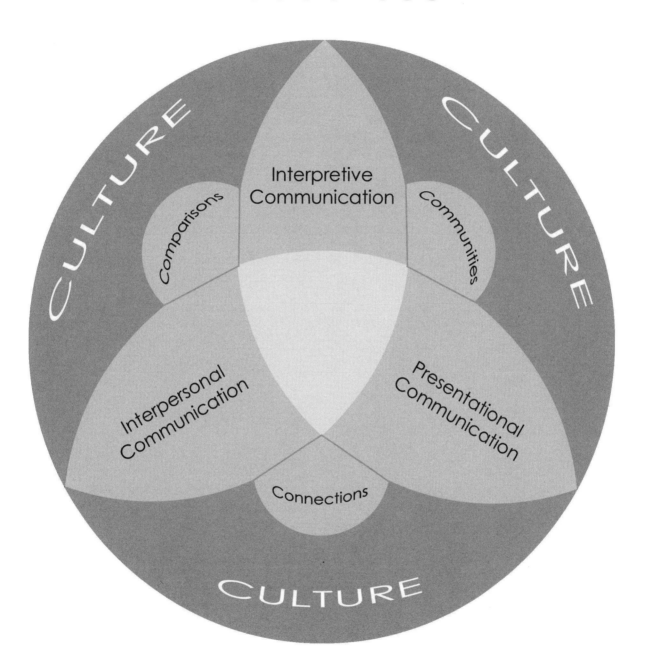

Resources

Curriculum Planning Template–Blank
Annotated Curriculum Planning Template
Key Questions: Thematic Topics
Wisconsin's Model Academic Standards for Foreign Languages
    Overview
    Content and Performance Standards
    Wisconsin Performance Guidelines
    Sample Student Performance Tasks
Language Functions: A Different View of Structures and Vocabulary

TABLE IV.1 Curriculum Planning Template
Thematic Curriculum Unit—Performance Assessment and Planning Guide

Key Question: Theme: Topic:

Targeted Proficiency Level:	Beginning	Developing	Transitioning	Refining
Communication Mode:	Interpersonal Interpretive Presentational	Interpersonal Interpretive Presentational	Interpersonal Interpretive Presentational	
Performance Assessment				
Wisconsin Standards: **Communication**				
Target Performance *(Key elements from the Performance Guidelines to consider in rubric development)*	Content: Accuracy:	Content: Accuracy:	Content: Accuracy:	

Communication Strategies:		Communication Strategies:		Communication Strategies:	
Cross-Cultural Applications:		Cross-Cultural Applications:		Cross-Cultural Applications:	

Links to Culture and the other Wisconsin Standards:

✓ **Connections**
✓ **Comparisons**
✓ **Communities**

Evidence (How these standards are incorporated in the instruction)

Structures and Vocabulary:

What needs to be taught for students to be successful in the performance assessment

Resources

TABLE IV.2 Annotated Curriculum Planning Template

Thematic Curriculum Unit—Performance Assessment and Planning Guide

Key Question:	**Theme:**		**Topic:**	
Choose from the four key questions (Table IV.3)	Select from themes relating to "Self and Community" or "Personal, Local, and Global Issues" (Table IV.3)		Identify the specific aspects of this theme on which the unit will focus	

Beginning	Developing	Transitioning	Refining
Refer to the Performance Guidelines (pp. 237–40) to determine the proficiency level of students			

	Beginning	Developing	Transitioning	Refining
Communication Mode: The three modes of communication are identified and described as the C of Communication in the Wisconsin Model Academic Standards for Foreign Languages (see pp. 228–30).		Interpersonal Interpretive Presentational	Interpersonal Interpretive Presentational	Interpersonal Interpretive Presentational
		The order of the communication modes for the unit assessment may vary from unit to unit. Identify the order in which students will demonstrate their communication skills. Circle here the mode of each performance assessment task below.		
Performance Assessment		*Describe the assessment task for each communication mode above (interpersonal, interpretive, or presentational). Students perform each task to demonstrate their achievement of the specific performance standards designated below.*		
Wisconsin Standards: Communication		*Identify the communication standard (from the Wisconsin Model Academic Standards for Foreign Languages on pp. 228–30) that each assessment task has targeted. Check that students will provide evidence matched to specific standards.*		

Target Performance (Key elements from the Performance Guidelines to consider in rubric development)	Content: *For each category of the Performance Guidelines (pp. 237–40), select the specific characteristics that apply to each performance task. If the category is not reflected in the task, leave it blank.*	Content:
	Accuracy:	Accuracy:
	Communication Strategies:	Communication Strategies:
	Cross-Cultural Applications:	Cross-Cultural Applications:
Links to Culture and the other Wisconsin Standards: ✓ *Connections* ✓ *Comparisons* ✓ *Communities* **Evidence** (How these standards are incorporated in the instruction)	*Refer to the four other C's of the standards (see pp. 231–35) to expand and enrich the unit, either as part of the assessment or as activities leading to the assessment. Document what students will do in the task or activity to provide evidence that these standards have been included. Don't force standards into the unit superficially; focus on the standards that are integral to the unit.*	
Structures and Vocabulary: What needs to be taught for students to be successful in the performance assessment	*Identify what the students need to know and practice to successfully complete the performance assessment tasks. These language components will form the basis for the practice pieces in the daily lesson planning. Consult the "Language Functions" (pp. 256–58) for descriptions of knowledge and skills across the four language levels, grouped by language functions.*	

TABLE IV.3 **Key Questions: Thematic Topics**

Beginning

Who am I?
Who are you?
Identify similarities and differences

Developing

What is my life like?
What is your life like?
Investigate similarities and differences

Self and Community

- Biographical Facts
- Interests/hobbies
- Family
- School/studies
- Friends/peers

- Geography, climate, political divisions
- Urban, suburban, rural
- Community, housing
- Stores/shopping/restaurants
- Travel, transportation

Transitioning

How do I look at the world?
How do you look at the world?
Share and compare perspectives

Refining

What do I think and feel?
What do you think and feel?
Discuss and defend opinions

Personal, Local, and Global Issues

- Intellectual and aesthetic pursuits
- Religion, Philosophy
- Cultural heritage, traditions, practices, celebrations

- Politics
- History
- Current events
- Ecology, environment
- Work/career

Wisconsin's Model Academic Standards for Foreign Languages

Jack Kean
Assistant State Superintendent Division for Academic Excellence

Susan Grady
Director, Content and Learning Team

Paul Sandrock
Consultant, World Language Education

Elizabeth Burmaster
State Superintendent
Wisconsin Department of Public Instruction
Madison, Wisconsin

Foreword

Wisconsin's Model Academic Standards for Foreign Languages were first published in 1997. They have changed local curriculum design and classroom instruction. Our work with the foreign language community has led to this first revision. The content standards remain unchanged, but we move from the original description of performance standards for elementary, middle, and high school students to a four-step-model: beginning, developing, transitioning, and refining. These standards still describe what is possible to achieve in a K–12 program of foreign language instruction. Only when students begin to learn a foreign language in elementary grades will they be able to achieve the "refining" level of these standards. However, because at the beginning of the twenty-first century very few students in Wisconsin study foreign languages at the elementary level, describing four levels of performance will help districts set their own appropriate targets for a sequential program, whether it begins in elementary grades, middle school, or senior high. The most critical factor in developing higher levels of proficiency in a second language is time. These four levels describe what students can do in a second language when they begin in elementary school.

Effective schools research tells us that one of the most important elements in improving the results of education is being clear about standards. Having clear standards for students and teachers makes it possible to develop rigorous local curricula and valid and reliable assessments. The data from such assessments tell us where we need to place our emphasis as we improve teaching and learning. Being sure the entire community has input into academic standards is essential if everyone is to have ownership in the education of our students. We are proud that we have developed challenging academic standards not only in areas traditionally associated with large-scale state and district assessment but also in subjects where assessment takes place primarily in the classroom.

We believe that these standards will continue to assist parents and educators in preparing students for the challenges of modern society. Although Wisconsin has traditionally led the nation in educational excellence, clear statements about what students should know and be able to do are necessary to maintain this strong tradition. My thanks to those of you in all walks of life who have contributed to this important effort and who are now implementing these standards in Wisconsin's schools.

Elizabeth Burmaster
State Superintendent

Acknowledgments

Wisconsin's Model Academic Standards for Foreign Languages would not have been possible without the efforts of many people. Members of the task force freely gave their time and expertise in developing the academic standards. In addition, their employing agencies generously granted them time to work on this initiative. The task force members are

Donna Clementi, Chair
Foreign Language Standards Task Force
French Teacher, District Department Head
Appleton West High School

O. Lynn Bolton
Spanish Teacher
Nathan Hale High School
West Allis

Jaci Collins
French and Japanese Teacher
Washington Junior High School
Lincoln High School
Manitowoc

Gale Crouse
Professor and Chair
Department of Foreign Languages
University of Wisconsin–Eau Claire

John Fortier
Academic Standards Consultant
Department of Public Instruction

Eileen Hesseling
Spanish Teacher
Pulaski High School
Milwaukee

Claire Kotenbeutel
Chinese and French Teacher
James Madison Memorial High School
Madison

Ellen Last, Director
Challenging Content Standards Project
Department of Public Instruction

Brigitta Ritter
German Teacher, District Department Head
Waukesha West High School

Judy Ulland
Latin Teacher
Logan High School
La Crosse

Special thanks to Greg Doyle, Kathy Addie, Donna Collingwood, Gail Endres, Amy French, Robin Gee, Connie Haas, Victoria Horn, Jill Ness, and Peg Solberg for their valuable contributions to this publication. Their talents and assistance are sincerely appreciated.

Overview of Foreign Languages

People today are connecting across cultural, political, and economic borders via the Internet and other information technologies. To meet the challenges of ever-increasing global connections and to be a front-runner in a global economy now and in the 21st century, students in Wisconsin must communicate in a culturally appropriate manner with people from around the world. Our students must be aware of different perspectives reflected in both the language and behaviors of other people. They must possess language skills and an understanding of other cultures to be productive members of the diverse communities in which we all live.

These Wisconsin standards for foreign language learning are based on an instructional program in languages other than English for all students beginning in kindergarten and continuing through 12th grade. These standards are not meant to reflect the status quo of language learning in Wisconsin, but are a bold statement of what parents and community members continue to request: a strong foreign language program beginning in the elementary grades. These standards do not neglect the teaching of basic language structures, but rather encourage the student to go beyond this knowledge to develop real-life uses for foreign languages. It is the role of parents, teachers, and community members alike to encourage and guide the development of these skills in our students as they strive to become responsible citizens.

Wisconsin's Model Academic Standards for Foreign Languages reflects the latest research in the field of second language instruction as presented in *Standards for Foreign Language Learning: Preparing for the 21st Century.*[1] This document, developed by leaders in second language education from across the United States, outlines standards for language learning. The Wisconsin content standards were adopted from this national document. The Wisconsin standards document adds performance standards that support each content standard. These were developed for students in Wisconsin by Wisconsin educators and citizens.

These standards are standards for all languages taught in Wisconsin schools, which at the time of printing include American Sign Language, Chinese, French, German, Hebrew, Japanese, Latin, Menominee, Norwegian, Ojibwe, Oneida, Russian, and Spanish. All of these languages have unique characteristics that may require some modifications in the standards to reflect their special traits. For example, Latin places a stronger emphasis on reading, while oral skills receive less emphasis. Non-Roman alphabet languages, such as Chinese, Japanese, and Russian, may require more time to develop reading and writing skills.

Five key words summarize the intent of these standards:

- COMMUNICATION: communicate in languages other than English
- CULTURES: gain knowledge and understanding of other cultures
- CONNECTIONS: connect with other disciplines and acquire information
- COMPARISONS: develop insight into the nature of language and culture
- COMMUNITIES: participate in multilingual communities at home and around the world

With communication and culture as the cornerstone for language learning, **the goal is for all students to learn how, when, and why to say what to whom.**[2]

[1]*Standards for Foreign Language Learning: Preparing for the 21st Century.* (Yonkers, N.Y.: American Council on the Teaching of Foreign Languages, 1995).
[2]*Ibid.*

COMMUNICATION
A. INTERPERSONAL: CONVERSATION

Students in Wisconsin will engage in conversations, provide and obtain information, express feelings and emotions, and exchange opinions in a language other than their own.

Rationale: Students must know how to use the language effectively in order to exchange ideas and information with other people in a culturally appropriate manner. This standard focuses on the goal of learning to engage in conversations.

Performance Standards

Beginning Receptive–Imitative	Developing Imitative–Reflective	Transitioning Reflective–Interactive	Refining Interactive–Initiative
A1: Conversations: Students will carry on a short conversation about personal interests, including what they have done, are doing, and are planning to do.	**A1: Conversations:** Students will sustain a conversation including descriptions on selected topics about themselves and their state or country.	**A1: Conversations:** Students will discuss and defend an opinion on selected topics from the local to the international level.	**A1: Conversations:** Students will discuss or debate a wide variety of topics from the local to the international level, hypothesizing, convincing, persuading, and negotiating to reach a conclusion.
A2: Questions: Students will ask and answer questions, including biographical information.	**A2: Questions:** Students will ask and answer a variety of questions, giving reasons for their answers.	**A2: Questions:** Students will ask and answer a variety of questions that require follow-up questions and responses for more information.	**A2: Questions:** Students will ask and answer a variety of questions that require elaboration and substantiation of opinions.
A3: Opinions: Students will state personal preferences and feelings.	**A3: Opinions:** Students will state personal preferences and feelings with some explanation.	**A3: Opinions:** Students will defend personal preferences, feelings, and opinions with more complete explanation.	**A3: Opinions:** Students will defend personal preferences, feelings, and opinions with substantive arguments.
A4: Problem-solving: Students will express personal needs.	**A4: Problem-solving:** Students will give possible solutions to a problem related to a personal need.	**A4: Problem-solving:** Students will suggest options for solving problems related to personal needs and needs of others.	**A4: Problem-solving:** Students will discuss options and negotiate to solve a problem.
A5: Comprehension: Students will ask for repetition and repeat to ensure understanding.	**A5: Comprehension:** Students will ask for simplification and clarification.	**A5: Comprehension:** Students will ask for clarification and suggest alternative words to ensure understanding.	**A5: Comprehension:** Students will ask for clarification and be able to paraphrase to ensure understanding.

COMMUNICATION
B. INTERPRETIVE: LISTENING AND READING
Students in Wisconsin will understand and interpret a language other than their own in its written and spoken form on a variety of topics.

Rationale: Students must develop strong listening and reading skills to interpret the concepts, ideas, and opinions expressed by members of other cultures through their media and their literature. This standard focuses on increasing the level of understanding as students listen to, read, or view materials in their new language.

Performance Standards

Beginning Receptive–Initiative	Developing Imitative–Reflective	Transitioning Reflective–Interactive	Refining Interactive–Initiative
B1: Listening: Students will understand spoken language on familiar topics that has strong visual support.	**B1: Listening:** Students will understand spoken language that incorporates familiar vocabulary and structures.	**B1: Listening:** Students will understand spoken language that incorporates more advanced vocabulary and structures.	**B1: Listening:** Students will understand spoken language on a wide variety of topics.
B2: Listening: Students will comprehend simple daily conversations on familiar topics and selected, age-appropriate authentic recordings, broadcasts, and videos.	**B2: Listening:** Students will comprehend the main idea and some supporting ideas of selected authentic materials including recordings, broadcasts, and videos.	**B2: Listening:** Students will comprehend the main ideas and supporting ideas of oral presentations, and selected authentic materials including videos, and radio and television broadcasts.	**B2: Listening:** Students will comprehend the main idea and supporting ideas of oral presentations and authentic spoken materials.
B3: Reading: Students will understand written materials on familiar topics that have strong visual support.	**B3: Reading:** Students will understand selected written materials on topics of personal interest.	**B3: Reading:** Students will understand more complex written materials on a variety of topics and formats.	**B3: Reading:** Students will understand written materials on a wide variety of topics and in a wide variety of formats.
B4: Reading: Students will comprehend the main idea of selected, short authentic written materials.	**B4: Reading:** Students will comprehend the main idea and some supporting ideas of selected authentic written materials.	**B4: Reading:** Students will comprehend the main idea and key supporting ideas, and begin to make inferences in selected authentic written materials.	**B4: Reading:** Students will comprehend the main idea and supporting ideas, and make inferences in a wide variety of authentic written materials.
B5: Strategies: Students will use previous classroom experience with the language to understand its spoken and written forms.	**B5: Strategies:** In addition, students will begin to derive meaning through use of prediction, prefixes, suffixes, root words, words similar to English, contextual clues, and word order.	**B5: Strategies:** In addition, students will use the dictionary to look up words that cannot be deciphered via previously learned strategies.	**B5: Strategies:** In addition, students will analyze the author's use of language to understand a written text.

COMMUNICATION
C. PRESENTATIONAL: SPEAKING AND WRITING
Students in Wisconsin will present information, concepts, and ideas to an audience of listeners or readers on a variety of topics in a language other than their own.

Rationale: Students must develop strong speaking and writing skills in order to communicate their thoughts, concepts, and opinions effectively to members of other cultures. This standard focuses on presenting information in a way that is appropriate for the audience.

Performance Standards

Beginning Receptive–Imitative	Developing Imitative–Reflective	Transitioning Reflective–Interactive	Refining Interactive–Initiative
C1: *Oral Presentations*: Students will dramatize student-created and/or authentic songs, short poems, skits, or dialogues.	**C1: *Oral Presentations*:** Students will present student-created and/or authentic short plays, stories, skits, poems, and songs.	**C1: *Oral Presentations*:** Students will present student-created works and excerpts of authentic literature.	**C1: *Oral Presentations*:** Students will present student-created works and authentic literature.
C2: *Speeches*: Students will write and present a short narrative about themselves.	**C2: *Speeches*:** Students will write and deliver a short presentation about their school or community.	**C2: *Speeches*:** Students will write and deliver a short speech on a topic of personal interest.	**C2: *Speeches*:** Students will write and present a speech on a topic that has been researched.
C3: *Directions*: Students will give simple commands and make requests of another person or group.	**C3: *Directions*:** Students will give simple directions to someone in order to complete a multi-step task.	**C3: *Directions*:** Students will give a series of directions to someone, coaching the person in order to complete the task.	**C3: *Directions*:** Students will give a series of detailed instructions to someone with suggestions on how best to complete the task.
C4: *Recounting Events*: Students will tell a simple story.	**C4: *Recounting Events*:** Students will tell a story incorporating some description and detail.	**C4: *Recounting Events*:** Students will recount a story with substantive description and detail.	**C4: *Recounting Events*:** Students will recount a long story with a wide variety of details and descriptions.
C5: *Forms of Writing*: Students will write personal journals and/or brief messages to friends (postcard, letter, E-mail).	**C5: *Forms of Writing*:** Students will write short compositions and letters.	**C5: *Forms of Writing*:** Students will write formal compositions and letters for a variety of purposes.	**C5: *Forms of Writing*:** Students will write formal compositions, research papers, and letters for a variety of purposes.

CULTURE
D. PRACTICES
Students in Wisconsin will demonstrate an understanding of the relationship between the practices and perspectives of the cultures studied.

Rationale: To fully understand another culture, students need to develop an awareness of another people's way of life, of the patterns of behavior that order their world, and of the traditional ideas, attitudes, and perspectives that guide their behaviors.

Performance Standards

Beginning Receptive–Imitative	Developing Imitative–Reflective	Transitioning Reflective–Interactive	Refining Interactive–Initiative
D1: Patterns of Interaction: Students will observe and imitate appropriate patterns of behavior (such as greetings or gestures) used with friends and family in the cultures studied.	**D1: Patterns of Interaction:** Students will interact with respect using culturally appropriate patterns of behavior in everyday informal and social situations.	**D1: Patterns of Interaction:** Students will interact with respect according to the social and cultural requirements of most social and some formal contexts.	**D1: Patterns of Interaction:** Students will interact in a variety of cultural contexts (formal/informal, social/work) with sensitivity and respect.
D2: Cultural Activities: Students will participate in and learn about age-appropriate cultural activities (such as games, songs, and holiday celebrations).	**D2: Cultural Activities:** Students will experience cultural and social activities common to a student of similar age in the target culture (such as holiday celebrations, school life, and pastimes).	**D2: Cultural Activities:** Students will compare and contrast activities from other cultures to their own in relation to home, school, community, and nation.	**D2: Cultural Activities:** Students will examine the role and importance of various social activities within the cultures studied (such as religious celebrations, historical events, rites of passage).
D3: Beliefs and Attitudes: Students will identify some common beliefs and attitudes within the cultures studied such as social etiquette or the role of family.	**D3: Beliefs and Attitudes:** Students will identify some common beliefs and attitudes within the cultures studied and compare them to their own beliefs and attitudes.	**D3: Beliefs and Attitudes:** Students will discuss and compare beliefs and attitudes within the cultures studied and their own in relation to home, school, community, and nation.	**D3: Beliefs and Attitudes:** Students will explain how beliefs, perspectives, and attitudes affect the target countries' position on global issues.
D4: Historical Influences: Students will identify reasons for different patterns of interaction.	**D4: Historical Influences:** Students will begin to be able to explain historical and philosophical reasons for different patterns of interaction.	**D4: Historical Influences:** Students will exhibit broader and deeper knowledge of historical and philosophical backgrounds that explain patterns of interaction.	**D4: Historical Influences:** Students will discuss historical and philosophical backgrounds that have influenced a culture's patterns of interaction.

CULTURE
E. PRODUCTS

Students in Wisconsin will demonstrate an understanding of the relationship between the products and perspectives of the cultures studied.

Rationale: To respect and appreciate the diversity of their world, students need to learn about the contributions of other cultures to the world and the solutions they offer to problems confronting them. Awareness of these contributions helps students understand how their views and other people's views of the world have been influenced.

Performance Standards

Beginning Receptive–Imitative	Developing Imitative–Reflective	Transitioning Reflective–Interactive	Refining Interactive–Initiative
E1: Objects and Symbols: Students will identify objects and symbols, such as flags or currency, that are used day-to-day and represent other cultures.	***E1: Objects and Symbols:*** Students will compare objects and symbols, such as flags or currency, from other cultures to those found in their own culture.	***E1: Objects and Symbols:*** Students will research the historic background of objects and symbols and how they came to represent certain cultures.	***E1: Objects and Symbols:*** Students will connect objects and symbols of other cultures to the underlying beliefs and perspectives.
E2: Contributions: Students will identify some major contributions and historical figures from the cultures studied that are significant in the target culture.	***E2: Contributions:*** Students will identify major contributions and historical figures from the cultures studied that are significant in the target cultures.	***E2: Contributions:*** Students will examine the role and significance of the contributions of other cultures in today's world.	***E2: Contributions:*** Students will examine the role and significance of other cultures on the target culture.
E3: Mutual Influences: Students will identify some historical and contemporary influences from other cultures that are significant in their own culture, such as explorers and settlers, music, and sports.	***E3: Mutual Influences:*** Students will identify some historical and contemporary influences from other cultures that impact today's society, such as the democratic form of government and environmental concerns.	***E3: Mutual Influences:*** Students will discuss how historical and contemporary influences from other cultures shape people's views of the world and their own attitudes toward issues facing the world.	***E3: Mutual Influences:*** Students will explain the impact of a culture's views on what is happening and could happen in the world today.
E4: Geography: Students will identify countries, regions, and geographic features where the target language is spoken.	***E4: Geography:*** Students will explain the impact of the target country's geography on daily life.	***E4: Geography:*** Students will explain the impact of the target country's geography on the people's beliefs, perspectives, and attitudes.	***E4: Geography:*** Students will evaluate the target country's geography with respect to the impact on politics, economics, and history.

The following six standards encourage students to go beyond their knowledge of and skills in language and culture to develop real-life applications for communication throughout the world. That is why these standards are presented in a different format, illustrating that they provide a context for the development of skills in communication and culture. Students at all levels of language development engage in similar types of activities in connections, comparisons, and communities; the difference is in the increasing sophistication with which students use their language skill and cultural knowledge.

CONNECTIONS
F. ACROSS DISCIPLINES

Students in Wisconsin will reinforce and further their knowledge of other disciplines through a language other than English.

Rationale: The conscious effort to connect the study of languages with other disciplines opens doors to information and experiences which enrich students' entire lives. Students can use information and skills learned in other classes to practice their new language. Conversely, language classes provide additional information to enhance what students learn in other disciplines.

Performance Standards

F1 *Speaking and Writing:* Students will use topics and skills from other school subjects to discuss and/or write in the language studied.
F2 *Reading and Listening:* Students will read material, listen to, and/or watch programs in the language studied on topics from other classes.
F3 *Accessing Resources:* Students will access resources in the language studied on topics being discussed or researched in other classes.

CONNECTIONS
G. ADDED PERSPECTIVE

Students in Wisconsin will acquire information and recognize the distinctive viewpoints that are available only through a language and its cultures.

Rationale: Being able to access information in more than one language gives students a much richer base of knowledge. Not only is there a greater choice of resources, but there is also the opportunity to analyze a topic from another culture's perspective, providing students with unique insights.

Performance Standards

G1 *Popular Media:* Students will read, view, listen to, and talk about subjects contained in popular media from other countries in order to gain a perspective on other cultures.
G2 *Accessing Resources:* Students will access information in the language studied in order to gain greater insight about other cultures and/or their own.

COMPARISONS
H. LANGUAGE

Students in Wisconsin will demonstrate understanding of the nature of language through comparisons of the language studied and their own.

Rationale: Students who study more than one language gain insight into the nature of their own language and can analyze the power of word choice. They can compare how different language systems express meaning and reflect culture.

Performance Standards

H1 Structures: Students will identify cognates (words similar to English), word roots, prefixes, suffixes, and sentence structure to derive meaning.
H2 Idioms: Students will identify expressions that cannot be translated word for word in order to derive meaning.
H3 Translation: Students will identify words and expressions that have no equivalent in another language.
H4 Cultural Characteristics: Students will identify cultural characteristics of language such as formalities, levels of politeness, informal and formal language.
H5 Phonetics: Students will compare the sound-symbol association of English to that of the language studied.

COMPARISONS
I. CULTURE

Students in Wisconsin will demonstrate understanding of the concept of culture through comparisons of the cultures studied and their own.

Rationale: Students who study more than one language continuously compare and contrast the practices of people in different cultures. This helps students understand themselves better and builds understanding of different responses to similar situations.

Performance Standards

I1 Cultural Variations: Students will discuss the meaning of perspectives, products, and practices in different cultures.
I2 Comparisons: Students will compare the form, meaning, and importance of certain perspectives, products, and practices in different cultures.
I3 Characteristics of Culture: Students will understand the concept of culture as they compare other cultures to their own.

COMMUNITIES
J. PRACTICAL APPLICATIONS

Students in Wisconsin will use the language both within and beyond the school setting.

Rationale: As businesses expand domestic and international markets and as people of the world meet each other more often through face-to-face encounters and/or the use of technology, the need for students to be proficient in other languages becomes critical in order for the United States to maintain international respect and economic competitiveness.

Performance Standards

J1 Service: Students will provide service to their school and community through such activities as tutoring, teaching, translating, interpreting, and assisting speakers of other languages.
J2 Outreach: Students will participate in activities where the ability to communicate in a second language may be beneficial, including business internships, exchange programs, and sister city projects.
J3 Communication: Students will exchange information with people locally and around the world through avenues such as penpals, E-mail, video, speeches, and publications.

COMMUNITIES
K. PERSONAL ENRICHMENT

Students in Wisconsin will show evidence of becoming lifelong learners by using the language for personal enjoyment and enrichment.

Rationale: Students who study another language are better prepared to be responsible members of their communities because of their global perspective. They have expanded their employment opportunities both at home and abroad and have access to a wider variety of resources where they can pursue topics of personal interest.

Performance Standards

K1 Media: Students will use various media in the language studied for study, work, or pleasure.
K2 Careers: Students will investigate careers where skills in another language and/or cross-cultural understanding are needed.
K3 Understanding: Students will deepen their understanding of other cultures through various avenues such as cuisine, sports, theatre, dance, and art.
K4 Further Learning: Students will look for opportunities to learn more about languages and cultures.
K5 Intercultural Experiences: Students will travel to communities where the language studied is spoken and/or host someone from a country where the language studied is spoken.

Wisconsin Performance Guidelines

These performance guidelines are designed to inform instruction and assessment. The performance standards describe how students will show achievement of the content standards and how the focus for learning will shift from the *beginning* to the *developing* level, then on to the *transitioning* and *refining* levels. The goal of the performance guidelines is to describe how well students are able to do what is described in the performance standards. The performance guidelines help students chart their progress by describing the elements for improved use of the language at four checkpoints, ranging from the focus for a beginning student through the description of a highly functional user of the world language. Growth described in these performance guidelines is possible when a world language program provides continuous instruction from the early elementary grades through 12th grade. Just as students continue to develop skill in their first language throughout their lives, the same applies to acquiring a second language. The description of the *refining* level implies lifelong learning.

The performance guidelines are a useful tool for analyzing students' strengths and areas needing improvement. Criteria are described within four categories: content, accuracy, communication strategies, and cross-cultural applications. The four criteria under "content" make it clear that what one says is as important as how accurate one's written or spoken skills are. The criteria under "accuracy" describe four areas that are important for improving one's skills in conversing, interpreting, and presenting. The criteria under "communication strategies" describe five aspects of engaging in conversation, of understanding, and of being understood. The three criteria under "cross-cultural applications" underline the importance of being able to adjust one's manner of communication to fit particular situations and expectations that may vary from one culture to another. Students and teachers need to remember as they evaluate language proficiency that each student will develop a unique profile across these criteria. For any individual student, skills may be at higher levels in some criteria and not as developed in others. By reflecting on this profile, students are better able to focus their attention on those areas needing additional practice.

In world language education, the term "proficient" is used to describe a language learner who has spent several years studying a language. To reach an advanced proficiency level, students need to begin their study in kindergarten and have continuous instruction through 12th grade. Because this understanding of the term is widely accepted by language teachers both in Wisconsin and nationally, it would be inappropriate to describe beginning and developing levels of student work as "proficient." Therefore, the student examples shown here represent work that is competent relative to the amount of time the student studied the language. Note the contrast between middle school and senior high programs, showing growth in what students can do in their second language.

WISCONSIN PERFORMANCE GUIDELINES: CONTENT

	Beginning Receptive–Imitative	Developing Imitative–Reflective	Transitioning Reflective–Interactive	Refining Interactive–Initiative
Complexity Sophistication	Relies primarily on memorized phrases and short sentences on very familiar topics in both oral and written presentations	Begins combining and recombining phrases into short strings of sentences on familiar topics in both oral and written presentations	Expresses own thoughts to describe and narrate using sentences and strings of sentences on familiar and some unfamiliar topics in both oral and written presentations	Reports, narrates, and describes using connected sentences with transitions to create paragraph-length discourse on a variety of topics in both oral and written presentations
Vocabulary	Uses a limited number of memorized words and phrases; relies on native language for unknown words and expressions; determines meaning by recognition of cognates, prefixes, and thematic vocabulary	Depends on vocabulary presented in class; may begin to use a dictionary to look up unknown words but will have difficulty selecting the correct translation; begins to use some common idiomatic expressions; may resort to native language to communicate unknown words and expressions	Uses vocabulary from a variety of topics; if precise vocabulary is lacking, can often find another way to express an idea/term; uses a dictionary as needed and selects correct translation most of the time; shows some understanding and use of idiomatic expressions; may invent a word or phrase in order to stay in the target language	Demonstrates control of an extensive vocabulary, including a number of idiomatic and culturally authentic expressions from a variety of topics; can successfully explain/describe a term or idea when the precise words are not known; supplements vocabulary by using dictionaries and reference books; will not fall back into native language to express self
Spontaneity	Responds automatically to high-frequency cues (i.e., hello, how are you, what's your name); can ask memorized questions (i.e., what's your name, how are you)	Responds with short answers to questions that have been rehearsed; asks simple yes/no questions, informational questions (i.e., who, when, where, what); begins to express reactions to responses (i.e., really, that's great, that's too bad)	Responds to unrehearsed comments, questions on familiar topics; asks a variety of questions and uses some expressive reactions and questions to elicit more information	Initiates and maintains conversations using a variety of questions and rejoinders
Situation	Accomplishes a task directed by the teacher; can meet limited writing needs such as a short message or note	Meets basic communication needs in a controlled setting; can meet practical writing needs such as short letters and notes	Meets communication needs on familiar topics in a variety of settings; can meet writing needs including letters, articles, short essays	Meets communication needs in a variety of settings; can meet a variety of writing needs including compositions, reports

WISCONSIN PERFORMANCE GUIDELINES: ACCURACY

	Beginning Receptive–Imitative	Developing Imitative–Reflective	Transitioning Reflective–Interactive	Refining Interactive–Initiative
Time/Tense	Can imitate any tense modeled and memorized	Begins to distinguish present, past, and simple future tenses with cues and modeling; can express own ideas in the present tense with some errors	Expresses own thoughts in present time with accuracy; with preparation can use present, past, and simple future times—some errors may be present	Comfortable expressing own thoughts in the present and simple future times; may exhibit some inaccuracies when using past tenses; begins using memorized patterns for hypothesizing, wishing, stating options
Ease	Expresses memorized phrases with ease and with few errors; may show evidence of false starts and pauses as topics expand beyond memorized dialogues	Restates and recombines memorized language with frequent pauses, hesitations, and false starts; many errors may occur as creativity increases	Creates with both familiar and new language; presents thoughts and ideas with some pauses and hesitations; errors may occur but do not interfere with communication	Expresses a wide variety of topics with few pauses and hesitations; errors may occur but do not interfere with communication
Pronunciation	Imitates sounds and intonation as part of a memorized process; understandable to someone accustomed to working with a language learner	May mispronounce words in a new context or words being read for the first time; understandable to a sympathetic native speaker, though this may require special efforts by the native speaker at times	Can use rules of pronunciation to pronounce correctly new words; converses with an accent and intonation that is understandable to a sympathetic native speaker, though this may require special efforts by the native speaker at times	Converses with an accent and intonation that is understandable to a native speaker, though this may require special efforts by the native speaker at times
Spelling/Orthography	Can copy with accuracy memorized language; will not notice errors	Will begin to notice errors in well-learned items and can correct high frequency items	Pays more attention to correct orthography	Can proofread to write the target language with few errors

WISCONSIN PERFORMANCE GUIDELINES: COMMUNICATION STRATEGIES

	Beginning Receptive–Imitative	Developing Imitative–Reflective	Transitioning Reflective–Interactive	Refining Interactive–Initiative
Comprehension	Understands short, simple conversations and narration with highly predictable and familiar contexts; relies heavily on visuals, gestures, facial expressions in order to understand; generally needs repetition, restatement, and contextual clues in order to understand; relies heavily on background information	Understands general concepts and some supporting ideas of short conversations and narration on familiar topics; relies on visuals, gestures, facial expressions; may need repetition, restatement, and contextual clues in order to understand; uses background experience to help anticipate meaning	Understands the main idea and some supporting ideas of conversations, lectures, and narration on familiar and some unfamiliar topics; uses contextual clues, inferences, key words and ideas, and text types to aid understanding; uses background knowledge to help understand the discourse	Understands the main idea and most supporting ideas of conversations, lectures, and narration on a wide variety of topics; uses organizing principles, inferences, contexts, background knowledge to aid understanding
Comprehensibility	Understood primarily by those accustomed to interacting with language learners	Understood by a sympathetic native speaker, though this may require special efforts by the native speaker at times	Understood by a sympathetic native speaker, though this may require special efforts by the native speaker at times	Understood by a native speaker, though this may require special efforts by the native speaker at times
Monitoring	May self-correct on high-frequency items	Self-corrects on well-learned items	Begins to notice incorrect language structure and/or need for idioms but may not know how to correct the structure	Can proofread to correct errors in structures and/or idioms when they are part of the student's prior learning
Clarification	Asks for repetition; may use gestures and facial expressions to show confusion	Asks for rewording, slowing of speech	May use paraphrasing, question-asking, circumlocution	Uses a variety of strategies to maintain communication
Impact	Focuses on successful task completion; uses gestures or visuals to maintain audience's attention and/or interest as appropriate to purpose	Asks follow-up questions; provides continuity to a presentation; begins to make choices of a phrase, image, or content to maintain the attention of the audience	Personalizes to maintain or reengage audience; able to provide comparisons and/or contrasts to reinforce message	Provides multiple examples to present a more convincing argument; varies delivery style in order to maintain attention of the audience

WISCONSIN PERFORMANCE GUIDELINES: CROSS-CULTURAL APPLICATIONS

	Beginning Receptive–Imitative	Developing Imitative–Reflective	Transitioning Reflective–Interactive	Refining Interactive–Initiative
Verbal	Imitates appropriate linguistic patterns (i.e., register, formal vs. informal address, intonation) when modeled by the teacher	Begins to recognize and produce linguistic patterns (i.e., placement of adjectives and adverbs, negation) appropriate to the target language	Recognizes and produces linguistic patterns appropriate to the target language	Recognizes and produces linguistic patterns appropriate to the target language; begins to show an awareness of the underlying meaning and importance of these patterns
Non-verbal	Imitates non-verbal patterns of behavior appropriate to the target culture (i.e., gestures, proximity, eye contact) when they are modeled by the teacher	Begins to use culturally correct behaviors outside the memorized context	Uses culturally correct behaviors to enhance verbal communication, showing some understanding of the implied meanings	Acts in a culturally correct manner in a variety of contexts with sensitivity and understanding of the implied meanings
Awareness	Understands a story line or event when it reflects a cultural background similar to own; begins to associate symbols, famous people, places, songs, etc. with a certain culture	Begins to use knowledge of own culture and the target culture(s) to help interpret oral and written texts	Recognizes differences and similarities in the perspectives of the target culture(s) and their own as they are expressed in oral and written texts	Applies understanding of the target culture(s) and its unique perspectives to enhance comprehension of oral and written texts

Sample Student Performance Tasks

Communication

A: Interpersonal: Conversation

Content Standard

Students in Wisconsin will engage in conversations, provide and obtain information, express feelings and emotions, and exchange opinions in a language other than their own.

PERFORMANCE STANDARDS: DEVELOPING LEVEL

A.1. Students will sustain a conversation including descriptions on selected topics about themselves and their state or country.

A.2. Students will ask and answer a variety of questions, giving reasons for their answers.

A.3. Students will state personal preferences and feelings with some explanation.

Sample Task

Pairs of students carry on a conversation that is recorded on audiotape. They are to discuss and ask about their daily lives and activities. Students are to ask questions of each other. They are also to provide additional information that is appropriate. Students continue their conversation as long as possible, up to two minutes. These conversations are not rehearsed, and students do not use a dictionary for help.

Samples of Student Work

Explanations of Ratings of Student Work

Middle School Example:
After One Semester of Instruction in Japanese

The students staged their conversation as a phone call. They greeted each other in a culturally appropriate manner and then continued by discussing a rock concert, homework, math class, and a weekend soccer game. Despite a very limited exposure to the language, the students were able to maintain the conversation without many pauses. While much of the conversation was memorized expressions, the speakers began to show some original combinations. They were able to discuss topics related to self and school as well as their likes and dislikes. Their pronunciation was clear and understandable. Although a few errors existed, their conversation was comprehensible.

Middle School Sample

― 「もしもし、レチャルさん。」
― 「お　元気ですか。」
― 「はい、元気です。お元気ですか。」
― 「おかげさまで。」
― 「ロックコンサートに行きました。」
― 「わすれました。」
― 「…3時半です。」
― 「そうです。」
― 「…しゅくだいをしましたか。」
― 「はい、…つまらないです。」
― 「数学はむずかしいでしたか。」
― 「はい、そうです。」
― 「週末は何をしましたか。」
― 「サッカー大会をします。」
― 「おもしろかったですか。」
― 「はい、そうです。…じゃまたね。」
― 「さようなら。」
　…

Senior High Example:
After Two Years of Instruction in Chinese

This conversation began with one student arriving to visit the other. She was invited in and offered green tea. They discussed the taste of the tea and she asked whether her friend was busy. She wanted to play Ping-Pong, but the boy plays poorly so she offered to teach him. He agreed, but he did not have a paddle. This was not a problem as she would bring an extra. They discussed a meeting time and he asked if she would like to eat Chinese food afterward at his house. She likes Chinese food, but refused as his father's cooking is always too hot. They parted, agreeing to meet at 3:30 at a friend's house. She promised not to be late. The conversation lasted two minutes with some pauses. The transitions from one topic to another by one student were easily followed by the other student. They had good pronunciation and the conversation could easily be understood by native speakers. The accuracy of tones and structures and the use of colloquial vocabulary and expressions made the conversation easy to follow.

Mary （玛丽）	Ian （宇生）
Knock, knock...	谁啊？
是我，玛丽。	请进，请进！
	请喝茶。是清茶——好吗？
很好喝。我最喜欢清茶。．．．	
你今天下午有没有空？	没有。有什么事？
我想去打乒乓球。你要跟我去吗？	好。可是我打的不太好。
我教你，好吗？	好。噢，我没有球拍！
沒关系，我带两个。	谢谢。几点了？
下午三点半，行吗？	行．．．．．．．
	．．．你喜欢吃什么饭？
我喜欢吃中国饭。为什么？	我想请你吃晚饭。
在哪儿？	在我家。行不行？
不行！我不喜欢你爸爸作的饭！是太辣的！	
一会儿见！	．．．．．．．一会儿见！噢，我们去哪儿？
三点半在小明家。别迟到了！	

Senior High Example:
After Three Years of Instruction in Japanese

The conversation began with one student explaining that he was very tired because of a weekend visit to the zoo with a friend for a biology class assignment. The students continued the conversation by discussing plans for after graduation, their reasons for studying Japanese, and finally their plans for winter break. The students maintained the conversation for the two minutes with few hesitations. They were able to provide transitions from topic to topic, reacting smoothly to each other's unrehearsed comments. They were able to use longer sentences with some complex language structures. Pronunciation was uneven, but could be understood by someone used to hearing non-native speakers of Japanese. The variety of vocabulary and structural accuracy made this conversation easy to understand.

Senior High Sample

- 「今日は、よしひこさん。」
- 「今日は、だいすこさん。」
- 「ねむいのようですね。」
- 「うん、とてもねむいです。」
- 「どうして。」
- 「週末は忙しかった。」
- 「週末に何をしましたか。」
- 「動物園へ行きました。」
- 「だれと一緒にいきましたか。」
- 「ジョンさんと一緒行きました。ジョンさんはちょっとへんな人だ。」
- 「どうしてへんですか。」
- 「うさぎを食べます。」
- 「そうですか。あなたもうさぎを食べたことがありますか。」
- 「いいえ、食べたことはありません。」
- 「わたしも。」
- 「ジョンさんはどうしてうさぎを食べますか。」
- 「「おいしい」と言いました。」
- 「どうして動物園へ行きましたか。」
- 「宿題でした。」
- 「何科目の宿題でしたか。」
- 「生物学の宿だでした。…だいすこさんは週末に何をしましたか。」
- 「週末は忙しかったです。えいごを見たり、本を読んだり、宿題をしたりしました。」
- 「大変ですね。…高校をすつぎょうしたあと、何をしますか。」
- 「まだわかりません。でも大学に行きます。」
- 「わたしも大学に行くつもりです。」
- 「どの大学に行きますか。」
- 「ミネソタの大学が好きです。」
- 「そうですか。…どうして。」
- 「…わかりません。」
- 「…だいすかさんはどうして日本語を勉強していますか。」
- 「日本語はおもしろい外国語ですから。」
- 「漢字が好きですか。」
- 「いいえ。…」
- 「わたしは漢字がとても好きです。」
- 「どうして好きですか。」
- 「…きれいだから。」
- 「そうですか。…毎日漢字の勉強をしますか。」
- 「いいえ、ときどきだけ。」
- 「でも、去年毎日勉強しましたか。」
- 「そうですね。赤い本の宿題をしました。」
- 「…冬休みには何をしますか。」
- 「スキーに行きます。」
- 「だれと一緒にしますか。」
- 「家族とやります。」
- 「わたしはスキーをしたこたはりません。」

Communication

C: Presentational: Speaking and Writing

Content Standard

Students in Wisconsin will present information, concepts, and ideas to an audience of listeners or readers on a variety of topics in a language other than their own.

PERFORMANCE STANDARD: DEVELOPING LEVEL
C.5. Students will write short compositions and letters.

Communities

J: Practical Applications

Content Standard

Students in Wisconsin will use the language both within and beyond the school setting.

PERFORMANCE STANDARD
J.3. Students will exchange information with people locally and around the world through avenues such as penpals, E-mail, video, speeches, and publications.

Sample Task

Students write a letter about how they spent their summer to a penpal from a sister school (from Wisconsin's sister states in Germany or Mexico, for example) using E-mail or fax. Students are told to describe their summer activities and to ask questions about their penpal's summer experiences, asking what the penpal did and what other people in that culture do. Students are to write their letter on a computer, if possible. For this sampling, no rewriting or dictionaries are allowed.

Samples of Student Work

Explanations of Ratings of Student Work

Middle School Example: After One Year of Instruction in Spanish

The student talked about swimming, eating, playing with her cats, and watching television or movies on days of bad weather. She concluded that summers are boring for her. Basically, the student was understandable. This student stayed in the present tense and used common vocabulary, so in spite of some errors in word forms, accuracy was high. The content of the letter shows evidence of communicating beyond the level of a beginning student: the student communicated basic information, asked memorized questions, and started to put expressions together in new ways. Few details were given. The student wrote in a conversational style using some slang expressions, appropriate for a penpal letter.

> En el verano, me gusta nadar. ¿Que hace en el verano? ¿Te gusta comer? Me encanta comer, pero vivo lejos de los restaurantes. ¡Que lastima! En el verano, me gusta tocco con mis gatos. y voy al centro commercial. En los días de mal tiempo, miro la television o voy al cine. Los veranos es muy aburridos para mí. ¿Y tú?

Senior High Example: After Four Years of Instruction in Spanish

This student described working as a lifeguard, assisting at an optometrist's office, and playing volleyball over the summer. She asked the penpal several general questions about summer activities. This student was very easy to understand. The writer used present and past tenses comfortably. Most of the errors were incorrect choice of vocabulary. When a word was not known, the student described what was meant. The student developed this familiar topic smoothly within the limited time for writing, providing some details. The student showed signs of complexity by combining structures and vocabulary creatively. Longer sentences, more description, and some use of clauses were signs of higher proficiency. The student maintained a conversational style.

Querida Lucía,   17 octubre

¿Cómo estás? ¿Cómo estaba tus vacaciónes del verano? ¿Hiciste muchas cosas?

Mis vacaciónes del verano estaba así así. Por mucho tiempo, trabajé todos las días entre los lunes y los viernes a dos trabajos. Mi primer trabajo era a la piscina de mi escuela. Allí miré a los niños que nadaron y enseñé a los estudiante como nadar bién. Me gusta eso trabajo mucho porque gano mucho dinero y trabajo con las personas cómicas. El trabajo segundo que tenía estababa con un doctor de los ojos en su oficina. Ayudé a los pacientes mucho cuando llegaron a la oficina. Allí también trabajé con las personas muy simpáticas. Por el resto de mis vacaciónes del verano jugué el vólibol en un equipo con mucho talento. También asistí un concierto grande con mi papá y mis amigos. Estaba muy divertida. Finalmente, visité las universidades para el año próximo con mis padres y mi hermana. Visitamos la universidad de Eau Claire, Wisconsin y la universidad de Madison, Wisconsin, la capital de Wisconsin.

Hacía mucho calor en Wisconsin durante la estación del verano. ¿Cómo hace el tiempo dónde vivas? ¿Qué cosas típicas haces durante el verano?

Yo ojala que tú tengas un año bien con cosas excelentes.

Con abrazos y besos,

Middle School Example: After One Year of Instruction in German

This writer began by describing her family. Then the letter talked about weather and her favorite summer activities of swimming, soccer, and visiting friends. It closed by asking about weather in Germany and the penpal's family and favorite animal. Even though there were some grammatical errors, the letter was quite clear and understandable. The student used only present tense and depended on vocabulary from class. The writer generally asked basic memorized questions and inserted an informal expression appropriately. At least one expression that is unique to German was used correctly. The student showed understanding of the German letter-writing form.

> Liebe Katja,
>
> Ich heiße Vroni. Ich bin 14 Jahre alt und wohne in Amerika. Ich habe 2 Brüder: ein ist 7 Jahre und ein ist 10 Jahre alt. Sie heißt Jimmy und Steven. Ich habe auch ein Hund, eine Katze und eine Ratze.
>
> Im Sommer, haben wir keine Schule. Hast du Schule? Ich schwimme gern und Fußball spielen gefällt mir. Was spielst du gern? Im Sommer besuche ich meine Freundin. Das ist Spitze! Manchmal sie schläft nach meinem Hause.
>
> Hier es ist oft sehr heiß im Sommer – nur 90° Farenheit. Wie heiß ist es in Deutschland?
>
> Hast du Geschwistern? Wo wohnst du? Was ist dein Lieblingstier? Mein ist ein Pferd.
>
> Schreibst mir!
>
> Deine,

Senior High Example: After Four Years of Instruction in German
The body of the letter tells of the student's trip to Germany and Switzerland this past summer, including descriptions of the host families. At the end, several questions are asked about the penpal's summer, such as if it is hard for the whole family to take a trip together. This student showed a higher level of proficiency by taking risks in trying to express thoughts, working around limited vocabulary knowledge. This led to several grammatical and spelling errors, but the content was still very comprehensible. The writer was comfortable using the present and future tenses and stayed consistently in the narrative past. The student successfully used some connecting words to create longer sentences. The overall tone was conversational, and provided some details, appropriate for this type of letter.

Liebe ?,
Guten Tag. Ich werde dir ein bischen ueber menen Sommer erzaehlen. Der letzte Tag des Schulejahres war 31. Mai. Am 3. Juni bin ich, mit 14 andere Schuelern, nach Frankfurt geflogen. Wir sind drei Wochen in Bayern geblieben. Es war Toll. Unsere 15 Schuler haben mit Familien in die Naehe von Eschenbach gewohnt. Meine Familie war ganz lieb! Sie haben zwei Toechter gehabt, Birgit - 10, und Maria -18. In nur drei Wochen waren wir beste freunde! Ich habe viele Freunden kennengelernt in Bayern (und viel Deutsch gelernt.) Am Ende die drei Wochen ist die amerikanische Gruppe zurueckgeflogen, aber ich bin in Europe geblieben. Ich bin nach Hessen fuer drei Wochen gefahren und habe mit einer Familie gewohnt. Sie haben zwei kleine Kinder gehabt. ich bin in viele Schulen in Hessen gegangen. Es war sehr interessant andere Schulen zu sehen. Die letzten drei Wochen bin ich nach der Schweitz gefahren. Alles war so schoen in die Schweitz. Hoffentlich kann ich sie in den nachsten 5 Jahren noch einmal besuchen. Ich bin am 4. August heim gekomen.
Was hast du diesen Sommer gemacht? Wie lange sind deine Sommer Ferien? Hast du in deinem Leben die Schweitz besucht? Was machen meistens die Deutsche Leute im Sommer? Ist es schwer fuer die ganze Familie eine Sommer Ausflug zusammen zu machen?

Communication

C: Presentational: Speaking and Writing

Content Standard
Students in Wisconsin will present information, concepts, and ideas to an audience of listeners or readers on a variety of topics in a language other than their own.

PERFORMANCE STANDARD: Developing Level

C.3. Students will give simple directions to someone in order to complete a multistep task.

Sample Task

One student is given a city map and asks a second student for directions on how to get to the post office. The city map has a circle and arrow indicating where he/she is standing in the city. The second student tells the first student how to get to the post office. The post office is indicated with an X on the second student's map. The second student coaches the first student on how to walk to the post office. The first student draws the route on his or her copy of the city map. They are given two minutes to communicate without the use of dictionaries. The task is videotaped; a transcript of the conversation is provided here.

Samples of Student Work

Explanations of Ratings of Student Work

Middle School Example: After Two Years of Instruction in French

Through a series of basically memorized commands, the coach accomplished the task. There was no added vocabulary to help the listener understand. The student following the directions did not check to make sure the right idea had been understood. The use of French is at a bare minimum, with several pauses.

- Où est la poste s'il vous plaît?
- Commencez la rue Pinel...
- Oui.
- Allez tout droit. Tournez à gauche, à la rue des Arts. Continuez... Tournez à droite à la rue Moulin.
- Oui.
- Tournez à gauche à la Boulevard Clichy.
- Oui (nods).
- Continuez à la deuxième rue.
- Oui.
- Tournez à droite...oui...oh! Continuez to the troisième rue...Excusez-moi, tournez à droite à la troisième rue, le Boulevard de Garibaldi. Continuez...la poste est...le post office est entre le Boulevard Garibaldi et l'avenue de Jeanne d'Arc, à gauche. Vous êtes ici.

Senior High Example: After Three Years of Instruction in French

Both speakers became involved in the activity and worked together to communicate. They responded to unrehearsed comments within this familiar task. The student who was asking for directions verified the directions at each step. There were a variety of errors, but the students could still communicate well enough to complete the task. Their conversation includes appropriate pauses, inflections, and vocabulary to accomplish the task. The speakers showed less hesitation, more spontaneity, and better imitation of French intonation compared to the middle school students.

- Alors Charles, commence à la rue Pinel.
- Rue Pinel...
- Euh. Tout droit comme ça à la droite. Et quand on arrive à la rue des Arts...
- Des Arts...
- Tourne à gauche.
- Gauche?
- A gauche. Et continue à la rue Moulin.
- Moulin.
- Et à la rue Boulevard Clichy.
- Clichy?
- Tout droit.
- Tout droit?
- Continue jusqu'à tu arrives à la Boulevard de Garibaldi. Est-ce que tu es là?
- Oui.
- Alors, tourne à droite...
- Tourne à droite?
- ...et continue...euh...continue tout droit presque...quand tu passesla rue Avenue de du Pont...
- Avenue du Pont?
- Regarde à ta gauche.
- Gauche?
- A ta gauche...regarde à ta gauche. Ne tourne pas! A gauche!
- OK?
- Quand tu passes à la gauche, il y avait une petite chose là-bas. Tourne à gauche dans la espace...
- Oui. Et je suis...
- Tu es à la poste.
- La poste? Poste...ici.
- Là-bas.

Communication

B: Interpretive: Listening and Reading

Content Standard

Students in Wisconsin will understand and interpret a language other than their own in its written and spoken form on a variety of topics.

PERFORMANCE STANDARD: DEVELOPING LEVEL

B.5. Students will begin to derive meaning through use of prediction, prefixes, suffixes, root words, words similar to English, contextual clues, and word order.

Comparisons

H: Language

Content Standard

Students in Wisconsin will demonstrate understanding of the nature of language through comparisons of the language studied and their own.

PERFORMANCE STANDARD

H.1. Students will identify cognates (words similar to English), word roots, prefixes, suffixes, and sentence structure to derive meaning.

Sample Task

Students are given a reading from an American magazine. Working independently, the students are to underline words which have Latin roots. On a separate sheet of paper, students list the English words they have found, underline the Latin root, and write a definition for the word based on the Latin root.

Middle School Example: After Thirty Hours of Instruction in Latin
Even after just over one month of studying Latin, this student was able to identify several English words derived from Latin. The student only defined the Latin word and did not use this to help define the English word.

English	Latin	Meaning
provocative	voces	talk
principles	princeps	leader or Emperor
advocated	voces	talk
interacts	intera	to ask
experiencing	explicare	to expect or explain
dead	mortua	to be dead
validity	valde	very
via	via	road
trade	tradit	to walk on
audience	audiunt	hear

Senior High Example: After One Year of Instruction in Latin
This student identified many more words with Latin roots compared to the middle school student. There was clear awareness of the role of prefixes. The student correctly translated the Latin root and applied this knowledge to defining the English word.

English	Latin	Meaning
Navigate	Navigio	to travel through from navigio meaning to sail
Glorified	gloria-ae f.	praised or admired from gloria = "glory praise"
Content	teneo / com	what is held within something from teneo meaning to hold and com meaning within
Navigational	Navigio	adjective of Navigate
Future	Futura	ahead in time, posterity from futura meaning future
Example	Examplia	something which shows meaning from examplia meaning example
Via	Via	road or way by means something is done from via meaning roadway
Unique	unos	trait which is particular to one person or thing from unos meaning one
Spectrum	specto-ere	what is seen from specto meaning to look at.

Resources

Imaginating	imaginis	what is thought up by the mind or image in the mind from imaginis meaning image
Advertisers	verto / ad	people who turn consumers to their product from verto meaning to turn and ad meaning to
Provocative	voco-are	based on voco meaning to call, provocative is an adjective which means something calls the attention of many people.
human-computer	humana	from humana meaning man.
advocated	ad/voco-are	from voco meaning to call and ad meaning to, advocated means to spoke for something.
Audience	audio	a group that hears or experiences something from audio meaning to hear.
Predicted	dicto-pre	tell before hand from pre meaning before and dicto meaning to say for every hundred from per- for every and onto = "100"
Fortune	fortuna-ae f.	sum of money or wealth from fortuna meaning
Script	scripto	a writing or something written from scripto a verb meaning to write
Database	Data	computer application which contains information from data meaning information
Unfortunately	fortuna	unlucky from fortuna meaning luck or chance with the prefix un meaning not
Addition	addō	something which is added from the verb addō meaning to add
Include Including	includō-ere	meaning to put in from includō meaning to shut in
Product	producere	something which is made
Access	accesso-ere	to go into

Language Functions: A Different View of Structures and Vocabulary

At the end of the curriculum development process, teachers will select structures and vocabulary on an as-needed basis to give students the tools they require to be successful at the performance assessment tasks. This chart helps in that selection process, providing a functional basis for identifying appropriate vocabulary or structures for instruction. These language functions provide the teaching focus in order to prepare students for the suggested performance assessment unit. They describe knowledge and skill for each language function category according to the targeted language level (beginning, developing, transitioning, or refining). Each succeeding level includes all previous levels' knowledge and skill (e.g., asking for clarification at the transitioning level means that the student learns and practices how to repeat words [beginning], select substitute words and ask follow-up questions [developing], and ask a series of questions and paraphrase to clarify meaning [transitioning]).

Language Functions and Related Tasks

Category:	Beginning:	Developing:	Transitioning:	Refining:
Ask questions	Ask yes/no questions Use tag questions Use question words (who, what, where, when, how)	Ask questions (who, what, where, when, how, how well, why)	Ask multipart questions	Ask questions with multiple clauses
Provide information	Use words, lists, phrases Connect memorized phrases into sentences	Use simple sentences Create with language by producing original sentences Report other people's speech (quoting)	Use simple sentences, connected sentences, strings of sentences Connect and extend discourse	Use complex sentences, connected sentences Narrate and describe
Ask for clarification	Repeat words Express a lack of comprehension with set phrases	Select substitute words, ask follow-up questions Explain one's lack of comprehension	Ask a series of questions, paraphrase to clarify meaning Pursue one's lack of comprehension by exploring what one thinks was meant	Use a wide variety of clarification strategies Pursue one's lack of comprehension by negotiating understanding
Maintain conversation	React to a limited number of formulaic questions Use simple leave-takings Extend greetings	Respond to simple direct questions Ask a few formulaic questions Use a variety of greetings Use a variety of leave-takings Get someone's attention	Initiate and maintain conversation Ask and answer questions Interrupt in a conversation	Initiate, advance, and/or redirect conversation Negotiate a solution to a problem
Describe people, places	Describe people and places (physical) Introduce self and a friend or family member Describe with adjectives	Describe people and places (character) Describe with adverbs	Describe people (psychological characteristics) and places (mood) Describe with adjective phrases	Describe people (motivation) and places (symbolism)
Tell a story, describe events	Use limited sequence words (first, second, later) Tell simple sequences (e.g., morning activities, school schedule) Describe simple past experiences and future plans	Use sequence and cause/effect words (at first, much later; therefore, because) Tell connected sequences (e.g., a summer vacation) Narrate simple past experiences and future plans	Use cohesive devices (in order to, rather than) Tell extended sequences (e.g., when I was young) Narrate past experiences and future plans	Use a variety of cohesive devices (linguistic and meaning-connectors) Tell well-developed stories

Language Functions and Related Tasks (Continued)

Category:	Beginning:	Developing:	Transitioning:	Refining:
Give and follow directions	Respond to classroom commands	Give and take simple directions (how to find a destination)	Coach someone through following of directions	
Express feelings	Tell likes, dislikes (concrete) Express support, praise with simple expressions	Tell preferences (more abstract) Express encouragement	Express a full range of emotions (excitement to upset) Express extended praise	Express sympathy and condolences Express apology
Express opinions	Use simple expressions to introduce a thought (e.g., I think that...) Provide one phrase or sentence to support one's opinion Agree/disagree using simple expressions	Use a variety of expressions to introduce a thought (e.g., Did you know that...; Guess what) Provide more than one sentence to support one's opinion Agree/disagree using sentences	Use impersonal expressions to introduce a thought (e.g., it is important that...) Provide examples to support one's opinion Agree/disagree using complex sentences	Use connected sentences to extend a thought Provide illustrations (stories) to support one's opinion Agree/disagree with fine-tuned precision across a wide range
Attend to cultural differences	Use appropriate gestures	Use formal and informal address		Choose vocabulary based on sociocultural requirements
Extend an invitation; Make arrangements	Make an appointment Use simple phrases to accept or reject an appointment	Present an invitation, providing some details Accept or reject an invitation	Convince someone to accept an invitation Explain an acceptance or rejection of an invitation	
State ownership	Use simple possessive words (my, your, our) Use possessive noun form (Mary's book)	Use a variety of possessive words (my, mine; your, yours) Use possessive expressions (belongs to, is part of)		
Offer alternatives	Use simple words to suggest an alternative (e.g., or)	Use different expressions to suggest an alternative (e.g., I think that...; we can)	Use different forms and expressions to suggest an alternative (e.g., conditional; we could) Express what is prohibited	Use forms and expressions to hypothesize (e.g., subjunctive; perhaps; it may be necessary to; I suggest) Express possibility, probability

Resources

Language Functions and Related Tasks (Continued)

Category:	Beginning:	Developing:	Transitioning:	Refining:
Take notes/ Summarize	List main ideas from oral or written prompts	List main ideas and subpoints		
Make requests	Make requests with simple expressions Ask permission with simple expressions Use polite expressions	Make requests with sentences Ask permission with sentences	Make requests with complex sentences Ask permission with complex sentences	Express wants, hopes, wishes
Use editing tools	Use an online spellcheck device	Use a bilingual dictionary	Proofread and/or peer edit	Analyze structure of paragraphs (to improve impact of writing)
Use context clues for comprehension	Use titles and other visual clues (e.g., pictures, illustrations)	Use main idea in order to predict possible meaning	Identify the story line in order to predict possible meaning (e.g., what might fit next)	Identify author's and/or cultural perspective in order to predict possible meaning
Use linguistic clues for comprehension	Identify cognates	Identify word roots, prefixes, suffixes	Identify verb forms Identify word order	Identify word form and placement in order to predict meaning
Meeting one's needs	Express thanks with simple expressions Make excuses with simple expressions Express apology with simple expressions	Express thanks with sentences Make excuses with sentences Express apology with sentences	Express thanks with complex sentences Make excuses with complex sentences Express apology with complex sentences	Make refusals Express anger or annoyance
Make comparisons	Compare two things Express equivalence	Compare three or more things Express equivalence and nonequivalence	Express extremes Compare quantities and ratios	